MW00513449

Advance Praise for *Life's Voyage*

What a remarkable voyage this is! Maurice Atkin's life has taken him, and takes us as fortunate companions, to every corner of the globe. His career was sometimes full of alligators and crocodiles, but it is the first-hand account of history that grabs the reader. From Israel's early days to work in the Soviet Union, Asia and Africa, Maurice Atkin made a difference in ways that few could equal.

—Michael D. Barnes
Former U.S. Congressman (D. MD.)

❖

Life's Voyage is a wonderful recounting of events and people which span more than half a century. Since I have known Maury Atkin through Bob Nathan and his consulting firm, Nathan Associates, Inc., my interest in *Life's Voyage* naturally went to encounters Maury had as part of this firm. Whether it was Maury's recounting of Prime Minister Kwame Nkruma of Ghana's justification for his cut of a new shipping firm going to his mistress's Swiss bank account, or the defeat of the cattle-hide embargo of the 1950s, or farming of alligators in Louisiana by a French Cajun, Maury's clients were amazingly diverse and demanding.

—John C. Beyer, President
Nathan Associates, Inc.

❖

In Life's Voyage, *Maurice Atkin offers a vivid account of his upbringing and longstanding 'love affair' with Israel. The story of his services to the newly born Jewish state brings to life the struggles and triumphs of those momentous times. Today's young people have much to learn from Atkin about how to put their professional training to work in the service of* tikkun olam.

—William A. Galston, Interim Dean
School of Public Policy, University of Maryland

❖

Maury Atkin's *Life's Voyage* is a fascinating series of vignettes from a life of Zionist dedication and creative commitment. Some depict an infant Israel filled with excitement, confusion, food shortages, and determination; some provide evocative insights into wary encounters between Israeli Diplomats and a skeptical State Department. Atkin's remarkable extracurricular and largely unsung role in helping Israel navigate turbulent Washington waters makes for intriguing and revealing reading.

—Samuel W. Lewis
U.S. Ambassador to Israel, 1977–1985

❖

Washington, D.C. is a truly unique place. For those who are interested in pursuing career paths that are stimulating and emotionally truly rewarding, it offers an opportunity to do just that, to make a difference. Maury Atkin made full use of that opportunity by advancing the worthy causes to which he applied his intellect and his energy. The activities that he recounts in his memoirs demonstrate his accomplishments in many countries that needed help in their economic development. But the one cause to which he has devoted most of his time and energy has been Israel. From his work, in 1948 for the Israeli Mission to the United States onward, Maury has engaged in a variety of activities that have served to strengthen the social framework on which the Jewish state rests. In Israel's early years, when the country suffered from serious food shortages, he negotiated the grant of U.S. Food assistance. Later he played a key role in the creation of Hadassah hospital. These are just two examples of the work he has done for Israel across the years. He has indeed made a difference.

—Richard Schifter
Former Assistant Secretary of State for Human Rights

❖

Maurice Atkin's book is a first-hand account that reveals previously unknown solutions to problems that threatened the founding of the new state of Israel. Readers will learn about the extraordinary ingenuity the author used to support the Zionist struggle to build Israel. Drawing on his previous experience at the U.S. Agriculture Department, he found a way to ship beef secured at 5 cents a pound, grains purchased at pennies per ton, and other foods to feed holocaust survivors fleeing to Zionist Palestine. Atkin reveals how, once President Truman recognized the state of Israel, he helped Israel shape its embassy and develop ties in Washington that have been so critical to its survival. Despite all that has been written about Israel, in reading this book, you will learn things you never knew.

—Janet L. Norwood
Former U.S. Commissioner of Labor Statistics

❖

Life's Voyage is the story of Maurice Atkin, from the time he was growing up in Washington D.C. between the two world wars and displaying a keen eye for entrepreneurial opportunities to his globe-spanning career advising for-

eign governments as well as domestic and foreign companies. Overriding his business interests was his 'love affair' with Israel. The vignettes of his many efforts on behalf of the new Jewish state make for lively reading. I had tears of laughter reading about how he solved the alligator problem in Israel. Looking back over nine decades, most of the 20th century, Maury dedicated his life voyage to making a difference. Indeed his story is one of how a profound difference was made. It is a worthy inspiration for young professionals as well as a great read for us all.

—James W. Kuhn
Professor Emeritus, Columbia University

❖

A parade of luminaries marches through Maury Atkin's fascinating memoir. We meet Israeli president Chaim Weizmann, Jerusalem mayor Teddy Kollek, and the economist Robert Nathan, not to mention a slew of alligators. But it is Atkin's own story that truly lights up the book, a life devoted to the Zionist dream. Then again, to paraphrase Herzl, if Maury Atkin wills it, it is not a dream.

—Franklin Foer
Author of *How Soccer Explains the World*

❖

Maury Atkin paints an affectionate, vivid, first-hand picture of Israel's birth and infancy. He tells the story—it reads like a friendly conversation— behind the headlines and his instrumental role in opening the first embassy in Washington, and helping to feed, clothe, house and nurture the infant Jewish state. It is a richly appealing story of people, from the famous to the unknown, through the eyes of one of the founding mishpacha. Particularly appealing is his detailed and intimate account of his first visit to Israel in 1951 with his wife Flora, whose delightful diary of that adventure is quoted extensively, much to the reader's enjoyment and enlightenment. This is a picture of Israel unfamiliar to the post-1967 generation, and the view of those nascent years through Maury's eyes is an essential part of knowing and understanding today's Israel.

—Douglas M. Bloomfield
Syndicated columnist and Washington consultant

❖

This book not only makes good reading, it also presents a little-known but vital part of the historic service that produced modern Israel. Maurice Atkin was indeed an unsung hero of that period and this book is an exciting and valuable record of his experiences.

—Ambassador Max A. Kampelman
Recipient of Citizens' Medal from President Reagan and
Medal of Freedom from President Clinton.

Life's Voyage

DEDICATED TO MAKING A DIFFERENCE

Maurice D. Atkin

*Graciously donated to JCA
by
Keller Publishing*

KELLER PUBLISHING
MARCO ISLAND, FLORIDA

Copyright © 2005 by Maurice D. Atkin

No part of this publication may be reproduced, stored in a retrieval system, or transmitted in any form or by any means—electronic, mechanical, photocopying, recording or otherwise—without prior written permission of the author.

ISBN 0-9674128-3-8

Composed in Adobe Warnock Pro by Hobblebush Books, Brookline, New Hampshire (www.hobblebush.com)
Printed in the United States of America

Cover photo © Jonathan Atkin

Published by

KELLER PUBLISHING

590 FIELDSTONE DR.
MARCO ISLAND, FL 34145

KellerPublishing.com

Contents

Illustrations

To Flora, my wife

The voyage has been smoother and the seas less stormy,
because of your devotion to our lives together these
past sixty-three years and, most recently,
to the production of this book.

&

In Memoriam

Fran and Mel Foer,
Sheva and Marver Bernstein,
confidantes and traveling companions
over many decades

Acknowledgements

Without my wife Flora's preliminary reviews and editing, this story would have been longer, and much less readable. Her suggestions, criticisms, diaries, and encouragement were invaluable. I am truly grateful for the time and energy she expended on this project—time and energy taken from her own writings.

Acknowledgements and thanks are also due to a number of persons who are no longer with us, who had a definite influence on my life and career.

Dr. Alan Gruchy, professor of economics, University of Maryland, taught me that economic activity and analysis involved more than mathematical formulae and resources; that nature and human activity frequently played significant roles in economic direction. Dr. Samuel DeVault, dean of the University of Maryland School of Agriculture, made it possible for me to continue graduate work when my personal world was being buffeted. Robert (Bob) Nathan, boss, mentor, partner, provided the resources and climate for my activities. He left me with a free hand to operate as I saw fit—but was readily available if and when I got into trouble. To them I owe a debt of gratitude.

And to Mel and Fran Foer for the wonderful memories of long discussions about everything and anything, to the many vacations together on land and sea, and to our extended scrabble games. They passed too soon.

Appreciation is due to my close friends and confidantes, Marver Bernstein, former president of Brandeis University and his wife, Sheva, who died in a hotel fire in Cairo. Probably more than any others they were aware of my activities with respect to Israel, provided encouragement and often excellent advice. More than thanks are due to Denise Tourover, Hadassah's official Washington representative, brilliant, dedicated, with strong views, and a welcome supporter in a clinch. I am grateful for having known and worked with Aaron Chilewich, whose ethical standards in business and life were an inspiration to all around him.

From the early days of my Israel Embassy activities, Saul and Sam Stern were there with encouragement and material help. And also, this memoir might have never seen the light of day except for their urging and encouragement.

Heartfelt appreciation is owed to my cousin Edward Cowan, retired *New York Times* correspondent and editor, for his many editorial suggestions. To Rabbi Stanley Rabinowitz, my religious mentor for many years; to Lorin Evans, my computer guru, whose patience and know-how surmounted technical problems that were baffling to me; and to Wade Keller, my Marco Island memoir mentor, editor and publisher for taking on this project, I am indebted. And much appreciation to my photojournalist son, Jonathan, for the cover picture and that of his grandmother, my mother, on page 4.

This memoir is primarily from current memory, with an occasional assist from letters, notes and documents when available. Accordingly, I ask forgiveness for errors in time and place, and even names and titles, or the lack thereof. These, and any other 'off course' mistakes, are solely mine. I hope that you will enjoy the cruise between the covers.

Maurice D. Atkin

Foreword

Maurice Atkin's memoir illustrates the validity of Socrates' axiom that an unexamined life is not worth living. Fortunately, he has lived long enough to look back upon a productive life, to affirm its blessings, and to identify the forces and influences that brought him to the point of recording his recollections. In examining life, he has described his relationship with the significant people who have made his life a remarkable adventure eminently worth recalling.

While his purpose in writing his memoir may have been to preserve a record of his achievements, he includes an account of his family origins so that his children, grandchildren and progeny will be enabled to trace their beginnings and to carry his memories into the future.

Since Maury's employment gave him what amounted to a ringside seat on history, the document provides a fascinating rehearsal of the origins and development of the State of Israel. In recording his own experiences he gives the reader an account of little known facts, usually ignored by the historian, but which add spice to the pages.

From his early associations with the pre-Israel Jewish Agency as a consultant, he found that his friendships enabled him to play a significant role in the perilous adventure that brought the State of Israel into being as it moved from crisis to crisis. Maury and his wife Flora traveled through much of the world from Asia to Africa and Europe dealing with such diverse commodities as ducks, alligators, and ostriches as well as ships, shipping and natural resources.

His work as economist and principal with Robert Nathan Associates, Inc. gave him an opportunity to view and record some of the more intimate and off the record foibles of many of the influential people who held positions of responsibility of the governments of both the United States and Israel.

Buffeted by external forces that made its subsequent acceptance as an independent nation virtually miraculous, he found his way between the obstacles of unfriendly officials in the United States and the demanding needs of an Israel struggling to protect and feed its citizens. He was forced to balance Israel's many requests for food with the rigors of Halachic Judaism.

Maurice Atkin has lived through as significant a period as any in the history of the Jewish people. His children and descendants are fortunate for his having the foresight and the strength to bequeath to them not only a clear description of the origins of their family but a fascinating description of the historic events and personalities that made up the cast of characters of this formidable period of Jewish history.

Stanley Rabinowitz, Rabbi Emeritus
Adas Israel Congregation
Washington, D.C.

Preface

In *Henry IV*, Shakespeare declares, "There is history in all men's lives." In the life of Maurice Atkin, the history of modern Israel is writ large—and runs deep and long.

From the early days that led to Israel's independence, Maury's life became deeply entwined with building the Jewish state. Maury's heart, talents, and skills were fully dedicated to this task. As the new nation was being born, he responded to the daunting, thorny challenges of the immigration and absorption of oppressed, tortured and displaced Jews the world over.

This historical nexus was preordained. From his late parents—Rose and Joseph Atkin, both ardent Zionists—he derived and fostered his love of Eretz Israel.

His affection for and bond with Israel were renewed and strengthened in 1946 at a Hadassah Ball in Washington D.C.—which Maury attended, "kicking and screaming (silently)." At this Ball he heard an impressive speech from James McDonald, U.S. High Commissioner for Palestine. Maury avowed that, "It turned out to be one of the major turning points in my life."

On the day following that speech, Maury, then a senior economist with the U.S. Department of Agriculture, initiated his close and meaningful association with the Jewish Agency for Palestine in New York. In these two years prior to Israel's independence, he placed his formidable capabilities at the disposal of Agency officials, counseling them on wide-ranging matters, particularly pertaining to the procurement of materiel vital to the emerging State of Israel. In this period, he advised and assisted Teddy Kollek in his fundraising and propaganda endeavors, and provided research support to American luminaries, Bob Nathan and Oscar Gass, as they drafted the critical economic, development and political analyses in advance of the United Nations debate on the creation of the State of Israel. These analyses gave significant and substantive support to Abba Eban's arguments before the United Nations.

On Israel's Independence Day, May 14, 1948, Maury accepted an appointment as Executive Officer and Agricultural Advisor of the newly created Israel Mission—later Embassy—to the United States, resigning from his secure position at the U.S. Department of Agriculture.

In his memoirs, Maury describes his job: "As E.O. (Executive Officer), it was my responsibility to set up a working establishment, hire local support staff, procure office furniture, buy cars, and see to 1,001 things that provided diplomats with a functioning office."

It was at this early juncture that Maury visited my brother Sam and me at our office furniture showroom, discussing his work and seeking our assistance. His zeal, dedication and ingenuity in the execution of his job responsibilities were amazing to observe—contagious and persuasive. From that first meeting, a friendship ensued—that was long and enduring. Over time it ripened through our mutual service on the boards of several community and national agencies. And for those of us who became activists for Israel, Maury's presence was a constant inspiration.

In retrospect, his job description seems mundane when contrasted with the foresight with which he carried out his vision and responded to the enormity and urgency of Israel's requirements to transport, house, feed, clothe, and provide essential services to its people—especially the monumental number of new immigrants.

In February 1950, under difficult circumstances, Maury resigned his embassy post and joined Robert Nathan Associates. Not withstanding this formal separation, Maury continued through the years ahead to perform his magic and wonders for Israel. In eighty-six trips, over five decades, with unflagging passion and concern, he ensured that numerous shiploads of potatoes from Maine, meat from Texas, and—through the Hadassah pipeline—tons of cheese, butter, dried eggs, corn, wheat flour, rice, and assorted food stuffs were shipped to feed a hungry nation.

Equally wondrous was Maury's negotiation of a congressional line-item grant of $5,000,000 to Hadassah to rebuild its hospital on Mt. Scopus. This was administered by the U.S. Agency for International

Development, along with programs that Maury supervised that procured generators, sheets and pillows cases, two full field hospitals, and a host of items that uplifted a struggling nation and its people—all at little or no cost to the government of Israel, or to Hadassah.

Throughout these decades, his loving, caring Flora was mothering three children, maintaining an active home, and busy with her own career, and joining Maury as a steadfast colleague in his Zionist endeavors. A partner on nineteen of his trips to Israel, Flora has provided her own fascinating account, "From Dan to Be'ersheva," about their first trip to Israel in 1951—belated, honored guests of a grateful government of Israel.

David Ben Gurion, the nation's first prime minister, often spoke of Israel as a land of miracles. It is rare for miracles to occur spontaneously. Behind them are hidden forces, invisible hands, and selfless persons. Through his contributions and devotion to the State of Israel and its citizens, Maurice Atkin has bequeathed to us all a glorious legacy of miracles.

Saul I. Stern

Introduction
to *Life's Voyage*

May the sun shine on your face,
and the wind always be at your back.

These words from a sailor's prayer, for the most part characterize the tenure of my life. Sure, there were some serious 'off course passages' that had to be overcome. But I was fortunate to have had parents who instilled in me values in life other than material ones. They taught me that one's energies and brains should contribute to the public good, as well as to personal satisfactions.

This anecdotal memoir was originally intended for my family, hoping that it would answer questions that might not even have been asked yet—but might be asked some time in the future. However, I have been urged by many friends to make it more widely available. It is a series of remembrances of individual activities, people, and events, by no means all inclusive.

Many times over the years I have been asked about my family background and about my fascinating career; about the international travel and contacts, and the events and activities in which I have had an opportunity to participate. Immodestly, I can say that overall my activities in many areas made a difference—for the better.

Economics is frequently referred to as the DISMAL SCIENCE. As a professional economist working in the domestic and international arenas, my work was anything but dismal. I have traveled widely in many countries, often accompanied by Flora, my wife. I have sat at the desks and even the tables of state and business leaders, and sometimes found myself involved in events that made headlines—particularly in Israel.

Often I am asked how I became so deeply involved with the Israeli scene. Here is the story.

I was a mid-level professional, a senior economist, in the U.S. Department of Agriculture and was bored as hell spending my working hours trying to figure out how the government could dispose of millions of tons of surplus farm products. Part of my boredom was a result of having to put up with several colleagues who were political appointees, basically uneducated, with an excess regard of their own importance, who managed to huff and bluff and puff and accomplish little or nothing.

In October 1946, Hadassah's Washington chapter held its annual Harvest Ball at the Mayflower Hotel. Flora's mother, Anna Blumenthal, was an active life member. Silently kicking and screaming, I agreed to attend this dress-up affair. The guest speaker was James MacDonald, the United States' High Commissioner to mandatory[1] Palestine. This occasion turned out to be a major turning point in my life.

MacDonald's speech about the situation in Palestine, vis-à-vis the Jews and the Arabs, and the British policy and program under the League of Nations mandate, had an immediate and profound impact on me. The next morning, I took an early train to New York City. My mother's sister, Marcella Kaplan, was the personal secretary to Gottlieb Hammer, the executive vice president of the Jewish Agency for Palestine. The Agency was responsible for spending funds raised by American Jewry for the resettlement and absorption of Jews in Palestine from all over the world, but primarily Holocaust survivors.

Marcella arranged an immediate appointment for me with Gott Hammer. I told him I was impressed with what I had heard the previous night and wanted to get involved in whatever way I could in the Jewish resettlement and absorption programs. I said I had a graduate degree in economics and talked to him about my work in agricultural economics. I told him I had learned a bit about low level arms in the U.S. Marines. I mentioned my Young Judea background and my parents' Zionist interests and activities.

Gott was interested and arranged for me to meet Rusty Jarko, head of Materials for Palestine, the group that was accumulating various types of "supplies" for shipment, often clandestine, to the Jewish agency in Tel Aviv. A meeting was also arranged with Teddy Kollek, who directed what was called the Hotel 14 operation. Teddy's function was to raise money, develop propaganda operations, and purchase much needed equipment for the settlements in Palestine. He had a small cadre of young, enthusiastic, highly devoted men and women around him carrying out various missions and operations. They were almost all in their twenties. Teddy later became a legend in his own time as mayor of Jerusalem.

Teddy quickly taught me that if one of the people around him had an idea that might facilitate the Hotel 14 operations, and if he liked it, that person had to be prepared to implement the idea. There were no spare bodies; no money to hire people to carry out other peoples' ideas. I also learned from Gott that Bob Nathan, one of the most respected economists in the United States, was a consultant to the Jewish Agency for economic and development policy. He, Oscar Gass, and Dan Kramer had recently published a report commissioned by the Agency entitled *Palestine, Problem and Promise*. It was an economic refutation of the British White Paper that argued that Palestine could not economically absorb 100,000 refugees. The report was later published as a book with the same title. Gott Hammer suggested that I should visit Bob.

Fortunately, I had direct access to him through my activities in the American Veterans Committee (AVC). I had been membership chairman of the Washington chapter, and later had had some membership responsibilities in the national organization. Bob was president of the Washington chapter and an officer and member of the board of directors of the national organization, so I had no trouble meeting with him. Bob Nathan was also president of a small group of economists that he had assembled as Robert R. Nathan Associates, Inc., one of the earliest economic consulting firms in the country.

Until May 14, 1948, the day that the new state of Israel was born, I remained an official of the U.S. Department of Agriculture, and made certain nothing in which I was involved outside of the office took any time from my government responsibilities. I also made sure that word of what I was doing on my own time got to the secretary of agriculture, Charles Brannon. He had no objections. Indeed, the understanding I had was that he approved of it. I never had a problem from that source.

From October 1946 to May 14, 1948, by moonlighting, I had an opportunity to work with Bob Nathan on several Agency economic analyses, reviews, and programs. I also worked with Oscar Gass, then part of Nathan Associates, on budget analysis to spend $125 million dollars appropriated by Congress for agricultural development in the Jewish settlements in Palestine. I also became involved with Gott Hammer and Teddy Kollek in minor projects, none of which took a lot of time.

Some projects with Bob required our traveling to New York together. These were exciting times to be with that great person, and great mind, and great heart. It was a tremendous learning experience for a young, wet-behind-the-ears, economist or idealist. One of the highlights of this period was assisting in the preparation of data for presentation to the United Nations by Abba Eban, Moshe Sharrett and others in the debate about the future of the British mandate in Palestine and the establishment of a Jewish state as envisioned in the Balfour Declaration.

It was a period of fierce debate at the UN between the friends of the Arabs and the friends of the Jews. Delegates, almost daily, signaled changes of position.[2] It was not at all clear that the Balfour Declaration would be honored and the Zionist dream of a Jewish homeland would become a reality if and when the British pulled out. In any case, there was a UN vote on November 27, 1947. The Arab bloc had an elaborate pleasure palace set up on the top floor of the New York Sherry-Netherland Hotel—girls, whiskey, food—everything that might be needed to influence the votes of the UN delegates.

The Jewish Agency had several suites in the same hotel. Agency representatives included Abba Eban, Moshe Sharrett, Eliahu Epstein (later Elath), Sy Kenen and others. Jewish Agency representatives fed the delegates a steady diet of statistics, political, economic, and social arguments, justifying the establishment of a Jewish State. This was fairly dry stuff relative to the hedonistic pleasures that the Arab bloc offered.

Despite almost hourly position changes by delegates the UN did vote to partition Palestine between the Arabs and the Jews. This decision did not provide even half a loaf—but it was the basis for establishing a Jewish state, alongside an Arab state. The plan was immediately accepted by the Jewish Agency representatives, and just as rapidly rejected by the Arab bloc. This Arab rejection meant war in Palestine.

With Gott Hammer's backing, I met with Eliahu Epstein at the Jewish Agency offices at 2210 Massachusetts Avenue, NW, Washington, D.C. several weeks before May 14, 1948, the impending date when the British would leave Palestine. As a result of that meeting, on that momentous date in modern Jewish history, I resigned on May 13, 1948 from the U.S. government, and went to work for the government of Israel as Executive Officer and Agricultural Advisor at the Israeli Mission. The State Department dragged its feet for almost a year before granting embassy and ambassadorial status to Israel's diplomatic office. This Mission/Embassy distinction was based on President Truman's prompt de facto recognition of the new State, rather than de jure recognition. Since I was not giving up my American citizenship, my second title was "agricultural advisor" rather than "attaché." The Mission took over the Jewish Agency building.

It was the beginning of many exciting experiences and a career of travel, meeting many wonderful, and some not so wonderful people and, as the saying goes, having a ball.

Although my principal international responsibility had to do with Israeli clients, over the years I worked in many other countries, including the Solomon Islands, the Philippines, Sri Lanka, Egypt, Sierra Leone, Ghana, Nigeria, Mexico, France, Italy, and Russia.

With a satisfying career, working with exceptional people, I believe I have had an impact on the lives of many people in various countries. The psychological returns to me were often more satisfying than the material ones.

Maurice D. Atkin

7/2/08

To VBRDE
with Thanks

Mary Attic

PART I

The Voyage Begins

1

Family Background

MY MOTHER, ROSE Abrams, was born on the lower east side of New York City. Her parents my maternal grandparents, Barnett (Beryl in Hebrew) and Gussie (Hassa in Hebrew) Saffron Abramowitz, came to the United States in 1881 from Riga, Latvia, as newlyweds.

When Barnett and Gussie arrived in the new world, they were accompanied by Barnett's mother and father, Zelda and Moses, as well as Barnett's brothers, Harry, Louie, Ike and Ben, and sisters, Mae, Tillie, and Bessie. Barnett was the eldest. For convenience, as was frequently done, Abramowitz was shortened to Abrams by all of the family except Barnett's brother Harry, who kept the original name. The change must have been made before my mother was born since her birth certificate shows her name as Abrams.

Gussie's mother, Geesa, had buried several husbands. Gussie had a younger half brother, Mendel Nonas, born in the United States. She also had a half sister, Elka, married to Mendel Atkin, my father's uncle who had come to the "Golden Medina" several years earlier. So both families were linked even before my parents knew each other.

Barnett and Gussie first lived in a typical lower east side New York cold water flat on Hester Street. They had six children, three of whom were born there.

David, their first born, was scalded to death as a toddler when he pulled a pot of boiling water from a stove on to himself.

3

Photo by Jonathan Atkin

FIGURE 1: The author's mother, Rose Atkin, circa 1981, age 85

Rose, my mother, was born in 1896, followed by Harry and Paula
(née Pearl). When Rose was four or five, the growing family, hoping to find better economic conditions, moved from New York City
to Hobart, N.Y., about 120 miles north of Manhattan. Rose's sisters,
Dorothy, Marcella, and Zelda were all born in Hobart. I, too, was
born there because my mother preferred the coolness of the Catskills
to the heat and humidity of Washington D.C. for the event. A village
of about 800 souls in Delaware County, Hobart is at the foothills of
the Catskill Mountains. The Delaware Creek, the headwater of the
Delaware Bay, ran through town and my grandparents' property. It
was at most seven or eight feet across. As a young boy, I used to visit

Hobart in the summer. My childhood recollection is of a huge, two-story, clapboard house with big, open porches all around, on a piece of land with a barn and a small farm. Some crops were raised on the property along with chickens. Actually, the 'crops' were vegetables for family consumption. They also kept a cow and a horse.

I remember jumping across the narrower part of the Delaware Creek, and climbing on the small dam near the center of the town. This dam provided a modest amount of electric power to the town. I can also remember the mournful sound of the milk train whistle as it made its early morning run picking up cans of milk from the numerous dairy farms.

Years later, when I was being interviewed for a job at the United States Department of Agriculture, when asked if I had ever lived on a farm, I replied, "I was born on a farm."

When I visited Hobart in my early thirties, I was amazed to see how small the house was, how close other houses were, and how small the porches were. But the Delaware Creek still ran right through the property.

In Hobart, grandpa Barnett engaged in various activities to support a growing family. These included buying poultry and produce from the local farmers and selling them to the summer vacation homes and hotels in the Catskills—possibly "buy for ten, sell for eleven, and make a one percent profit."

Unfortunately, Barnett was not the world's best businessman and life was a constant economic struggle, particularly with a growing family—even though Gussie had a vegetable garden and chickens.

My mother, Rose Abrams, at birth was named Rachel. But her Aunt Bessie said that she looked like a rose, and from then on she was Rose. She was very bright, winning many awards in school for spelling, literature and math. Most of the awards were books of poetry and literature. I still have some of them.

After graduating from Hobart High School, Rose went to Stamford Teachers Institute in Stamford, N.Y., received a teacher's certificate and taught elementary school in Hobart.

My mother, like my father, spent a lot of time in Washington Zionist affairs, particularly in the Pioneer Women's Organization. She took great pride in organizing the Golda Meir Club. On at least two separate occasions she was elected Rosh (president) of the chapter. The name of the organization was later changed to Na'amat.

My Father's Family

Joseph Atkin, my father, born in 1891, grew up in the *shtetl* (small village) of Cherea, Russia, about 80 kilometers southwest of Vitebsk in what is now Belarus. His parents, Shlomo (Solomon) and Rivka Atkin,[3] my paternal grandparents, operated a small distillery and general store. Reportedly, the Atkin family lived in the only two-story house in the village. Cherea, of course, was in 'The Pale.' This was the only area where Jews were generally permitted to live under Czarist Russia. Most of this special area is now part of Poland.

In Czarist Russia only two percent of Jewish boys, and none of the girls, were permitted to attend 'gymnasium' or high school. Joseph was among the privileged few Jews to be graduated from 'gymnasium.' In addition to Russian, Joseph spoke Yiddish, Hebrew, Polish, and several gypsy dialects. Gypsies were frequent travelers through the pale.

Joseph's *lantzmann* (immigrants from the same town), whom I met when I was a young boy, told stories of his leadership of the teenage Jewish youth in anti-pogrom activities. Family legend has it that Joseph in a defensive fight with a band of Russian Cossacks was shot and left Russia with a bullet wound in his thigh.

On April 5, 1911, Joseph Atkin, age 20, a new immigrant from Russia, arrived at Ellis Island aboard the *USS President Grant* from Hamburg, Germany. He was met at the Ellis Island ferry by his uncle Mendel Atkin who lived in Kingston, N.Y., about eleven miles from Hobart. It didn't take long for Joseph to meet his Aunt Elka's niece Rose.

In Hobart, while learning the English language and American ways, Joseph peddled merchandise to local farmers and farm products to hotels and summer homes. At first, transportation was by horse and wagon, or in the winter, by horse and sleigh. In a short time he bought and used a motor truck.

In 1915 Joseph, at age 24, went to Washington, D.C. to seek his fortune. He opened a small grocery store near North Capitol and

Thomas Streets, N.W. and lived in the back of the store. His partner, a Mr. Waldman, many years later became general foreman of Joseph's wholesale butter and egg business.

It was love at first sight between Rose and Joseph. In 1916, they were married in Brooklyn. The newlyweds honeymooned in Washington and stayed there. Their first apartment was on Thomas Street, N.W., just north of Florida Avenue.

FIGURE 2: The author's father, Joseph Atkin, circa 1931, age 40.

After a year in the store, Joseph took a job as a salesman with an old-line wasp dairy products distributing firm—Golden Company[4]— selling butter, cheese, and eggs to the Jewish mom and pop stores. Joseph did well. When a Mr. Sachs, who ran Golden Company, died in the flu epidemic, Joseph was able to buy the business, renamed the firm 'Joseph Atkin', and took over its established Elk Grove brand of butter, which enjoyed a superior local reputation. In subsequent years, and particularly when the Broadway musical *Big Butter and Egg Man* was popular, Joseph Atkin was frequently referred to in Washington business circles as the Big Butter and Egg Man.

The business prospered. At one time the firm ran a fleet of twenty-six trucks, brightly painted butter yellow with a large picture of a buck elk painted on the side panels, the same picture that was on every one pound carton of butter.

In the 1920s, the population of Washington was only 300,000 to 400,000 persons. So, Joseph Atkin, Butter, Eggs, and Cheese was a large business. Most of the grocery stores in the area were either small chain stores (A&P, Sanitary, which later became Safeway, and Piggly-Wiggly) or mom and pop stores located throughout the neighborhoods. Most of these were Jewish-owned, and the largest wholesaler of butter, eggs and cheese was Joseph Atkin. The firm also sold to hotels, restaurants, delicatessens, and occasionally had large government contracts.

With the depression in the 1930s, came massive unemployment. Grocers, hotel owners, and businessmen were unable to pay bills. Bankruptcies were epidemic. Firms, such as Joseph Atkin became victims of their customers' economic problems. Having substantial inventories with no market, Joseph's business suffered. He refused to take Chapter XI, or personal bankruptcy, as the easy way out. Unlike today, bankruptcy then was a stigma. Business was picking up by 1934. However, in that year a stomach ailment was diagnosed as cancer of the bladder, a long, painful, agonizing illness, which my father fought for the next four years. He died in August, 1938.

While Joseph's vocation was in business, at heart he was an intellectual with a prodigious memory. He was able to quote at length from the Talmud, as well as the works of Sholom Aleichem, Gorky, and other Russian writers. Often he debated Biblical points with local rabbis, frequently being the devil's advocate for the sheer joy of the debate. Religiously he was agnostic, but proud of being a Jew; and he was an ardent Zionist. He and Zalman Henkin, also a Russian Jewish immigrant, were responsible for organizing Paole Zion in Washington.

My father had a penchant for bright colors, his favorite being fire-engine red, particularly in automobiles. Fortunately this was tempered by Rose, who incidentally, was one of the earliest women drivers in the city.

He was also an aficionado of opera and musical comedies, frequently taking trips to New York to see the latest. He loved fishing, golf, and bridge and was good at them.

Joseph had three brothers, Philip, Israel, and Grisha and two sisters, Gita, and Shulama. He brought his brother, Philip, to the United States in 1915. Except for his uncle Itzek who had arrived about 1921, the rest of the family remained in Russia. In 1931, twenty years after his arrival in the U.S., Joseph visited Russia to see his family. At that time he learned about the well kept secret of Soviet Jewish purges, official pogroms, and the near starvation conditions in Stalin's 'peoples' paradise.'

In the year 2000, following more than a fifty year search, I located my father's cousins in Moscow and St. Petersburg. It is interesting to quote parts of family history sent to me by my first cousin, Abram Mazo, concerning Joseph's leaving Russia in 1911, and in 1931 when he visited as a tourist.

> Josif's mother would often tell stories about Josif . . . how the military tribunal sentenced him to hard labor for distributing revolutionary pamphlets among the Tzar's soldiers in 1905. He decided to flee and came home to his parents one night under cover of darkness. They hid him in the hay loft for several days, and then one day the police chief arrived. Grandma and grandpa were able to reach an understanding with him, certain transactions took place, and instead of hard labor Josif was given three days to get out of town. There was only one place to go— America.
>
> In 1931, Uncle Josif came to visit us in Lenegrad. My mother then took him back to Chereya to see his mother. He had been greatly impressed by what he had seen in Lenegrad, par-

ticularly by the model kolkhoses (collectives) but his euphoria quickly evaporated when he reached Chereya and saw the fruits of collectivization unadorned. The local peasants, whom he had known since early childhood, came to see him, barefoot and hungry, and complained bitterly of their fate. My mother accompanied him to the Polish border where he abandoned Russia a second time.

❧

August 18, 1938, my father, only 47 years old, died. In December, 1938, my grandfather Barnett Abrams died unexpectedly of a heart attack at 65 years. My grandmother, Gussie lived until age 91. Joseph, Barnett, and Gussie are buried in side-to-side graves in the Tifereth Israel section of the Columbia Lodge Cemetery in Anacostia, D.C. abutting both Adas Israel and the Washington Hebrew Congregation cemeteries. My mother died on October 30, 1990 at the age of 94. She is buried at Judean Gardens in Olney, Maryland.

2

Growing Up

I WAS BORN ON July 9, 1917. My mother had returned to the Abrams family home in Hobart, to her mother for the birth. I was named Maurice David, after my maternal great grandfather, Moshe Abramowitz, and David Abrams the first born of my maternal grandparents Gussie and Barnett, scalded to death as a toddler. At the end of August, 1917, Rose returned to Washington with her new-born.

FIGURE 3: Two-month-old Maurice D. Atkin

One of my earliest recollections, when I was only three or four years old, was living at 505 Columbia Rd., N.W., very near Soldiers Home. I remember vividly my parents' bedroom, the large second floor front room with its off-white furniture and especially the rocker that I guess was my security blanket. I also recall picnics on the grounds of Soldiers Home with my mother, and sometimes my father or a domestic. What fun it was to play on the rolling hills around the large duck pond, feed the ducks and pick violets.

When I was four or five years old, my grandparents, Barnett and Gussie, moved from Hobart to Washington with their brood: Harry, Pearl, Dorothy, Marcella, and Zelda. They resided with us temporarily in the Columbia Road house. Shortly thereafter, Barnett bought a large house on Quincy Street, N.W. just east of 14th. In Washington, Barnett was in the scrap metal business in a small way.

In addition to the immediate Abrams family, there were other relatives living at the Quincy Street house as boarders, including cousin Morris Abrams (great-uncle Harry Abramowitz's son) from Bridgeport, Connecticut. He was working and attending law school. He and my uncle, Harry Abrams (Rose's brother), shared a room. I can still hear the verbal battles between those two.

About 1922–23, my parents bought a new house around the corner from my grandparents' home on Quincy Street, at 3821 13th St. N.W., and we moved from Columbia Road. This 13th Street residence was my home—along with assorted pets (dogs, cats, pigeons, fish, etc.)—for almost 20 years.

In 1927, Barnett and Gussie, and their children moved to 1307 Randolph St., N.W., about a block away, still near our home.

Our next door neighbors, the Dave and Stella Walsh family, were devout Irish Catholics, and good neighbors. We remained friends for many years even after moving away from that area. On the other side of our house was a German Catholic family named Wintermeyer with whom we had little contact.

When we first moved to 13th Street, the paved road ran only to Spring Road. We lived two blocks further north. When it rained the dirt road in front of our house became a sea of mud. When I was about nine or ten the road was paved. As this was done in the summer all the neighborhood kids enjoyed the water sprinklers set up to keep the top of the cement wet while the bottom set. This substituted for the non-existent neighborhood swimming pools that summer.

As a youngster, I had the usual childhood illnesses including chicken pox, mumps, mastoiditis, and measles, and also wrist and nose fractures. When I was about fourteen, I had a very serious case of nephritis, from which at one point it was expected that I would not recover. My body was bloated with fluids and my blood pressure was astronomical Our own family physician had thrown up his hands. Fortunately, our neighbors, the Walshes had told their physician, Francis Xavier Courtney, about my condition.

Dr. Courtney asked my parents if he could examine me. They welcomed him. He placed me on an extremely rigid diet, the main part of which was to drink several gallons of plain water a day to try to force flush the kidneys. In addition there was to be absolutely no salt or meat of any kind in my diet, and very little roughage. I could not have fatty foods, nor carbonated drinks. It was not easy to drink gallons of water a day. But after several days, I became a conduit and the blockage was broken. After a couple of months I was given a tablespoon of mashed and pureed boiled chicken breast. It was the most delicious food that I have ever had.

Dr. Courtney, who had no children, was on the board of the Georgetown University Medical School. He wanted me to study medicine and was prepared to see that I had a scholarship to do so. However, I had no desire to be a doctor, and let this opportunity go by.

When I was a teenager I was very active in Troop 73 Boy Scouts of America. For one year I was Scoutmaster of 73, the only Jewish Boy Scout troop in Washington. Some members of the troop were Sol and Eugene Love, J. Leon Helfgott, Sol Oremland, Aaron Yockelson, the brothers George and Marvin Tievsky, Jack Kay, Burt Pear, Jessie Weinstein, and Martin Myers.

In addition to the Scouts I was also active in Young Judea, and the Olympians—a sports/social club. The Olympians included Sonny Abramson, Allen Henkin, Mel Werksman, Ellis Burka, and Dave Chiome. The Jewish Community Center at 16th and Q streets, N.W. was the meeting locale for all three groups.

In the 1920s and 30s, Washington was a southern town with two school systems, one was for whites, one for blacks. The facilities for blacks were run-down old buildings, and their books were those cast off by white schools. Theaters, movies, hotels, restaurants, amusement parks, and swimming pools all observed the southern practice of separation. Even in government buildings, rest rooms were labeled "colored" and "white." This was also true at the soda fountains in every drug store. Such was the culture in which I grew up—and which bothered me very much

In the summer much of my time was spent out of doors, frequently swimming in the Severn River and the Chesapeake Bay. My exposure to the summer sun meant rapid and deep tanning to the point that I was darker than some African-Americans. With my deep tan and dark curly hair, I often was exposed to anti-Negro racism. A few incidents follow.

On one occasion my cousin Morris Atkin and I were returning from a trip downtown. Morris was very blond and fair skinned. I was just the opposite, as I had just come back to the city from Boy Scout camp and was deeply tanned. We boarded a crowded streetcar for the trip home. (No busses and no subways then.) One seat was available. I took it. My seat companion was a lamplighter. (At that time the street lights were gas lit. Every evening a gas lighter would make the rounds and light the lamps. In the morning a lamplighter would turn off the lights.)

As I sat down, this man got up and not realizing that Morris and I were together, whispered something to him. Morris laughed, but said nothing to me. Later I asked him what the man had said to make him laugh.

"He said that I could have his seat. He wasn't going to sit next to no nigger."

Another encounter! I was thirteen and had just returned to the city, deeply tanned, after several weeks at Camp Roosevelt, the Boy Scout camp on the Chesapeake Bay. On the Saturday after my return to the city, I was in the ticket line at the Earle Theater on 13th street, Northwest, between F and E streets. This is now the Warner. It was one of the old style plush art deco movie houses of the area.

An usher, resplendent in a red and gold uniform, called me out of the line.

"We don't sell tickets to Negroes." he said.

With some degree of chutzpah and anger I demanded to see the theater manager. There was some stalling, but finally an assistant manager came out to see me. I told him what had happened, then removed a wrist band from my wrist and showed him the two inch wide stripe of white flesh where the wrist band had been. I said I was going to report the incident to my father, who knew the owner of the movie house. The assistant manager was most apologetic and I was admitted to the movie free. Later, I received a batch of complimentary tickets.

The incident did not do much for racial equality, but it gave me more insight into what black teenagers had to put up with.

The American Veterans Committee (AVC), a liberal post-World War II veterans organization, believed in, and actively fought for racial equality. For several years I was membership chairman of the Washington chapter. This was where I first met Robert R. Nathan, who was president of the chapter.

⋟

My sisters, Shulamith Zelda and Greta Ruth, were both born in Washington, in 1923 and 1928 respectively, at Sibley Memorial Hospital then located on North Capital Street near L Street. Shulamith, whose name came from the Song of Songs, which our father loved, later legally changed it to Shom. Greta's middle name was from the Book of Ruth. When Greta was born our father bought her a beautiful, limited-edition, illustrated copy of "The Book of Ruth." Both Shom and Greta were named after deceased sisters of our father.

When I was about nine years old, my parents purchased a plot of land at Herald Harbor, Maryland, on the Severn River, on which they built a small summer cottage. This is where I acquired my first boat and developed a love for the water and fishing, particularly fishing with my father from a small rowboat.

Growing up in Washington, I attended Petworth Elementary School, McFarland Junior High, and Central High School. Washington was a southern town. Its school system was segregated. Division I was for whites, Division II was for blacks. In addition to my public schooling, I attended Adas Israel Congregation Sunday School, first in the synagogue at Sixth and Eye Streets, N.W., and later when the

Sunday school needed more space, at the Jewish Community Center at 16th and Q, N.W. I also attended after-school cheder (Hebrew school) at Tefereth Israel synagogue, 14th and Euclid Streets, N.W. three days a week. An old time would-be rabbi tried to teach me to read Hebrew. His methods were so old-country that I developed a reading bloc against what I have later come to recognize as a beautiful and expressive language.

In elementary school, my third grade teacher, Miss Thompson, was an especially inspiring instructor. I also remember another teacher who was a purple-headed anti-Semite. Following the practice of the day, I was pushed ahead one and a half years. As a result I was younger than most graduating from elementary school.

In junior high, I was on the track team, played in the band, wrote for the school newspaper, and was president of the school museum. At Central High, I also played in the band, wrote and photographed for the school newspaper, and was active in several school clubs. It was also at Central that I entered an essay contest sponsored by the political opinion magazine, *Foreign Affairs*. The prize was a four year college scholarship. My topic was "Japan and the Open Door Policy." I won first honorable mention. Close, but no cigar.

In June 1934, I was graduated from Central High a month before I turned 17. I applied for admittance to Harvard and Antioch, and was admitted to Antioch. Harvard turned down my application for the Littauer School, but indicated that if I reapplied for a business course, I would be admitted. Unfortunately, during the last months of my senior year in high school, my father was stricken with an agonizing bladder cancer. I changed my plans. Just before the semester started I enrolled at the University of Maryland's College Park campus.

In college, I enrolled in a liberal arts curriculum. I wrote for the campus newspaper, *The Diamondback*, played a cornet (poorly) in the marching band, joined Tau Epsilon Phi fraternity, and played intramural baseball. As I needed to pay my own way through college, I worked weekends, vacations, and often during the school week at a wide variety of jobs. And of course, like most normal teenagers, I had a well rounded social life, including parties, dances, picnics, theater and concerts.

Four years later, 1938, I received a Bachelor of Science degree with honors. I was then awarded the university's largest graduate fellowship, $800 per year, plus tuition, and even a space in the School of Agriculture's parking lot.

Four months later, and two months after my father's death, Dean Samuel DeVault called me in to his office and told me that my fellowship was being rescinded. I was shocked, and not a little disturbed. I thought that I had been doing well in my studies and in my assigned teaching. In the next thirty seconds, Dr. DeVault smiled and said that I was being given an appointment as Assistant Land Use Planning Specialist for the State of Maryland, salary $2,000 per year plus tuition. My duties were to continue my graduate courses and to be available to assist Jim Coddington, the State Land Use Planning Specialist on anything where I could be helpful. Wow! This was a position with a salary. It also alleviated some of my immediate financial problems.

I was awarded the degree of Master in Business Administration, majoring in cooperative economics in 1941.

In May, 1938, I had turned down an offered blind date with a Flora Blumenthal for a Tau Epsilon Phi fraternity dance. She came to the dance with Eli Elvove, a close friend of mine. That same evening I told her I was going to marry her. One can imagine what she thought of me then.

Perseverance paid off. On December 25, 1941, she became Mrs. Maurice Atkin. We wanted Eli to be my best man. However, Lt. Col. Elvove was then serving on General Douglas McArthur's staff in the Philippines.

Flora, too, had her experiences with anti-Negro racism.

Shortly after she and I were married in 1941, while teaching at private schools and a community center, she applied to teach modern dance at several colleges and universities in the Washington area. The dance instructor at Howard University, a 'colored' school, was pregnant and would not return the next semester. I suggested that she apply there. She did, and was immediately offered a position.

Although the opportunity was enticing, Flora had been raised in a socially conservative family whose contacts with Negroes were mainly with the *schwartzes* (colored maids) that worked for them as house servants. At Bennington College, in Vermont, where she had been enrolled in a modern dance program the summer before we were married, the dormitories were mixed, as was the student body. And in AVC we had several Negro friends with whom we enjoyed socializing.

If Flora taught at Howard, "What would the family think?" This was something a nice Jewish girl did not do. "What would the family's friends think?" And more importantly, would she be denied job offers at other schools, as a result, particularly the better private ones?

At that time, Flora was also directing the dance department at the Jewish Community Center in Washington. "What would her boss there think and do?" These were real gut-wrenching questions, considering the social structure of the community. Flora discussed it with the executive director, the indomitable Eddie Rosenbloom. His answer was "It's all right to work there, but don't tell anybody." She took the job, and did not keep it a secret.

A year later, Flora initiated a dance symposium at the JCC and invited groups from all the recreational institutions in Washington, including the Juanita K Nye House, which catered to blacks primarily. The program and audience were obviously mixed, but all went well, and the symposium was most successful. The ice was broken. Flora had moved Washington one small step towards desegregation.

I am pleased to report that my encouraging Flora to take the Howard job was good for both of us. For her, it was pushing the social envelope in the community. It was also a most interesting and satisfying experience. She learned that African-American students are students, just like those on any other campus. For me it was an extension of my beliefs, and the extra paycheck Flora brought home didn't hurt.

3

Roots of a Professional Career

GROWING UP IN Washington, D.C., during the 20s and 30s, I worked at various week-end, after-school, and vacation jobs. It was what young and teenage boys did.

While in elementary school I earned my spending money by selling subscriptions to popular publications—*The Saturday Evening Post, Ladies Home Journal,* and *Boy's Life.* I paid three and a half cents, and collected five cents for most of the magazines. In order to collect, several visits to the customer were often necessary, not always easy. In addition to our earnings though, we 'salespersons' were awarded, depending upon our sales volume, coupons of various colors which entitled us to prizes. Ten brown coupons could be redeemed for a canteen. We could get a Swiss knife or a tent for a given number of 'greenies' or 'goldies.' A good salesperson who pursued it long enough might earn enough points for a bicycle.

Along with Morris Atkin, my father's first cousin, but my age, I delivered groceries and other packages in my red coaster wagon. We went from the Arcade Market, on 14th Street near Park Road, N.W. to peoples' homes for a distance of three or four blocks for whatever tips they were prepared to pay—usually ten or twenty cents. A quarter was a bonanza. This remuneration method taught me the value of negotiating and setting a price before the act. Arcade Market was the precursor of contemporary malls. It was a large enclosed area containing about 100 stalls with all types of meats, vegetables, fruit, baked goods, flowers, fish, and other food stuffs. Each of the stalls was operated by a different owner. I can still smell the wonderful aromas. The market was about eight blocks from where I lived. Rather than take the wagon home each night we arranged overnight storage at the A & W Root Beer near the market. This stand, the first one of its type, was operated by a young man named Willard Marriott, the founder of the Marriott hotel and food empire.

In addition to selling magazines and delivering groceries, I shoveled snow in the winter and in the summer mowed lawns.

High school and college years brought other part-time job opportunities, including lifeguarding at Herald Harbor, Maryland, a summer resort on the Severn River where my parents had a cottage. At a Sears Roebuck store I first worked assembling bicycles, and then as a sales clerk. Starting at twenty-five cents an hour, after a short time, I was given a ten percent raise to twenty-seven and a half cents an hour, which I thought was great. At my father's wholesale dairy products plant I packed and wrapped prints of butter in specialized parchment paper. I could wrap as fast as any of the full-time employees. Even before I was old enough to have a driver's license, I often drove one of my father's delivery trucks. One of the most sought after, best paying jobs—a dollar compared to twenty-five and thirty cents an hour for other jobs—was sorting and delivering U.S. mail during the Christmas rush. These vacation jobs supplemented a rather meager, sometimes allowance.

During my undergraduate college years at the University of Maryland, 1934–1938, my varied jobs included part-time truck driving (I had a permit by then), weekend lifeguarding, tutoring high school students in geometry, and slaving, in May 1936, in the dairy department of the first Giant food store in Washington, making $15 a week for ten hour days. I was rescued from this drudgery by Dr. Phillip Hauser, an official in the U.S. Census Bureau (later director). Phil later married my mother's sister Zelda. When Flora and I were married in 1941, Phil was my best man. He was instrumental in getting me a temporary summer senior clerk's job in Dr. Ed Berman's economic analysis shop at the Department of Labor. The salary was $30 a week with benefits. Berman was one of the country's leading labor economists. At the end of the summer, he asked me to stay on. I thankfully declined and returned to full time classes. This summer work was an exceptional experience for a young college student.

In 1936, while still in college, I worked for the *Washington Post* newspaper, first soliciting subscriptions by telephone, and later writing obits, and covering small accidents and fires. I started at $14 a week. Within three weeks this was raised to $18. I was on cloud nine. For the work, I needed a car. The *Post* paid me a car allowance sufficient to buy a much used 1932 Plymouth coupe for $125.00. A consequence of that job was that it qualified me to become a member of the E-street Club, people who had worked at the *Post* when it was located on E street, N.W.

Altogether these experiences provided the wherewithal for a teenager to do things that otherwise might not have been possible, particularly during the Great Depression years, 1930–1934, when unemployment reached record levels of twenty-five percent and people were curtailing their expenditures, even for food. A gallon of gasoline was 12 to 15 cents, a hamburger and root beer at the local (Marriott) Hot Shoppe 25 cents, a double-decker ice cream cone 5 to 10 cents, first-class postage was 2 cents, a seat in the National Theatre second balcony 55 cents, and a new car could be bought for $700.00. A top government salary was $10,000.

It was in my sophomore and junior years in college that I hit my big economic successes. The *Jewish Ledger,* now the *Jewish Week*, used to publish pages and pages of New Year and Chanukah greetings from individuals to all their friends for one dollar per message. Payment for a high percentage of these had not been made, and in my sophomore year in college, I responded to an ad in the *Ledger* for an ad collector. There was no salary, no guarantee, just 25 percent of the amount collected. With little exception, people paid when I knocked on their doors. They had not bothered to pay because writing a check and mailing it was a hassle, and many families did not have checking accounts.

The *Ledger* then asked me if I wanted to collect for delinquent general advertising, with a graduated commission, up to 90 percent, depending upon the age of the delinquency. Within a month I was making $50 to $60 a week, and could not handle the volume alone. I enlisted several of my fraternity brothers (Tau Epsilon Phi) as collectors. My take from them was 25 percent of what they earned. I was in economic heaven. With little effort I was making almost $100 a week for the six or seven months that this operation kept going.

At the end of my sophomore year I bought my first convertible, a 1936 Plymouth, for six hundred dollars. It had a radio, heater, and was only a year old, and it looked like a cream puff. It also had a rumble seat. This was an arrangement where the hatch on the rear storage area opened from the front instead of the rear, revealing a seat, making the car a four-passenger one instead of a two-passenger. In good weather it was a great ride.

The big "hit" of my junior year, 1937, had to do with the packing and storage of the seasonal spring egg abundance to insure supplies during the fall and winter shortage. Eggs were delivered to grocery stores, hotels, and restaurants in 30 dozen wooden crates. The crates were divided into two sections. Each section held five layers of three dozen eggs separated by soft cardboard fillers and flats. (Today eggs are generally packed in cartons of different sizes—one dozen, eight eggs, six eggs.)

Generally, the merchants trashed the empty crates. So, I borrowed one of my father's trucks in the summer, fall and winter, and when not in school, I would visit the retail stores and restaurants and offer to take the empty crates, fillers and flats off their hands. Keeping only the clean ones I was able to accumulate and fill five garages that I rented for $5.00 per month per garage. Come spring and high seasonal egg producing period, egg packers and shippers had a huge appetite for clean crates, fillers, and flats. Guess who cleaned up.

These successful acquisitive spurts had to be put aside upon graduation in June, 1938. It was time for graduate school and to start a professional career. My immediate concern about my future was sharpened when I lost my father two months later in August, 1938. I was 21 years old, had a widowed mother and two sisters ages 15 and 10. For some unfathomable reason, my father who covered many business risks with insurance had refused to buy life insurance. The net value of the business, just coming out of the depression was not much. My father's extended illness strained family finances and there were large, unpaid medical bills.

The doctors and hospitals had great compassion and settled my father's outstanding bills for a fraction of their face amount. To meet day to day costs my mother opened our home to a few of the college graduates who were flooding into Washington in 1939, to work in the

1940 census. The Jewish Community Center had a roster of Jewish homes available for Jewish young men and women. All of her boarders were intelligent and serious people. Dinner table discussions were stimulating and often fun though many of them had to do with the war brewing in Europe. Several of these young men and women became my lifelong friends.

In 1940, I applied for and received a position in the U.S. Department of Agriculture as a junior agricultural economist, salary $2,000. I suspect that the appointment was made partially in recognition of the cooperative work that my father had done with the Department in improving methods of poultry and dairy marketing. He was the first to market eggs in cartons, each carton stamped with the date that the eggs had been graded, he was the first to cooperate in setting up poultry marketing cooperatives in Virginia and guarantee a better return for the farmers than they had been receiving. In 1941, when I received a Master of Business Administration degree in agricultural economics and cooperatives, I was promoted to an associate economist salary, $2600.

Though I had a military deferment due to my responsibilities in the Department of Agriculture, in December, 1942 I enlisted in the United States Marine Corps Reserve. I was honorably discharged four months later. My discharge stated, "By Special Order of the Commandant."

Early part time jobs gave me invaluable insights, experience, and contacts that were the building blocks which led to a satisfying career. During that career, I believe I made a positive difference to hundreds of thousands of people. The psychological riches were tremendous, even more important than the material benefits.

FIGURE 4: Flora and Maury, 1943

FIGURE 5: Family: Jonathan, Joseph, Carol, Barrie,
Maury, Flora. Circa 1968 on Lake Michigan

PART II

Love Affair with Israel

4

Life in the Embassy

MAY 14, 1948! As anticipated, the British Mandatory Government of Palestine lowered the British flags and departed. David Ben Gurion, secretary general of the Jewish Agency proclaimed the rebirth, after 2,000 years, of the State of Israel. In Jerusalem, Tel Aviv, and Haifa Jews danced in the streets. There was also dancing in the streets of New York, Baltimore and Washington.

In Washington, D.C. the Jewish Agency for Palestine had a political office at 2210 Massachusetts Avenue, NW. Eliahu Epstein, a professor of Middle East Studies at the Hebrew University, Jerusalem, headed up this office.

FIGURE 6: Left, Joey Atkin assists Ambassador Elath in planting a tree at the first Israel Embassy in Washington

On May 14, 1948, the Jewish Agency building became the government of Israel Mission to the United States. Although President Truman had promptly extended recognition to the new state of Israel, the office was neither an embassy nor a legation. This recognition was "de facto" not "de jure." It should be remembered that the personnel then dealing with the mid-east at the U.S. State Department, were almost all Arabists. The Mid-East Activities Section did everything possible to drag its feet in setting up diplomatic relations with the new entity—Israel. Not until six or eight months later was the status changed from Mission to Embassy with Eliahu Epstein as ambassador rather than head of Mission.

By pre-arrangement, on the 13th of May, 1948, I resigned my position as a senior economist from the USDA and reported to Eliahu Epstein (later changed to Elath) to assume my duties and responsibilities as the executive officer (EO) and agricultural advisor to the new Israel Mission to the United States. As an American citizen, technically I could not use the diplomatic term 'attaché.' However as far as the Mission was concerned, and the authorities in Israel, I was the agricultural attaché, and treated as such—in addition to my more demanding, at that time, role as executive officer. I took a significant salary cut, as well as gave up job perks to join the Mission.

What was the executive officer? What was my function? The executive officer basically was responsible for the mission's operation from the economic or business standpoint. The EO hired and fired local non-diplomatic staff, arranged for furniture, heat, light, telephones and vehicles. The EO's office was also responsible for arranging adequate office space for the expanding diplomatic staff. Keeping in mind that most of the arriving staff and families had had no previous experience in the United States, let alone in Washington, it was often necessary to assist in finding housing, locating schools, and securing medical service. How to get a driver's license, what were fair and reasonable prices to pay for such items as TV sets, cars, clothes and a million other items that arriving strangers needed, or thought they needed, fell within the purview of my office.

Often budgetary considerations interfered with Embassy operations. Some of the diplomats thought they were entitled to perks that their counterparts in other embassies enjoyed, such as better office facilities and personal housing. For the most part this was a minor annoyance. The Israelis were generally understanding and accepting, although there were instances of complaints and griping mostly from the wives. We did everything possible to make their stay in America as comfortable as possible.

Setting up the Embassy

For ease of writing I use the term Embassy, although for most of the first year we were a Mission.

On the historic May 14th, 2210 Massachusetts Avenue had very limited personnel. On site were Eliahu Elath and his wife Zahava, two secretaries, an African—American couple who performed as janitor/cook/cleaners and often provided soothing encouragement to the diplomatic staff when the military situation in Israel looked dark. There was also a small press office staffed, temporarily, by the son-in-law of Jorge Garcia Granados, the Guatemalan ambassador to the United Nations. Garcia Granados had been most instrumental in bringing about the affirmative vote of the UN in November, 1947. His intense interest in Israel and concern about fairness to the Jews were much the result of his association with his neurosurgeon, the late Dr. Harvey Ammerman, a committed Zionist and a mensch. There may have been one or two other Israeli staff persons, but I do not remember them.

The first days at the Embassy were terribly busy. Eighteen-hour days and Saturday and holiday work were not unusual. The Washington Jewish community was most helpful in acclimating and welcoming the staff. Israel had no Embassy residence for the ambassador. Judge David Bazelon graciously lent his lovely home on Linnean Drive in northwest Washington. Joe Cherner, the largest Ford dealer in the area, arranged discount purchases of a Mercury sedan for general office use, and a Lincoln limousine as the official Embassy car. Saul and Sam Stern of Stern Office Furniture were very helpful in helping us acquire office equipment. Abe Kay, owner of Indian Spring Country Club, extended complimentary memberships to the staff.

Funds for operating the Mission were practically non-existent. Among the first items on my agenda was opening a bank account. In the first four or five months no funds whatsoever came from Israel or from the Jewish Agency in New York to pay staff salaries or buy supplies. We operated without any payroll transfers being made for quite some time. When I complained by cable and telephone to Israel I was told "The Commander in Chief of the air force has no planes. Find the money locally." The money we urgently needed was about thirty-thousand dollars. By begging and borrowing from local Jewish Zionists, such as Abe Kay, Joe Cherner, Isador Breslau and Isador Turover, I was able to meet the payrolls and stay financially current. Later, a system of fund transfers and budget approvals was worked out and the immediate problem was alleviated, although there was never really enough money to be able to do the job that needed to be done. That was one of the challenges of the operation.

As expected, Israeli staff started to arrive.

The first new arrivals were Uriel Heyd, the first secretary, comparable to minister counselor, with his wife Shoshana, and two very blond sons, Michael and David, aged 5 and 3. My office arranged for a rental residence on Olive Street in Silver Spring, Md. for the family as well as for driving lessons for Uriel and Shoshana. Once they passed the D.C. driving test I helped them purchase a car.

Uriel, before coming to Washington, had been a professor at the Hebrew University, Jerusalem, working closely with Eliahu Epstein. His sons, Michael and David, many years later also were professors at the Hebrew University. The Heyd and Atkin families became very fast friends which continued with their children even after Uriel and Shoshana had both died.

About six months later Col. Ephriam Ben-Artzy, military attaché, arrived with his wife, Victoria. As a member of the famous Jewish Brigade, he had received his military training from the British, and honed it in the Haganah. Ben-Artzy was promoted to Brigadier while on duty at the Embassy. He brought his own one-man staff, a young man by the name of Friedman, who was also in the army. I never knew his rank but he was a devoted and loyal operator for Ben-Artzy.

"Haizie" Zinder came as the press attaché. Haizie was an American who had made aliyah to Israel. He had worked in the Jewish Agency's UN delegation during the trying days of the debates in New

York. He and his wife, Chemda, a sabra (native born Israeli), also had two children.

A second secretary, Arthur Liverhant, arrived with his mother. Arthur, a bachelor, was very orthodox. He initially objected to the use of Hebrew for commerce or casual conversation, preferring Yiddish for such purposes. However, he soon got over this. Occasionally, however, his orthodoxy caused some intra-staff friction that was more amusing than harmful.

The African-American couple, mentioned earlier, lived in the building. They were somewhat older than anyone else on the staff with the possible exception of Eliahu. They were the building's housekeepers and also prepared staff lunches. In true democratic fashion, generally all the staff ate lunch together in the embassy. They were excellent meals. The staff was small, cohesive, and loyal.

Two Areas of Special Importance: Arms and Food.

In the early days the political and military security of the new State of Israel was far from assured. On Independence Day, five Arab armies, intent upon throwing the Jews into the sea invaded the Jewish territory. There were times when it appeared doubtful that the undermanned, under-supplied Israel defense forces could hold off the combined Arab onslaughts. The world was surprised when the Israel Defense Force, previously the Haganah, was successful in defeating all five Arab armies.

Like others in the embassy, as well as in Teddy Kollek's Hotel 14 group, and in Rusty Jarko's Materials for Palestine, I had some responsibility for obtaining and paying for some of the arms for the under-armed, under-manned military force. Having been in the U.S. Marine Corps, although only for a short time, I was familiar with the small arms that were available. Working with my old friend Rusty Jarko, I helped locate, ship and pay for the type of arms that were most needed. These came predominantly from the U.S. (clandestinely), Mexico, Czechoslovakia, and France.

One miserable March evening, while we were living in Silver Spring, Maryland, there was a knock on our door. I opened the door to two men shivering on the front stoop. They showed me U.S. Treasury papers and badges identifying themselves as Treasury agents. They said they wanted to ask me some questions, and since they had no search warrant I was free to refuse. Having no reason to do so, I invited them into the house.

As soon as they came in and looked around the living room, one of them said, "This doesn't look like the house of a millionaire." I agreed with him, and told him it certainly was not the house of a millionaire. He asked how I explained fairly recent bank deposits in several Washington banks of varying amounts totaling several million dollars. My name was the only name on the account.

I immediately told them that not a penny of the deposits was mine, that these accounts were funds collected privately from American Jews to support the Israel defense forces. They thanked me, and left.

The next morning I went to the executive offices of the White House and saw David Niles, one of President Truman's advisors. I told Mr. Niles about the episode. He said, "Not to worry." That was the last I heard of it.

As soon as the State was established and the Arab armies attacked, well intentioned people all over the United States sent packages to the Mission containing handguns, rifles and odd lots of ammunition. These were appreciated gestures, but for the most part generally useless as equipment for Israel's needs. A military group requires a high degree of standardization. It would have been an impossible situation if the personnel in a unit were equipped with varying types of firearms and calibers of ammunition. Nevertheless, these items were shipped to the Ministry of Defense in Israel for its judgment as to disposition.

We also received large quantities of "Physicians Samples" of medicines and drugs. These samples usually had two or three pills in a sample box. The cost of shipping these few pills in their sample containers would have been prohibitive. To have removed them from the sample containers and accumulate meaningful quantities of the different individual drugs would also have been very expensive in terms of time, even if done by volunteers, and extremely costly if done with paid workers. Medically, it would have been unwise to repackage without costly professional supervision. These too, were sent to Materials for Israel for disposition.

At one point, before Col. Ben-Artzy was on scene, the commander of the Israel Air Force asked Ambassador Eliahu Elath to get some information about an aircraft called the Berliner Aircoupe, and specifically could one safely solo in the craft after twenty minutes of instruction as was advertised. The plane was built in a facility at the College Park, Maryland airport, just outside of Washington.

Eliahu asked me if I would go to College Park and "check it out."

So, dutifully, I went to the Berliner plant, with Uriel Heyd along for moral support. The plane was a small single engine low speed craft of stretched and varnished canvas over wooden and aluminum frames. The controls were very simple. It had a tricycle type landing gear. It was very light weight. And yes, after fifteen minutes of flying instruction, I soloed in the advertised twenty minutes. Uriel agreed with me that for Israel's needs it was not a practical aircraft. But I enjoyed the experience.

Uriel and I shared many embassy experiences together. On one occasion, the ambassador had been invited to visit a "chalutz" training farm in New Jersey. He asked me to make the visit as his representative. Uriel agreed to go with me after I suggested that his rank would be much more impressive than mine to the boys and girls who were planning for a life on an Israeli kibbutz. When we arrived we were dismayed at the almost slovenly conditions in which the livestock as well as the personnel were living. While thanking the group for the invitation, and encouraging them to learn as much about modern agriculture as possible before making aliyah to Israel, we not so gently told them that the conditions on the farm were a far cry from how cattle were raised and people lived in Israel. On the drive home, Uriel expressed shock at the concepts that these young people had about kibbutz life.

Food

Once the Embassy's operating structure was functioning, I turned to the problem of alleviating the acute shortage of food in the new state. The population was increasing dramatically on a daily basis as the

Jewish refugee camps in Europe and Cyprus were being emptied. The food problem became even worse with the large migrations of Jews from North Africa, Yemen, and to a lesser extent, South America and South Africa. My ten years in the U.S. Department of Agriculture proved invaluable.

The "land of milk and honey," except for extensive acreage in citrus groves, was basically sand and rock spread over almost all of the area that the Jews claimed as Israel. Some grains were grown in the Negev. Some vegetables were grown in the Hulah, mostly by Arab farmers. Some of the *kibbutzim* (socialist collective farms) and *moshavot* (small land holders cooperative farms) had vegetable patches, poultry and dairy cows.

The sudden influx of hundreds of thousands of new, generally penniless, immigrants created an immediate demand for large increased supplies of foodstuffs. Domestic production capabilities were totally inadequate. With a shortage of local production, a practically nonexistent treasury, and new immigrants arriving daily, there existed the potential for a food crisis. Dov Josef was appointed food czar. His responsibility was to establish a food rationing program and techniques for the local population and to locate sources of food that would provide the calories, protein, carbohydrates, etc., needed— preferably, at concessional prices.

Eliahu Elath discussed the problem with me. Fortunately, I had some ideas. Much of my work as agricultural advisor required close cooperation with the Jewish Agency for Israel—both the New York office and the one in Jerusalem. Responsibility for immigration and absorption fell to the Jewish Agency. With tens of thousands of new immigrants arriving from different parts of the world, there was intense pressure to develop industry and agriculture to provide jobs and food. I went to New York to explore the problem with Gottlieb Hammer who, as executive vice president of the Jewish Agency for Israel was responsible for finding funding for Agency activities. A major activity was immigrant absorption—including feeding and housing.

A fairly immediate partial solution came to mind, and was eagerly accepted by both Eliahu and Gott. This involved taking advantage of the U.S. Department of Agriculture's surplus food program. Under this program non-profit groups such as CARE, CARITAS, and Church World Service were eligible to receive large quantities of free surplus food stuffs from the bulging American government stocks. See the chapter "Life with Hadassah" for the story of Israel and surplus foods.

The Agency allocated substantial resources to agricultural development that would provide jobs for immigrants and an early cash return on the investment. Accordingly, several thousand fresh (pregnant) heifers were purchased in the United States for shipment to Israel. These were almost all Holstein-Fresians, heavy milk producers. The first shipments were made through Norfolk, Virginia aboard a Liberty ship, a new inexpensive and quickly constructed freighter. The vessel's open holds had been converted into a 'barn' with stalls and stanchions. As an experiment, another shipment was made by air using large propeller-driven planes with stalls for the cattle. This experiment demonstrated that airlifting was not only technically feasible, but economically advantageous. All future shipments went by air.

Poultry husbandry lent itself to the quick development of cash producing marketable products. I was directly involved in these operations. The Jewish Agricultural Society of America, established during the period of large eastern European Jewish immigration to the United States, had been most helpful in the development of a poultry industry in Jewish Palestine. With the emergence of domestic food needs in the new State of Israel, millions of day-old chicks were being shipped to Israel to kick-start poultry production. Most of the chicks were white leghorns, an excellent egg producing breed, but also very short on producing salable meat. It took me some time before I could convince the powers that be to shift to cross breeds that would provide both eggs and poultry meat with little or no increase in production costs.

In a few short years Israel would become a producer of eggs and poultry meat greatly in surplus to domestic needs. Israel rapidly developed export markets for eggs, meat, day old chicks and fertile eggs in Europe and parts of Asia and Africa. Iran, under the Shah, was a particularly lucrative market for day old chicks.

Israel also was importing breed turkeys and eggs from the U.S.

upper Midwest. These birds were predominantly very large broad breasted varieties, excellent birds and efficient converters of feed to growth. However, there was hardly any household in Israel with an oven large enough to roast a large turkey. Accordingly, turkey meat was generally sold as parts. With gentle persuasion, the turkey growers in Israel gradually shifted to a smaller breed of broad breasted birds—which became very popular.

Much of my time at the embassy involved working with the Government of Israel Supply Mission in New York. That office had the responsibility for commercial procurement of large quantities of foodstuffs for human use and feed for animal consumption. Of course, the Supply Mission was also responsible for procuring many types of "hardware."

The food requirements for a rapidly growing population included large amounts of grains, vegetable oils, and meat proteins. My function was to examine U.S government programs that might be "exploited," and recommend acquisition programs and procedures frequently implementing such recommendations myself. I also provided a liaison between officials of the USDA and the GOI Supply Mission in New York. Thousands of tons of foodstuffs, principally grains, were procured and shipped under the various programs.

Almost all food was severely rationed in Israel. The financial and social price of absorbing the inflow of nearly penniless immigrants and refugees from various parts of the world had put a strain on the almost non-existent Israeli funds, as well as on the resources of social agencies such as the Jewish Agency. The Hadassah food program that I had set up was literally a life saver to the new country. The program went very well. We were shipping hundreds of tons of much needed foodstuffs to Israel. These had been procured at extremely low cost.

Although the embassy employed a competent social secretary, Ethel Ginburg, responsibility was mine for the smooth running of social affairs as executive officer.

The 1949 Independence Day celebration was almost a disaster. The affair was held at the Statler-Hilton Hotel at 16th and K streets. Discussions with the maître d' indicated a knowledge by the hotel staff of kosher requirements. "No ham, no bacon, lots of fish. No problem. We do lots of kosher." Questions about the number of bars, number of waiters, what drinks, how embassy-supplied spirits would be handled and, of course, costs were all settled satisfactorily in advance.

Came the day of the affair. Fortunately, Flora and I arrived at the hotel early to check that everything was in order. It was beautifully arranged, but—a big BUT! Included with the fish were the most luscious looking shrimp, oysters, and miniature crab cakes. Very, very tref—not kosher. A panic call to the maître d'. Within fifteen minutes all was changed. Thirty seconds later the Ambassador and Mrs. Elath arrived and commented how nice everything looked. Only Flora and I knew about the near disaster.

Before I left the embassy in March, 1950. Dr. Eliezer Samuel and his wife Mira and children arrived. Eliezer had been appointed as a full-time agricultural attaché, a move which I applauded. Prior to coming to Washington he had been teaching agricultural economics at the Volcani Institute in Israel. It was my pleasure to introduce Dr. Samuel to my contacts in various U.S. government offices in Washington. Flora and I maintained a warm friendship with the Samuels long after they returned to Israel. In fact, the Samuels were our first official hosts on our trip to Israel in 1951 as guests of the government. This invitation was issued by Pinchas Lavon, then minister of agriculture, at the suggestion of Michael Palgi, chief of the meat division, with whom I had had a close working relationship.

Mexican Meat Caper

Red meat was a rarity during the early days of the State of Israel. Poultry was the basic meat supply. As stated previously, eggs and poultry meat could be produced in a fairly short time. Poultry husbandry also provided a quick cash crop for the flood of immigrants being settled on kibbutzim and moshavim. Generally, the only beef available was from male calves produced from the rapidly growing herds of dairy cows. Under a Jewish Agency program thousands of fresh heifers were being sent to Israel from the United States by plane and ship. Beef cattle were not introduced into the Israeli agricultural economy until many years later.

Funds for imported foodstuffs were in extremely short supply. Israel had no money to buy beef at world market prices. But the demand for meat proteins was growing rapidly.

Fortunately for Israel, in 1949, the U.S. government was just setting up, along the Texas-Mexican border, the mechanics of a program to prevent the spread of a Mexican hoof and mouth disease epidemic. This scourge threatened much of Mexico's beef population. The Texas cattle industry could be wiped out if the disease spread north across the Rio Grande.

The program called for establishing a twenty-five mile wide quarantine strip along the entire Texas-Mexican border in which no cattle could be moved in or out except under close supervision by the U.S. and Mexican authorities. All the cattle in this quarantine swath were to be slaughtered in existing as well as new abattoirs. A schedule of payment arrangements to the Mexican cattle owners was established. Several new modern abattoirs were built south of the border and the program was ready to roll. There was no question what-so-ever about the quality of the meat and its freedom from disease. The slaughtering, inspection, and packaging standards were stringent and exacting.

One of the problems facing USDA planners however was how to dispose of the quality meat to be produced under the hoof and mouth disease program without destroying or having a major impact on the price of commercial beef in the U.S. and/or Mexico.

Just about this time the question of meat availability for Israel was raised. Gottlieb Hammer asked me about the possibilities of procuring surplus meat under one of the U.S. government programs.

My initial inquiries were met with much enthusiasm by officials in the Foreign Agricultural Service of the U.S. Department of Agriculture. The government of Israel (GOI) was a potential buyer of some of the beef, and shipments to Israel would definitely not displace normal commercial world trade. On behalf of the GOI, I offered a ready, willing, and able outlet for substantial quantities of canned and chilled meat—and certainly without competition to the U.S. meat exporting interests.

An arrangement was negotiated to purchase about 15,000 tons of canned and chilled beef for Israel at the price of five cents per pound delivered to port at Houston, Texas or Mobile, Alabama. Very satisfactory shipping charters were also arranged on a provisional basis. Funds for the purchase and shipping costs would come from the Jewish Agency. These were the easy parts!

Of course the beef had to be kosher. I did not expect a problem here. The abattoir that would process our beef was a brand new facility. It was located in Ciudad Juarez, just across the Rio Grande River from El Paso. The only meat that would be processed there, until our 15,000 tons were shipped, would be kosher beef.

And of course, I thought there would certainly be many kosher slaughterers—schochtim—as well as supervisory rabbis-mashgiach—available. How wrong I was!

Naively I obtained the name of the slaughterers' union from the New York Rabbinical Council. I called the union office and spoke to some one who identified himself as an officer. I explained who I was and what I needed. Oh, yes, they would be glad to arrange for the needed rabbinical stamp of approval—the *hecksher*—and it would only cost ten cents per pound. I asked how many ritual slaughterers I would get for ten cents per pound. "None, that is for the certificate only." The schochtim would be extra as would be their costs of going to Texas and living there for several weeks. Explaining that this meat was not for commercial sale, that it was for Israel, and that we had no money did no good at all. It was take it or leave it. I could see the proposed program collapsing.

Disheartened and expecting a similar result, I next called the office of the Rabbinical Council in Chicago. After all, a great deal of kosher slaughtering went on in the then meat capital of the world. To my surprise I was met with enthusiasm. Yes, they would like to participate in the program. There would be no cost for the kosher certificate, only for the out-of-pocket costs of the ritual slaughterer going to Texas for a few weeks.

Through contacts in Dallas, Texas, we located a rabbi in El Paso, Texas. Yes, the rabbi was available and would be pleased to participate. Further, there would be no charge for his supervision.

All the pieces were assembled. Live cattle were moving to the abattoir. The packing of the canned and chilled meat, with kosher certification, commenced. Rail cars to take the products were lined up. The refrigerator vessels for the chilled beef as well as the break-bulk carriers for the canned beef were in port, ready to load and set sail for Israel.

This was all too good to be true. We expected something to happen, to interfere with the program. Nothing did.

Everything worked fine—except that the New York slaughterers' union was most unhappy. They sent cables to the religious authorities in Israel protesting the training and background of the Texas rabbi and the schochet from Chicago. They claimed that the meat was trefe—not kosher—and that the rabbi and the Chicago slaughterers were not properly trained. Aside from asking me for details of the back-ground of the people we used, the Ministry of Trade and Industry in Israel ignored these New York complaints. I was probably bothered more by these complaints than were the Israeli government authorities.

But the story was not over. Then as now, the government of Israel was a coalition of several political parties. One of these parties was from the religious bloc—almost always a swing party in the Israeli political structure.

The first shipment of canned beef arrived in Haifa harbor on the eve of Rosh Hashanah, the Jewish New Year, a holy day. With the vessel's arrival, the religious bloc of the coalition, taking a cue from its New York cohorts, walked out of the government. The coalition collapsed. The government fell.

I was terribly mortified and embarrassed. Had I done such a wrong thing? Were the New Yorkers right? Or was this a sleazy economic move by a powerful union concerned with feathering its own nest?

As soon as I could, I sent a cable to Moshe Sharret, prime minister of Israel, apologizing for any harm I had caused, and submitting my resignation as a member of the embassy staff in Washington.

A cable promptly came back, "Keep resignation. Send more meat."

As far as Israel was concerned, the U.S./Mexico hoof and mouth program was a great success.

"The American Cheese—Is It Kosher?"

During the course of the Hadassah surplus food program under Section 416 of the Agricultural Act of 1948, my office, while I was still at the embassy, arranged the shipping of approximately 10,000 tons of cheddar cheese from East Coast ports to Israel.

American cheddar, a first-rate cheese, was the same product being sold in the best groceries and delicatessens in the United States, and was being used abundantly in America's school lunch programs. The cheese was packed in round fiber-board or wooden tubs. Each tub contained a solid block of cheese weighing about 56 to 60 pounds.

Shortly after the first shipment arrived in Haifa port, Ambassador Elath received a cable from Rabbi Isaac Herzog, the Irish born chief rabbi of Israel. Rabbi Herzog was the father of Chaim Herzog, later president of Israel, and Vivian Herzog, minister counselor at the Israel Embassy, Washington, shortly after I left.

"The American Cheese, Is It Kosher?" the Rabbi cabled.

Ambassador Elath asked me to reply to the cable. I replied with a phone call to the chief rabbi's office in Jerusalem.

Hard cheese, such as American cheddar and Swiss cheese, is made using rennet as a starter in the milk. Rennet is a chemical distillation of the enzyme 'rennin' from the stomachs of calves. It is also found in much smaller quantities in certain plants.

I told Rabbi Herzog that the cheese was one of the most nutritious food products produced in the United States, that it was sold in Jewish stores throughout the country, including ones that advertised that they were kosher. I also indicated that while some of it, particularly the cheese produced in Vermont and New York states, was probably made with vegetable rennet, the bulk of it, however, was made using veal rennet, and as such would not be 'glat kosher.'

"Is it a nutritious food for children?" was the next question. There was not only a shortage of food staples in Israel, there was an even greater shortage of protein foods in the diet.

Without any qualms whatsoever, I said that it was an excellent, clean and nutritious food for children, and that it was served extensively in the American school lunch programs.

Within the next several days, Rabbi Herzog issued a ruling that the American red (cheddar) cheese was to be considered kosher for consumption by children who had not reached their fifteenth year.

End of problem.

In a slightly different vein, the Agency absorption staff had another problem feeding Jewish immigrants from Yemen at the ATLIT absorption center near Haifa. These Sephardic Jews, were accustomed to a rice, oil, onion, and lamb diet. These foodstuffs were not available.

Using the available dried skim milk, the Yemenites were taught how to make various cheeses by Jewish agency personnel. From personal experience I can attest that the product produced was good. But it was totally foreign to the Yemenites and they, in the beginning, even refused to try to eat it. Some that did try it actually became ill from the strange food. Probably a psychological reaction. Some would take their cheese allotment, go to Haifa—a short distance—and trade it for foodstuffs, if available, more attuned to their culture. This procedure, against all rules, was heartily discouraged. Not necessarily with success.

However, over time, the immigrants from Arab countries became, on a per capita basis, heavy consumers of dairy products.

FIGURE 7: Maury Atkin, circa age 25

Weizmann's Ribs

Just hours after Israel's declaration of independence on May 14, 1948, Harry Truman gave official recognition to the new state, followed almost immediately by the USSR.

In 1949, Chaim Weizmann, Israel's first president, came to Washington at the invitation of President Harry S. Truman. It was the first official meeting of the two presidents since the State of Israel had come into being.

FIGURE 8: Dr. Chaim Weizmann, first president of Israel
Painting by Meron Sima

Weizmann had arrived in Washington a day earlier than the official visit time table. It became my responsibility, as executive officer of the Israel Embassy, to work with the U.S. State Department in making arrangements for the Israeli presidential party during the period prior to the official visit.

After arrival by train from New York, President Weizmann went to the Presidential Suite of the Shoreham Hotel along with his secretary, David Kimche, and his military aide, Col. David Arnon. The next day they were to move to the Blair House, the United States' official residence for distinguished foreign visitors.

Of course, the welcoming committee of prominent Washington Zionist leaders and a smattering of rabbis was on hand at the Shoreham to greet the president. I was there in my liaison capacity.

After about an hour of talk, and not a little noise, it became evident that the president, not a young man, was tiring. Accordingly, Kimche and I started requesting the visitors to leave so that Weizmann could get some rest.

When the suite was cleared of the local dignitaries, Weizmann came over to me. He was a tall, heavy set man with very thick glasses that made his eyes look huge. He looked down and questioned me. "Nu Moshe, have all the "machers" (big shots) left?"

I told him that only Kimche, Arnon, and I were still there.

"Good," he said. "I remember that there used to be a very good rib place near here."

"Yes, that would be Arbaugh's. It is still here and their ribs are excellent," I replied. Arbaugh's, then and now, was located on Connecticut Ave., just around the corner from the Shoreham Hotel.

"Fine. Let's go and get some ribs" said the president of Israel.

"Mr. President," I said. "I can go and get ribs. Kimche can get ribs. Arnon can go and get ribs. But you cannot go to Arbaugh's and get ribs."

For a few seconds he stared at me through those thick lens, and then with a smile, said "You are right. Kimche, you go get us some ribs."

So that was how I came to eat a ribs dinner with the first president of Israel.

Before I left for the night he autographed and gave me a copy of his book, *Trial and Error, An Autobiography of Chaim Weizmann.*

On the morning of the official visit, after President Weizmann had moved to the Blair House, President Truman walked across Pennsylvania Avenue to the Blair House. Here he met the president of Israel on the front steps of Blair House. While photographers were scrambling for vantage positions, President Weizmann presented President Truman with a Torah scroll. Pictures of this presentation were on the front pages of newspapers in all major American cities.

The story is told that at this meeting of the two presidents, Truman congratulated Weizmann on being president of a new country. Weizmann responded that while Truman was president of almost 200 million people, he, Weizmann, was president of almost five million presidents.

5

Goodbye Embassy—Hello RRNA

F ROM THE DAY when I reported for duty at the Israeli Mission, I worked ten to twelve hour days, sometimes longer, often on weekends and on Jewish and secular holidays. With a few exceptions the rest of the staff also put in similar hours. I worked hard, but enjoyed almost every minute of it. I was assured by my colleagues and superiors that I was doing an exemplary job.

I was shocked and hurt when in January, 1950, Haim Raday, secretary general of the Israel Ministry of Foreign Affairs, notified Ambassador Elath that my salary of $8,100 per annum should be reduced to $5,200.

Raday, who had never been in the United States, wanted to divide the positions of executive officer and agricultural consultant into two positions—a concept which I thought made sense. He also wanted the positions filled by Israelis who would accept the offered salary, but have many perks and benefits paid in Israel. Despite vehement protests by Ambassador Eliahu Elath and Minister Counselor Moshe Keren, Raday's decision regarding the salary stuck and so I submitted my resignation effective April 1, 1950.

I started to look for work that would support my family that by now included three children. Following usual job hunting procedures, and a tip as to where my professional experience might be useful, I filed a form 57, job application, at the United States State Department, along with a copy of my resignation from the government of Israel staff.

Shortly, several senior State Department officers called me for interviews. To my pleasant surprise I was offered the position of Assistant Chief of International and Functional Intelligence. The salary would be higher than it had been at the Israel Embassy. I accepted. My responsibilities would be analyzing economic intelligence reports coming from around the world I was told.

I agreed to a swearing in on April 1, 1950, appropriately, April Fools Day, but it was not to happen.

On March 23, in Wheeling, West Virginia, the non-lamented late Senator Joseph McCarthy (R. Wisconsin), went on an uncontrolled rampage. As the chairman of the Senate Committee for Un-American Activities, he made one of his usual demagogic speeches to the effect that he held in his hand the names of twenty-three employees of the State Department who were card-carrying Communists, a claim later proven to be absolutely false.

The next day I received a call from the State Department personnel office saying that all personnel actions were being held up for the time being, and that I would be called when I could be sworn in.

In the meantime, I had not been exactly idle. At the time of my resignation from the embassy, I was deeply involved with a massive program of acquiring foodstuffs from U.S. government agencies under advantageous prices and arranging for their shipment to Israel. I was also involved in the structure and operation of the distribution system in Israel which I, with Hadassah, The Women's Zionist Organization of America, had established.

It had been my intention to use accumulated leave for a well deserved and needed vacation during the month of March before reporting to the U.S. State Department on April 1. However Eliahu and Moshe implored me to continue working on the food project as a consultant until I was called for a swearing in.

Expecting it to be a short consultancy I agreed to do so and suggested an arrangement with a per annum fee three times my Israel government salary, plus expenses. Both readily agreed and so informed Otzar, Israel Ministry of Finance. This anticipated short consultancy turned into a major part of my subsequent career in association with Bob Nathan.

I had earlier rented two empty rooms in Bob's economic consulting office and set up a working operation to handle procurement and shipping for the foodstuffs program while still on the embassy staff. Space in the embassy building was not available. Felix Putterman, on recommendation of Stanley Frosh, a Washington lawyer, neighbor, car pool associate, and friend, joined as my assistant. Felix was extremely knowledgeable about an immense amount of trivia, which was often useful in our operation. He also had good political skills and a sense for what might be doable in problematical areas.

During this interim period of about six months, in addition to my government of Israel consultancy, I was available to handle various matters for clients of the Nathan firm. While waiting to hear from the State Department I successfully served some of Nathan Associates' clients along with a growing list of new Israeli oriented clients of my own.

In September, I was called to appear for swearing in on October 1, 1950. Bob suggested that I forget the State Department, and the probability of having to testify before unfriendly Congressional committees, as well as being frustrated with government bureaucrats. He invited me to join his firm as a principal. With just a handshake, I did so. This was the start of a wonderful relationship that continued even after my retirement. In retrospect I owe much thanks to the paranoid senator from Wisconsin and Haim Raday.

No. 3 Thomas Circle

Despite moving to more spacious and elegant quarters over the years, the offices of Robert R. Nathan Associates, Inc. at No. 3 Thomas Circle, N.W., Washington, D.C. were always, to me, the flagship location of RRNA. That was where Nathan Associates started. That was where I first became involved with the firm several years before joining it. And that was where I enjoyed learning about and really getting to know Robert Nathan, a legendary figure at the time.

The building was a World War I brick house in a row of three similar structures, located on a prominent point where Rhode Island Avenue, Massachusetts Avenue, and 14th Street met at a circle dedicated to Civil War General George Thomas sitting proudly on his horse. No. 3 was three stories high with a partially finished basement which had been remodeled into offices. The entrance from the backyard parking lot was through Bob Nathan's office—not always a convenient situation.

Robert R. Nathan

After his stint as deputy director of the War Mobilization Board, and one as a private in the Army, Robert 'Bob' Nathan, in 1948, established the economic consulting firm of Robert R. Nathan Associates, Inc. with offices at 3 Thomas Circle, N.W. in Washington, D.C. Bob Nathan, originally from Dayton, Ohio, had been pictured on the cover of *Life* magazine as deputy director of the War Mobilization Board. He was a protégé of Simon Kuznets, a Nobel Laureate in Economics. Bob had been his assistant in developing a new concept measuring a nation's economic growth, National Income Studies. Bob had also been a principal advisor to the French government in developing the Monnet Plan for the economic recovery of France after World War II. He was the author along with Oscar Gass and Daniel Creamer of "Palestine, Promise and Problem," a seminal study rebutting the British White paper which claimed that the land of Palestine could not economically absorb 100,000 Jewish refugees from the European concentration camps. His book, *Mobilizing for Abundance* was a postwar treatise on how to use America's huge productive capacity to stimulate and insure economic growth. For many years he was on the cutting edge of American social and political policy. It could be truly said that Robert Nathan was a household name. In short, he was the giant of American postwar economic policy planners.

FIGURE 9: The author with his mentor and friend, Bob Nathan

Indeed, he was a giant in other ways. In his late teens, he had been afflicted with a condition that caused excessive growth of bones and body. His height went to 6′2″, much taller than his twin brother Larry (who was exactly my 5′8″). Bob's hands became huge, as did his head. He looked like a tough heavyweight prize fighter. In fact, one of the several pictures in the *Life* magazine story showed him with boxing gloves and a fighter's stance. Despite his pugilistic appearance, Bob was soft and gentle. He was a big teddy-bear, with an enormous intellect, an off-the-chart IQ to match, and a large generous heart. True, he could and did often cuss like a trooper. But I soon learned this was a front.

His office was always filled with smoke from an ever present pipe, plus, in the winter, a wood burning fireplace. As a boss and associate he was tough. His standards were high. Through his toughness he was a great teacher. Along with his toughness, he was generous. Generous to charities, and to his staff and friends.

I first came to know Bob Nathan through the American Veterans Committee, a liberal organization whose motto was "Citizens First, Veterans Second." Bob was on the National Board as well as chairman of the Washington chapter. I was membership chairman. At the time it was the only veterans organization in the country that did not discriminate racially.

During the UN debate on Palestine in November, 1947, Bob and I were sharing a room in the Sherry-Netherland Hotel in New York. During the night I got up to use the bathroom, and didn't want to turn on the light and disturb him in the other bed. I tripped over something.

As he turned on the light I discovered I'd tripped over his back brace. It was the first time that I knew that this big, physically imposing man had a bad back and almost always wore a heavy leather and metal brace.

Bob was extremely helpful to me with ideas and contacts during my period as executive officer of the government of Israel Washington Mission.

The Staff

The small, but dedicated staff, in addition to Bob, included two professionals: Sidney Lerner and Ajay Creshkoff. In addition there was

Ruth Aull, Bob's efficient and devoted secretary—a statuesque Swede who wanted to have a child without the encumbrance of a husband, and did. When Ruth left, her position was taken by Lucy Baglia, whose talents were better suited and used for office administration and bookkeeping than secretarial, and Wilson Harris, our general messenger, mail room clerk, and office man. Mr. Harris was the epitome of a gentleman, well spoken, always prompt, well groomed, proud of himself and his achieving family. He and his wife, Hannah, each had an individual dignity and poise that anyone would be proud to equal. He was a pleasure to have as a colleague. After Wilson retired many years later we always welcomed Hannah and Wilson at the firm's annual holiday party. During the next months the staff expanded considerably with the addition of several extremely competent economists.

Sidney Lerner

A University of Wisconsin trained economist, BA 1936, MA 1938, Sid was the second ranking staff member, having joined Bob Nathan in 1946. Immediately prior to joining the firm Sid had been an economist in the Munitions Division of the War Production Board. He had previously organized and administered the foreign department of a large metal-trading firm.

Sid had worked his way though school as a court reporter and was a shorthand whiz. He had a knack for asking tough questions in a rapid fire manner, boring in for answers. A good analyst and writer, his mind worked very fast. This was reflected in his speech. Sid also had the linguistic habit of interjecting "You see" two or three times in any verbal paragraph, much as today some people tend to use "you know." It was useless to tell him "I see." He seemed to be unaware of the "you sees." Eleanor, his wife, was a talented artist. She had an unusual flair for decor and color. We took advantage of her skill in our home and in the decor and furnishing of my very elegant new office when the firm moved to the Ring Building at 18th and M Streets, N.W.

In the mid fifties, Sid left the firm to become a vice president at Commercial Metals Co. (CMC), a big-board Dallas based international scrap metal firm and a client of Nathan Associates. When Sid went to Dallas, CMC became my responsibility within the Nathan firm.

Ajay Creshkoff

Ajay was an academic economist. A Philadelphia native, he was a graduate of the University of Pennsylvania. His inquiring curiosity about a problem took him down many analytical roads. He was tenacious in following a lead. This was great for analysis, but death to the balance sheet bottom line. Ajay spent much of his professional time at RRNA backing up overseas teams—a most useful, indeed necessary, function not always recognized by the government agency with which RRNA had a contract. In this work he flourished. He also spent on average one day a week in New York working with the Jewish Agency economic office. His wife, Marcia, worried excessively each time that Ajay flew to New York. If the plane was a few minutes late she was calling Flora and the airlines.

Always cheerful and always with a pleasant smile he was fun to work with. For some years, as he lived in Chevy Chase, he was a passenger in my carpool. Ajay left Nathan Associates to teach international economic development at the University of Pittsburgh after many years with the firm.

Franz Wolf

Shortly after I joined Nathan Associates, Franz Wolf, a very competent, classical economist, with a doctorate in economics from the University of Freiburg, Germany came on board. When he left Germany in 1935, he was associate editor of the *Frankfurter Zeitung* and chief of the Information and Statistical Department of the Dresdner Bank in Stuttgart, Germany.

Prior to his joining Nathan Associates he had held positions as director of Research and Statistics and deputy director of the Office of Economic Policy, Office of Price Stabilization; commodity editor of the *Journal of Commerce;* and statistician and economist with Bear, Sterns and Co., in New York.

Franz was almost never without a pipe in his mouth, smoking Balkan Sobranie. His office maintained a permanent blue smoke screen. In telling a story, and he had many to tell, he was anything if not thorough. No detail was ever left out. As he was part of my car pool we heard many a story.

As an economist he was among the best, both thorough and imaginative. His wife, Ilk, was one of our favorites. Unfortunately, she was a cancer victim too early. Franz retired from RRNA after many years of superior service. In 2000, we participated with the Wolf family in celebrating his 100th birthday. Franz, who died at age 104, was a model of a gentleman and a scholar.

Ed Hollander

Ed Hollander, a graduate of Hanover College, had had extensive high level experience in a variety of government agencies. This included secretary of the Planning Committee, War Manpower Commission; chief of the Bureau of Labor Statistics Division of Price and Cost of Living; and labor economist on the staff of the Council of Economic Advisors. Just prior to joining RRNA he had been assistant chief of the Planning Division of the War Manpower Commission. In 1944–45 he saw sea service in the Navy.

An excellent economist and an elegant writer, he was one of those who helped the firm develop its enviable reputation for quality output. Unfortunately, cancer took him much too early.

Lou Walinsky

An excellent economist, Lou Walinsky spent most of his time with RRNA directing the Nathan team in Burma.

Oscar Gass

Oscar, one of the co-authors of *"Palestine, Problem and Promise"* rented space in the lower level of No. 3 Thomas Circle. He was not a member of the firm, and ran his own consulting office, the Jewish Agency being his principal client at the time.

Oscar was a big man—obese. About five feet five, he weighed at least 250 pounds. A "straight A" graduate of prestigious Reed College, Oscar was truly brilliant. His ability to articulate at length was buoyed by an impressive vocabulary. He seemed to have great disdain for anyone with lesser intellectual capacity than his.

His office was strewn with statuettes of hippopotami. Many had been given to him by Edna, his Nissei wife, also a Reed College graduate.

6

Life with Hadassah

HADASSAH, THE WOMEN'S Zionist Organization of America, with a membership in 1948 of around 250,000 was a powerhouse in the American Jewish cultural scene. It was also a powerhouse in Israel where it built and operated a world class hospital. Hadassah also played an active part in various Zionist policy bodies. It had been founded in 1919 by Henrietta Szold, a Baltimore social worker who had visited Palestine and was appalled by the health conditions she found there.

According to *Lost Love: The Untold Story of Henrietta Szold,* by Biela Round Shragela, based on compilation of Miss Szold's journals and letters, Benjamin Hartogensis, a prominent member of the Baltimore Jewish community and one of Flora's distant relatives, proposed to Miss Szold. He was turned down. She was madly in love with lawyer Louis Ginsberg, a renowned rabbinical scholar for whom she had been translating for years. Unfortunately for her he married a younger woman. Miss Szold remained Miss Szold—fortunately for Israel and Hadassah.

Denise Tourover

Early in my work at the Embassy of Israel I had frequent contacts with Hadassah, most particularly with Denise Tourover, a national vice president of Hadassah and its first official Washington representative. In this volunteer capacity Denise monitored the Washington political and legislative scene for items that might be of interest or importance to Hadassah. There were of course many. When I left the embassy in 1951, Hadassah retained me as a consultant and advisor on Washington matters. This continued until I retired from Nathan Associates in 1980.

Denise Tourover and her sister, Yvonne Kushner, had an extensive Reform Jewish background although they had attended a con-
vent school in Louisiana. They were both tireless in their activities
in the Washington Jewish community, Denise politically and Yvonne
through the dramatic arts.

FIGURE 10: Mother Superior accepting food shipment from
Denise Tourover, Hadassah national board member

As Washington representative for Hadassah, Denise exhibited a
dedication above and beyond the call to duty. Denise had a law degree, and was fond of throwing legal phrases into conversation and
in her letters and reports. She was extremely bright and had a nimble
mind. She was most articulate, a characteristic reflected in her vo-
luminous correspondence with friends, associates, and anyone who
might cross her. Strong willed with strong opinions, she also wrote
long letters to congressmen, senators, and other administration officials. Often intolerant of others' opinions, she frequently clashed
with the Hadassah National Board, of which she was an outspoken
member. I must say she was right much more often than she was
wrong—but went about expressing her opinions and ideas without
regard to other peoples' feelings. Many was the letter I received from
her tearing me apart for perceived slights. She could be extremely

sweet, or extremely angry—no middle ground. Some of our office staff, in private, referred to her as "Madam Menopause." Rebecca Schulman, president of National Hadassah, once said to me privately, "Your job is to make Denise look good." This was an invitation to potential confrontations.

Such was the personality with whom I worked over several decades. In short, it was a wonderful experience and despite frequent clashes I had great admiration for her. I think this was reciprocated. We saw eye to eye on most of the policy matters which she tried to get the Hadassah Board to adopt. However, most of the time in those years the board had a singular tunnel vision for sheets and pillow cases and refused to see or use the potential political clout that almost 300,000 members across the country possessed. Denise and I tried to change this. Our efforts must have had some impact as in later years Hadassah developed an active program related to American affairs.

Public Law 480, Section 216, Surplus Foodstuffs

One of my first activities with Hadassah was establishing a surplus food supply pipeline from the United States to Israel. This was a major function of my responsibilities as the Embassy of Israel's agricultural advisor. Establishing this food stream required the cooperation of Israeli government offices, New York and Jerusalem offices of Jewish Agency for Israel, and, of course, Hadassah.

FIGURE 11: Arab orphan girl receiving canned beef
under the Hadassah administered program

To support farm prices declining almost since World War II, under authority from Congress, the U.S. Department of Agriculture had been purchasing and storing vast quantities of foodstuffs, surplus to American domestic or commercial foreign market outlets. These foods varied from time to time, but included dried skim milk, cheddar cheese, butter, butter oil, dried eggs, cottonseed oil, rice, corn flour, wheat flour, sometimes beans. Dry and cold storage facilities in the U.S. were bulging with government owned surplus foodstuffs. In addition, overseas the U.S. military had huge quantities of stored foodstuffs surplus to any possible postwar requirement. These latter could not, by law, be returned to the United States for resale.

The American domestic welfare and school lunch needs could absorb only a small part of the surpluses filling warehouses across the country. A lack of space for additional price support purchases, plus growing political problems of waste and spoilage, demanded that steps be taken to reduce these surpluses.

The Agricultural Act of 1948 included a program under Public Law 480 of that act making these foodstuffs available to Registered Volunteer Agencies (RVA). The bags, crates, and cans of food were free to the RVA agencies. However, it was necessary to demonstrate that food received under the program and shipped abroad would be distributed only to the needy, and would not displace normal and usual commercial transactions in the recipient country. As the U.S. government had no interest in displacing normal commercial agricultural exports with concessionally priced surplus supplies, food shipments authorized under the PL 480 program had to be demonstrably "over and above" commercial imports and domestic production in the recipient countries. Ocean freight had to be paid by the recipient agencies. At least half of the shipment had to be in American flag bottoms, vessels flying the American flag and American owned.

To participate in a PL 480 program it was necessary to have the cooperation of an American voluntary agency working in overseas relief programs. Two immediate agencies came to mind, one was Hadassah and its Hadassah Medical Organization. The other was the Jewish Agency for Palestine, renamed after May 14, 1948, the United Israel Appeal (UIA). The UIA was responsible for immigrant absorption into Israel. Its funds came from an annual nation wide appeal by the United Jewish Appeal (UJA).

CARE, (Committee for American Relief to Europe), CARITAS, (Catholic Relief charities), Lutheran World Relief, and a few smaller charitable organizations were making use of these foods and shipping surplus foodstuffs to their overseas installations such as schools, hospitals, and church soup kitchens.

Israel's food needs, over and above normal commercial trade, were gigantic. The American surplus food program seemed to be a perfect fit—if Israel could meet the qualifying conditions.

As Israel's agricultural advisor I was invited to attend a UIA Board meeting in New York City early in 1950. where the problem was discussed. UIA, along with the Joint Distribution Committee was a constituent of the UJA, the fund raising arm of American Jewry. Also in attendance was Gottlieb Hammer and Moshe Boukstein, able counsel to the UIA, representatives of Hadassah and other Israeli oriented organizations.

Having been involved with the Surplus Food program when I was in the USDA, I thought I had a partial solution to the problem. But an American registered voluntary agency, approved by the appropriate office of the U.S. State Department was required as the recipient, distributor, and controller of any surplus foods obtained. Hadassah seemed like the ideal partner to the UIA and the government of Israel. It had an operating infrastructure in Israel, with hospitals, schools, and some feeding stations. It had already established programs to ease the problems of absorbing thousands of new citizens into a new culture, language and environment. It was an American organization that operated and made policy for its Israeli operations. It had a history and reputation for humanitarian activities.

To participate in the program the American Voluntary Agency had to be registered with and approved by the Advisory Committee on Voluntary Foreign Aid of the International Cooperation Administration (ICA), an arm of the Department of State. The ICA was later reorganized as the Agency for International Development (AID).

Back in Washington, I discussed the situation with Denise Tourover. Denise instantly grasped the value and potential of such a program for the development and security of the state of Israel as well as providing Hadassah with an opportunity to enhance its posture among American Jewish women. However, up to that time Hadassah had not registered as an RVA.

The first step was to convince the Hadassah National Board in New York that registration with the Advisory Committee was a good thing to do. This was not easy. This would be an operation foreign to anything Hadassah had ever done. Hadassah leadership was concerned about Hadassah's responsibilities, methods of control, warehouse and distribution systems, and, of course, costs to it—all legitimate concerns. Denise took on the job of persuading the board. She had able assistance from Moshe Boukstein who explained to the Board legal exposures, liability risks, and the importance to Israel of the project. The Hadassah Board had total confidence in Moshe's judgment.

Still fearful of unknown problems, the Hadassah National Board reluctantly agreed to file for registration. Along with Denise, it was my responsibility to prepare the registration application, including the economic justification for the program. This was the easy part.

The office of American Voluntary Foreign Aid within State's Economic Cooperation Administration set up every obstacle it could think of to hinder if not block the process. First it was necessary to demonstrate that Hadassah facilities in Israel were under the direction and *control* of the American organization—that Hadassah was not just a conduit to funnel money to an Israeli structure. This was not difficult to do. Then we had to show that Hadassah had capable staff to supervise distribution of surplus items and that this supervision was under the direction of an American citizen.

Fortunately, Hadassah had several extremely capable members in Israel who were active volunteers in the organization. These included, among others, Rose Vitelis and Rhoda Cohen, American citizens, who had made aliyah, were well organized, and had administrative talent. In addition, Hadassah had full time Israeli administrative staff available to work with the volunteers. They included Yehuda Dekel and Schlomo Yoeli, both in the purchasing department.

After several months and many meetings Hadassah was approved as a Registered Voluntary Agency entitled to receive surplus commodities for relief distribution abroad.

Hadassah staff in Israel compiled lists of schools, children's homes, old age institutions, refugee feeding centers, immigrant reception centers, and churches with feeding programs. Christian, Moslem and Jewish institutions were included. The lists showed name of institution, address, and number of participants. Many of the new immigrants had already been moved out of reception centers to housing around the country, and had very small stipends furnished by the Jewish Agency. In view of this, I took the position that almost the whole country could qualify for relief. Moshe Boukstein backed me up on this concept. The compiled lists were submitted to the Advisory Committee on American Foreign Aid. I set up our administrative operation for the program in the Nathan Associates office building. Over several years, in Hadassah's name, we applied for, secured, shipped, and distributed thousands of tons of foodstuffs, often in full shiploads. Each package carried the legend "Donated by the People of the United States." A second statement said "Not for Resale."

The voluntary agency had the responsibility of paying the ocean freight, handling and warehousing costs in the recipient country. The recipient agency also had to have a system of controlled distribution to insure that the products were distributed to the needy.

Under the arrangement that was worked out the Jewish Agency for Israel arranged to pay the ocean freight charges for the shipments that Hadassah was to make. The products were to be distributed to absorption centers, welfare agencies, schools and hospitals—Jewish and Arab—throughout the country. The recipient welfare agencies in Israel were authorized to repay their proportionate share of the out-of-pocket costs, meaning freight, administration, warehousing, etc. There was to be no profit to anyone. Given the vast quantities being shipped against the tremendous need for food stuffs in Israel (this was during the *Tsenna* [scarcity] period of 1951–55), it was almost impossible to keep some of the products from being resold by some of the recipients.

The magnitude of the operation we set up for Hadassah, is shown in the following data for 1951 and 1952:

- 26 million pounds of dried skim milk
- 4.5 million pounds of dried eggs

- 18.6 million pounds of butter
- 4.4 million pounds of cheddar cheese
- 10 thousand tons of Maine potatoes

The aggregate wholesale value (in 1953 dollars) of shipments in 1951–1953 was well over $20,000,000. Shipments in subsequent years almost equaled this level.

Other commodities subsequently added to the availability list included rice, wheat flour, vegetable oil, beans, corn, corn flour, and bulgur (par-boiled cracked wheat).

There were two interesting incidents relative to the inclusion of bulgur in the program. When Senator Hubert Humphrey made a statement on the Senate floor about the inclusion of bulgur the *Congressional Record*, reporting the speech, wrote the words in Hebrew letters. As far as we know this was the only time that Hebrew has been in the *Congressional Record*. The second incident was in Israel when cereal made from bulgur was offered to Arab school children. They refused to eat it, fearing it was second rate or spoiled wheat.

The actual handling of the procurement and shipping was done by a small but dedicated staff that I had hired. Felix Putterman, and later Joe Napolitano, were in charge of this part of the operation. I have forgotten the names of most of the five or six people that worked on this, but Rose Sturm comes to mind.

The arrangement was that the foods would be distributed to the various schools and institutions in Israel without charge for the product. However, where possible, the recipient agencies were expected to reimburse Hadassah a small unit amount to cover Hadassah's out-of-pocket shipping, warehousing and distribution costs. On this basis some grocery stores in poor neighborhoods were given allocations of food for distribution with the understanding that these surplus foods were to go only to qualified relief recipients. This recovery of distribution costs, amounting to a few agarot per unit, was approved by the U.S. government. One hundred agarot equaled an Israeli pound, the Israeli basic currency unit. A pound was equal to $.366.

After several years of smooth operation I received a call from Ray Ioanes, assistant chief of Foreign Agricultural Services of the U.S. Department of Agriculture, to come to his office to discuss something quite serious.

After shipping about twenty-five million dollars wholesale value of product, the Department of Agriculture, following complaints, called Hadassah on the carpet regarding the "illegal resale of surplus food stuffs through commercial outlets."

I had known and liked Ray from many years of working together on various projects. He was a good, fair, and innovative administrator and had been most helpful to us on the food programs. This was also true of his two assistants, Tom Street and Patrick O'Leary. On the other hand, we had been helpful to the Department of Agriculture in finding an outlet for substantial quantities of surplus food.

Early on during the distribution period, both Ray and Tom had spent a week in Israel with me examining the operation of the program: how the pipeline worked, the way foodstuffs reached the people, the controls for accountability, and the value of the program to the people. They had been quite satisfied with what they had seen, and all records, books and distribution information were made available to them.

Upon receiving the call from Ray, I immediately went to his office. Ray showed me a report sent to Washington by the American Embassy in Tel Aviv to the effect that most if not all of the Hadassah foods were being sold on the open market by grocers at below retail prices, but well above the approved small agorot reimbursement intended. We later found out that there had been complaints filed by Arab sources.

If true, this was a serious violation of Hadassah's commitments to the USDA and to State. Also if true, and bruited about, it could have tremendously damaged Hadassah's American image, its reputation with the U.S. government, and possibly even jeopardized its tax exempt status. This was indeed a serious matter. Ray was sympathetic to our situation and said we should take our time, get the facts together and come back to see him.

Of course I was stunned. The first thing I had to do was to report this to Denise and to Hadassah. Denise took the news fairly calmly and analytically. Not so other senior Hadassah officers. The ladies of Hadassah went ballistic. They blew up—particularly Rebecca Schulman, then national president.

An immediate meeting was called in New York with the officers of Hadassah, including Denise, Moshe Boukstein their lawyer, and myself. Of course, I was on the carpet. I had promoted the program. I had directed it. Denise was also on the carpet for not watching more closely what I was doing. Actually she watched it like a hawk. Hadassah officers accusing her of dereliction was just not fair.

Moshe was calm and deliberate. He had been supportive of what I had done from day one. His lawyerly approach was: "Let's get the facts. What was going on in Israel? Who had authorized the sale of the products at above minimum handling costs? What would Hadassah strategy be in replying to the USDA to avoid a huge penalty and public disclosure?"

We found out that, yes, many of the food stores were selling butter, cheese, skim milk, and flour, at prices well above the approved levels. We also found out that this was with the acquiescence of the Ministry of Finance of the Israel government. This further complicated the situation.

All we needed was an international situation that could be exploited by Israel's many enemies.

Getting the facts together we found that we could demonstrate and document that most of the AID foodstuffs did indeed go to approved outlets and well within the parameters of cost and usage intended in the program. We also discovered that a not insubstantial amount had been diverted through means we never found out—possibly we didn't want to know—to normal commercial channels and was being sold on the open market still with the markings "Gift of the People of the United States—Not for Resale" and with the handclasp logo.

At our next meeting with the USDA authorities, Rebecca Schulman, president, and Faye Schenk, treasurer, along with Denise represented Hadassah. Moshe Boukstein attended as their lawyer. I was there for obvious reasons. In addition to Ray Ioanes of USDA there was a stony faced representative from State who was a deputy director of that agency. His name was Charles Taft, the son of Senator Robert Taft (R. Ohio) and no friend of Israel. There were also a representative of the USDA solicitor's office, and one or two other government officials. To say that this phalanx scared the daylights out of the Hadassah people would have been the understatement of the year.

Ray presented the problem and asked for Hadassah's reaction. Before that could be given, Taft made a statement that seemed to the women present to be accusing them of grand larceny, high treason, and a few other crimes.

Moshe spoke for Hadassah. He stated firmly that there was no intention or activity by Hadassah to do anything improper; that the American Embassy in Tel Aviv was constantly informed about everything Hadassah did under the program. We had to acknowledge that there obviously had been some leakage which should not have happened, but did, but that according to our information it was relatively minor.

Taft pushed and referred to a possible fine of $20,000,000, one helluva lot of money. The Hadassah women paled. We left, saying we would review the problem and would ask for another meeting. I met a few days later alone with Ioanes to discuss the situation. He indicated that he did not see the situation as Taft did. He also indicated, as I remember it, that USDA solicitor's office did not see it the Taft way either. Communications between the New York office of Hadassah, and Hadassah in Israel, as well as between Hadassah and the government of Israel were fast and furious.

We soon learned where the problem had arisen. It was caused by over zealous Israeli government officials who thought they could "handle the Americans"; that they could get around American regulations and quietly gave "the wink" to food stores about prices for the surplus products.

In a subsequent meeting between Ioanes and me, he was fairly firm that some penalty would be required, and that if it were promptly settled, there would be no publicity. This was something we very much desired. Taft had talked about $20,000,000. At a private discussion with Ray I was informed that a penalty around $1,000,000 or more would be expected.

After getting approval from the necessary Israeli government entities, a formal meeting to make an offer was set up. This was attended by several Hadassah senior officials, representatives of State, representatives of the USDA solicitor's office, Moshe Boukstein and myself. Taft did not attend. The offer of $1,000,000 was made—and accepted. It was agreed that there would be no publicity. There never was. Even with this payment, the operation was a huge success from the nutritional, psychological, and cost benefit standpoints.

Hadassah sent the USDA its check. The government of Israel reimbursed Hadassah. Food shipments continued, but with much closer scrutiny by Hadassah's Israeli staff. The program continued through 1955. It literally saved Israel from severe nutritional imbalances and hardship. With the huge abundance of foodstuffs in Israel today, both domestic and imported, it is hard to conceive of a time that food was rationed, and that even with rationing it was often difficult to obtain one's allotted ration.

Much of the credit for the success of the operation in Israel goes to Rhoda Cohen, Hadassah's Israel representative assigned to handle warehousing, record keeping and distribution, for the surplus commodity program. With little or no background in an operation of this type, Rhoda did a yeoman's job. In this work she epitomized the acme of volunteerism: dedicated, scrupulously honest, smart, tactful and innovative. She was a gem in the project of feeding Israel during those years. In this work, she had the able assistance and cooperation of Hadassah Hospital's professionals in the purchasing department, Shlomo Yoeli and Yehuda Dekel.

Rhoda's husband, Rabbi Jack Cohen, was director of the Hillel House at the Hebrew University in Jerusalem, and professor of Jewish Ethics. A remarkable man, he has spent many, many years trying to bridge the cultural, economic, and social gaps, between Arab and Jewish students. On our various trips to Israel it was always a pleasure to be with Jack and Rhoda Cohen. The stimulating, innovative and often dramatic discussions in their home were something to which we always looked forward.

In addition to the obvious nutritional and financial value of these surplus shipments there were occasionally some interesting by-products of the overall program. One sticks in mind at the moment. The flour and some of the bean products were shipped in white muslin bags with the AID shield, hand clasp logo and the gift legend mentioned above. Israeli institutions being textile and dollar short, and not ready or willing to waste anything, took the bags, cleaned them and made them into dresses, smocks, shirts, aprons, purses, and coats. Accordingly, on several of our trips we saw young women wearing short white skirts, with the AID logo and the gift legend prominently displayed. These bags were used not only in Israel, but for shipments to CARE and Lutheran World Relief and Church World Service and other voluntary agencies all over the world. As one could expect, it was not long before the fashion of re-tailoring these bags made its way back to the United States.

Note: It would be remiss to leave the impression that all food aid to Israel came through Hadassah. In addition to the Hadassah program, the government of Israel, through its Israel Supply Mission in New York, was purchasing and shipping large tonnages of various grains financed through credits made available by the Commodity Credit Corporation, a USDA agency, These credits were repaid in Israeli currency. I was also a consultant to the Supply Mission, and was involved in negotiating many of the purchase contracts and preparing the economic justifications for Israel's participation in the program.

In addition, the Jewish Agency, in its program to provide employment for new immigrants and build the agricultural economy of the new nation, was buying and sending by ship and plane, thousands of fresh Holstein-Fresian heifers, and day old chicks. I was also a consultant to the Agency on these programs.

Rebuilding the Hadassah Hospital on Mt. Scopus

During the 1948 War of Independence, the hospital on Mt. Scopus, the pride of Hadassah, suffered extensive damage. Even though they tried, Arab armies failed to capture the Mount. However, for all practical purposes it became unavailable. Arab armies surrounded the small enclave on Mt. Scopus which included the hospital, some Hebrew University buildings, and a small but historic cemetery. A less than company-sized military unit was based there to maintain an Israeli presence. These soldiers were periodically rotated. This rotation involved great risks. The road to Scopus was blockaded by Arab gunmen and incidents were not uncommon. These incidents often proved fatal to those who attempted to run the blockade. In April 1948, just before the War of Independence, one convoy, supposedly with British army protection, tried to reach Scopus. It was ambushed. Dr. Haim Yassky, administrator of the Hadassah Hospital on Mt. Scopus, was killed along with over sixty other doctors, nurses, and other Hadassah personnel.

During the nineteen years that the Mt. Scopus facility was not available Hadassah built a larger and more modern hospital at Ein Karem. This location, in the western and newer section of Jerusalem, was personally selected by David Ben-Gurion, then prime minister.

In June, 1967 during the Six Day War, Israeli troops captured all of east Jerusalem opening the route to Mt. Scopus. I visited the Scopus campus during the truce in late June, 1967. It was a shambles. Windows out, doors hanging loose, concrete and glass debris in hallways, rooms, and operating theaters. Hadassah had to make a decision whether to rebuild it or tear it down. As there was much history in the building, it was decided to rebuild it. However, funds for this purpose were sorely lacking.

Fortunately, the U.S. Agency for International Development (AID) administered a program entitled, "Aid to American Schools and Hospitals Abroad." The major beneficiary of this program was the American University of Beirut in Lebanon, which received ten to twelve million dollars annually. In fact, the whole program had been established for the benefit of that institution.

Congressman Otto Passman (D. Louisiana) was the sponsor and guardian of the program. The people at AID responsible for administering the program hated it. Passman, however, was chairman of the House Foreign Affairs Committee, and of the sub-committee on Appropriations. He was a congressional power house. A hard drinking southern bachelor of the old school, he ran the committee with an iron hand. AID officials feared him, and catered to his every wish, including making sure that he had adequate supplies of bourbon on his frequent overseas trips. It was also rumored that he was slightly anti-Semitic.

Denise Tourover knew about this program. She discussed with me the possibility of having Hadassah become a participant. I spent some time talking to AID administrators about this. Ice water was thrown on the very concept of expanding the program to include additional schools or hospitals. Arturo Constantino, the AID administrator of the program, was sympathetic but far from encouraging.

I met with Bill Gaud, administrator of AID, to discuss the idea of

Hadassah's participation. Gaud, who was a fair and competent chief of the agency and with whom I had good rapport, was very blunt, "Over my dead body," he said. He hated the whole concept of the program and wanted to scuttle it. Passman would not let him.

My reaction was, "Bill, I don't want you to have a funeral, but I am going to get Hadassah to participate in that program." I pointed out that as I read the law establishing the American School and Hospital Program, it seemed to me that Hadassah was a perfect fit for the purposes and intent of the Act.

We marshaled our forces, estimated our strengths, and laid out a strategy. A powerful committee went to work. We were Si Kenen, the amazingly successful, quiet-spoken lobbyist for Israeli causes, and the founder and director of the American Israel Public Affairs Committee (AIPAC); Faye Schenk, then national president of Hadassah; Denise Tourover, and myself.

Si Kenen had entree to almost any member of Congress, knew the legislative process, and enjoyed the respect of most of the senators and representatives in Congress, even those who disagreed with him. Properly organized and motivated, 300,000 voting Hadassah women could also have powerful clout.

With Bill Gaud's challenge, we set the wheels in motion.

Working with Denise, I prepared many documents for submission to AID requesting participation for Hadassah. Prominent Hadassah members from communities that members of the Foreign Affairs and Appropriations committees came from were brought to Washington to meet with their representatives.

While working the AID offices, we also set up congressional bridgeheads. Denise organized a campaign for individual members of Hadassah to write to their representatives and senators. The National Board of Hadassah was a bit squeamish about this, as it feared that Hadassah might lose its tax-exempt status if it engaged in "politics." The board instructed its members to write as individuals, not as Hadassah representatives. Never before had Hadassah attempted to use its potential political clout. Its attorney, Moshe Boukstein, assured the board that writing letters to Congress was every American's right and privilege.

Si Kenen set up meetings with influential members of Congress, to whom we presented documents and arguments as to why Hadassah should participate. He also arranged for Faye Schenk to testify before the appropriate committees of Congress. I wrote her testimony. She was an excellent witness and made a very good impression. Si also arranged meetings for me with Senator Inouye (D) of Hawaii. He was chairman of the Senate Foreign Relations Committee, and was most helpful. We also met with Congressman Passman. He had received many letters from his own constituents in Louisiana and recognized that it was better to be liked by 300,000 women than otherwise.

The upshot and bottom line of all the effort was that both the House and Senate inserted a line item in the AID budget providing for a direct grant of $5,000,000 to Hadassah to rebuild the Mt. Scopus Hospital.

Hadassah was ecstatic. With this, Bill Gaud knew he had lost. He called me with congratulations. AID started to cooperate in administration of the grant.

However, every imaginable roadblock was put in our way. We had to demonstrate that the operation of the hospital in Israel was directed and controlled by American citizens; that policy was entirely in the hands of Americans; that Hadassah was not just a money funnel to transmit funds to Israel. We had to document that Hadassah was a solvent organization. This process took many months and many meetings. It took many revisions of the documentation, each time to overcome the additional objections of AID.

On a beautiful spring morning in 1975, the rebuilt hospital on Mt. Scopus was formally rededicated. Israeli flags waved in the breeze as a band played appropriate music. An audience of Hadassah and government of Israel dignitaries, along with representatives of the American Embassy and several hundred Israeli and American members of Hadassah and their spouses assembled. The festivities opened with a procession, At the head of the procession alongside Faye Schenk, national president, and Dr. Kalman Mann, general administrator of Hadassah's medical programs in Israel, Flora and I marched into the renovated campus. It was a proud moment for Hadassah and certainly for us.

Ann Eden, president of the Washington chapter of Hadassah, was sitting in the front row of the attending audience. When she saw us in the march her mouth dropped open. She had had no idea of my work with national Hadassah and was surprised with our VIP treatment at the dedication. My activities for the National Board of Hadassah were generally not known by the Washington chapter.

Subsequently, until I retired, I prepared applications for Hadassah institutions that resulted in annual grants ranging from $300,000 to $3,500,000.

Surplus Hardware

In addition to providing food to RVA agencies, there were also U.S. government programs whereby RVA agencies could obtain a wide variety of U.S. surplus equipment for use overseas. These items came from the military, from Veteran Administration hospitals, from FEMA, and many other agencies.

The surplus goods ranged from sheets and pillow cases to D-8 Caterpillar tractors. All had been declared 'surplus' to the needs of some government installation. In theory, other U.S. government agencies and domestic (U.S.) charities had first crack at such 'surplus' items. From that point, there was a pecking order of claimants, with the overseas agencies near the bottom of the list. However, the 'theory' did not always work. Much very good, often new or near new, material became available.

Our office was constantly on the lookout for surplus items that might be of use to Hadassah. We found many. These included hundreds of new or nearly new blankets, sheets, and pillow cases, dental chairs for Hadassah's dental school, medical instruments, two full U.S. Army field hospitals with all the ancillary equipment, trailer mounted water tanks, electric controlled hospital beds including Schtrieker beds for orthopedic patients, portable x-ray equipment, and large emergency generators. Many of these items came out of dismantled Veterans' Administration hospitals that had been built and equipped, but never used. Many came from U.S. military bases when supply officers decided they wanted something new or different. Two full Army field hospitals, never used, came from American bases in Europe. Each had cost the Army over a million dollars. These hospitals included beds, blankets, sheets, pillows, operating room equipment, x-ray machines, and all the medical instruments that a field hospital would need. Nothing was omitted.

My administrative assistant, Molly Tatel, who had started in 1962 as my secretary, was extremely helpful in many ways. She had a major responsibility locating useful surplus equipment, handling railroad and truck movements of commodities, and keeping AID happy with reports and documents required. When we started moving surplus commodities other than food, such as generators, tractors, blankets, hospital supplies from military and Veterans' Administration facilities, Molly did yeoman work with officials of the U.S. Army Mechanicsburg (Pa.) Depot, a major military materiel depot, to procure and ship these items

Our major contacts in Hadassah for surplus hardware were the old stalwarts, Yehuda Dekel and Schlomo Yoeli, in the Hadassah purchasing department in Israel.

＞

Over the years I made many trips to Israel in connection with my work for Hadassah and other Israeli clients. I had the psychic satisfaction of seeing the actual physical results of my efforts. I could see and touch buildings and equipment that I had had a major responsibility in their being there. I thrilled to see the vigor and health of people and institutions that had benefited from my efforts. And they were good. I had made a difference.

Interesting Incidents

HALLOWEEN

Flora accompanied me on trips to Israel on nineteen different occasions. On one of these in late autumn we were invited by Dr. Kalman Mann, administrator of the Hadassah Hospital, and professor of medicine in the medical school, to a dinner at his home. The date was October 31. We arrived to find that the dinner table was decorated with orange and black tablecloths and napkins. The date was Halloween in the states.

When we mentioned how appropriate the decor was for the date our hosts were most surprised. They had never heard of Halloween, and the decor was pure coincidence and happenstance.

Also invited were some of the senior department chiefs of the hospital, including several world-renowned surgeons.

After drinks and hors d'oeuvres and much discussion of Israeli politics, we sat down to a sumptuous dinner. The main course, in our honor, was a turkey. But what a turkey!

After the appetizers and soup, Dr. Mann's wife brought out a beautiful well browned whole tom turkey. She explained that this was an experiment since she had never before cooked a whole bird.

Then Dr. Mann looked at the surgeons present, and asked, "Which of you will carve the turkey?" There were no takers. Not one of the doctors or other guests present had ever carved a turkey.

Then Kalman looked at me. "Do you know how to carve a turkey?"

"I have carved one or two," I said.

So guess who performed surgery. It was great fun. We also educated the guests about Halloween. The turkey and the evening were delicious.

WAITER—WAITER

Hadassah holds a national convention each year, the high point of the Hadassah year for its members. Every other year the convention is held in some major American city. On alternate years it is held in Israel.

In 1965, the convention was at the Waldorf-Astoria Hotel in New York. The featured speaker at the major convention banquet was Vice President Hubert Humphrey. The VP was known as an eloquent speaker. He never used notes. His speeches were not known for their brevity.

Prior to the dinner, the Hadassah Executive Board entertained the VP at a private reception in one of the Tower suites of the hotel. Flora and I were invited as Hadassah's guests to the reception and the dinner. We declined the invitation to sit on the dais. Rather we, together with the then husband of Hadassah president Charlotte Jacobson (they were soon divorced) and several other prominent members of the Hadassah family elected to sit at a table immediately in front of the stage and dais. We were in 'black tie.'

Humphrey gave his usual rousing speech that the ladies loved. It was a long one. The liquids I had drunk at the reception and dinner were making themselves known. The longer Hubert talked the more uncomfortable I became.

Finally, he stopped. Or seemed to. I arose and proceeded through the audience heading for the nearest rest room. As I arose, somehow a white napkin got caught on my arm. I was unaware of this. As I went through the Waldorf's huge ballroom I passed a table where Rose Tepper, current president of the Washington area Hadassah chapter, was sitting. She greeted me and asked what I was doing there. I realized that with my tux, and the draped napkin, she thought I was a waiter.

Playing the part, I said, "Well Rose, you know how it is. Sometimes times are tough." And I proceeded to the restroom. Several days later, her husband, Lester, who did know of my various Israeli involvements called me. When Rose got home she had told him that things must be bad for the Atkins as I was working as a waiter in the Waldorf. He set her straight.

FIGURE 12: Seated, Charlotte Jacobson, President of Hadassah, and Bill Gaud, Administrator AID. Standing L–R, Denise Tourover, Hadassah Official Representative to Washington, Maury Atkin, Hadassah consultant, and Faye Schenk, National Hadassah Treasurer. Celebrating Mount Scopus $5 million grant.

Figure 13: Standing L–R, Harry Hemmerich, AID, Dr. Martin Foreman, AID, Denise Tourover, Washington official representative of Hadassah, Maury Atkin, Faye Schenk, national Hadassah treasurer, Helen Lortz, AID. Seated Herb Waters, Assistant Administrator AID and Charlotte Jacobson, national Hadassah president signing one of numerous Hadassah-AID agreements securing much needed funds for Israel.

POTATOES—POTATOES—POTATOES

Never a dull moment! The shipment of 10,000 tons of potatoes to Israel was quite a story.

With thousands of new immigrants into Israel each month during the first years of independence, the need for increased supplies of foodstuffs escalated geometrically. Among the staples in short supply were potatoes.

In the winter of 1950, the Embassy of Israel in Washington, received an inquiry from Israel about the possibility of acquiring potatoes under one of the U.S. government programs. A visit to the U.S. Department of Agriculture determined that the U.S. government indeed had a problem finding outlets for huge surplus stocks of Maine potatoes—particularly from Aroostook County. They would be available for sale to qualified recipients at prices considerably below market provided that they would move outside of normal U.S. market areas. In other words they could only be sold to recipients not likely to buy potatoes on the open market.

The Department of Agriculture had other problems with these potatoes too. They were in storage in Aroostook County, the northernmost county in Maine. The nearest shipping point was Searsport, Maine, about 150 to 180 miles from the Aroostook potato bins, and it was winter. Temperatures were running well below zero degrees F. The high water content of Maine potatoes made them tricky products to load in rail cars and ship in such temperatures. Anticipating that large quantities of bagged potatoes could be safely delivered to Searsport in specially heated rail cars, they would then have to be loaded into ships' holds without freeze damage. Assuming this would be successful, there was the remaining problem of a ten to fifteen day ocean voyage from cold water to warm water areas, with the risk of overheating and spoilage.

At the time that these problems were under discussion, the Spanish government, just a few weeks earlier, had in fact loaded five vessels at Searsport with Maine potatoes. Freeze losses from Aroostook to Searsport were at acceptable levels, but losses from Searsport to Spain were disastrous—well over seventy percent of the potatoes were garbage upon arrival. The losses were thought to have been the result of the vessels going from very cold to warm waters resulting in heavy sweating on the steel members of the ships' holds. The sweating caused fast developing rot which spread throughout the cargo.

Concerned because of the Spanish experience, I met with the technical people in the Potato Section of the Department of Agriculture's Fruit and Vegetable Division. Various procedures, albeit experimental, were discussed. With my fingers crossed, I made the decision to go ahead with a potato procurement program.

Accordingly, Hadassah, which had the right to purchase surplus potatoes at concessional prices, signed contracts to purchase 10,000 tons of Aroostook County potatoes to be delivered to Searsport alongside ship. The price was one cent per hundred pound bag. My office in the embassy negotiated, on behalf of Hadassah, charters for two Danish vessels, the Benny Skou and the Jytte Skou. The chartering document was a typical General Condition (Gencon) Charter. One of the standard provisions of such a charter is that if commodity delivery from dock to ship is to be by elevator, loading costs were on the account of the charterer. According to industry standards, that meant a grain elevator.

Transport of the spuds from Aroostook to Searsport and ship loading was scheduled for mid January, 1951. As it involved so many new techniques, I went to Searsport to be available to troubleshoot and to see that all went smoothly.

Maine's weather is always nasty in January. Usually potatoes were loaded aboard vessels using open slings and nets, but when it became apparent that Maine's weather was going to be especially nasty, on the advice of the Department of Agriculture, a piece of equipment with an endless moving belt generally used to load hay into barns, was brought in. We had a covered framework built over this conveyor to minimize exposure of the bagged potatoes to the frigid winds.

To avoid a repetition of the Spanish debacle we bought packing tape and as many rolls of brown wrapping paper that we could find in grocery, hardware, and general stores in towns near Searsport and Bangor. They had the paper for packaging but we used it to cover every piece of steel in the vessels that the bags might touch so that there would be no contact between sweating steel and burlap bags.

We also bought a supply of pine planks and electric fans. The planks were used to build forms that permitted air to flow through the cargo. The fans were to insure that there was moving air available, particularly when the vessels reached warmer waters.

The rail cars arrived in Searsport more or less on time. To protect the bagged potatoes from the bitter cold, every freight car had low level heaters. Using the covered conveyor, the Benny Skou was loaded as planned and departed for Haifa.

The stevedores started loading the Jytte Skou using the covered conveyor. Suddenly, the captain stopped the operation. He claimed, on advice from his home office, that the conveyor was an elevator, and therefore Hadassah was liable for loading costs. I argued that in the Gen Con charter the term elevators meant grain elevators, not the type of conveyor we were using, but to no avail.

With a couple of thousand tons of potatoes arriving, and the impossibility of getting another vessel in port before they rotted, and a certain lawsuit against Hadassah for costs, I decided that Hadassah would be the plaintiff and sue the Skou Company rather than be the defendant. A quick call to New York resulted in loading costs of $30,000 being transferred, under protest, to the owners of the Jytte Skou. The loading continued without further incident.

I am delighted to report that both ships arrived in Haifa, cargoes intact with about a two percent loss, considered normal for any shipment. The potatoes were off-loaded, along with the lumber, and fans. The potatoes went into Israel's food pipeline. The lumber and fans were sold at a good profit. Much of the credit for the success went to the Department of Agriculture's Potato Section. The people involved could not have been more helpful. Utilizing their ideas and suggestions, many of which involved experimental shipping techniques, resulted in a most successful operation.

With the vessels docked and unloaded in Haifa, on behalf of Hadassah, I filed a suit against the Jytte Skou owner. After several months a judgment for full recovery was received. As the owner was abroad, and the ships were not American registered, the judgment had to be served on the owner or to a captain on one of his ships. It had to be served in the United States.

All seaports on the Atlantic and Gulf coasts were notified about the judgment. We requested the courtesy of notification when a Skou vessel might be in any of the ports. Almost a year later I received a midnight phone call from the manager of the Port of Philadelphia telling me that a vessel resembling the lines of the Jytte Skou was in port, although it carried a different nameboard. I took an early train to Philadelphia, met with the local port authorities, determined that the vessel was indeed the Jytte Skou, and "nailed the mast" (presented the judgment to the captain). We put an armed guard on board to prevent the ship from leaving until the debt to Hadassah was paid. We had a certified check that afternoon.

          ❧

While at Searsport I experienced a Maine snow storm which was no fun. After two days drifts were piled up ten to twenty feet high. It was impossible to get out of the rooming house where I and several other dock people stayed. The proprietor soon ran out of food, except for scallops and lobster meat in the freezer. That and cans of evaporated milk were our breakfast lunch and dinner for two days. It took a while before I was prepared to order these sea foods again.

CARAVANS—CARAVANS

It was 1972. Through pressure from the United States, as the Jackson-Vanik Trade Bill was implemented, the Soviet Union reluctantly began to permit Jews to leave the "workers' paradise." This was the culmination of years of effort by the government of Israel, agencies of the United Jewish Appeal, and the American Committee for the Release of Soviet Jews. The bill liberalized U.S. commercial trade with the Soviet, provided that the USSR lifted restrictions on Jewish emigration. The Jewish Agency (the Agency) in Israel had representatives in the major Russian Jewish population centers. These agents provided transportation, counseling and, in general, whatever assistance was needed for those who wanted to leave, and who could get a Russian exit permit.

Congress had voted and the president approved $125 milion for Soviet Refugee Relief. It was anticipated that the refugees would be going to Israel. Seven hundred thousand Jews were able to take advantage of this window of opportunity and left.

The first groups, organized and paid for by the Agency, left by train for Austria. They were met by Agency personnel and escorted to a receiving base, the once elegant, but old, almost medieval, Schaumburg Castle near Vienna. In addition to meals and lodging for a few days, the refugees were exposed to the Hebrew language, Israeli culture, programs to assist new immigrants in absorption into Israeli society, and information on employment opportunities.

Some of the arrivals in Vienna, often those with relatives elsewhere, were siphoned off to Italy. From there they went to the United States, Canada, and Australia. Much of this activity was sponsored by the Hebrew Immigrant Aid Society based in New York. Gaynor Jacobson, the executive director, attractive, smart and personable, wanted an allocation of part of the $125 million. This grant had been orchestrated by Gottlieb Hammer and lobbied by him and myself in the State Department, with the assistance of the American Israel Political Action Committee (AIPAC) in the Congress.

The arrival of over thousands of new aliyot presented Israel with a major housing problem. While apartments and settlements were being constructed at a feverish pace, the flood of new-comers was greater than available housing could handle, and the Russian immigrants were dissatisfied with the tent and cinder block camps that the earlier arrivals in 1948–50 had put up with.

As most of the absorption responsibility was on the shoulders of the Agency, Russian housing was a prime topic at a United Israel Appeal board meeting I attended in the spring of 1972.

Gottlieb Hammer asked me what help might be possible from the U.S. government over and above that already granted for Soviet refugee resettlement.

I found that the Federal Emergency Management Administration (FEMA) had purchased three thousand state-of-the-art, new, fully equipped mobile homes. These were furnished with beds, chairs, sofas, kitchen equipment, air conditioners, TVs, and even blankets, pillows, cutlery, and plates.

FEMA had bought them for emergency housing of the homeless after a disastrous flood season near Wilkes-Barre and Johnstown, Pennsylvania. Less than one hundred and fifty had been used for the victims. FEMA was receptive to a negotiated sale to a registered voluntary organization, and Hadassah was once again called upon to participate in the mobile home program. Hadassah contracted with FEMA for the homes. The UIA supplied the funds for acquisition, shipment, and establishment of mobile home sites in Israel. In addition to negotiating the arrangement and planning the operation, the implementation became my responsibility

The final contract provided for FEMA to make 125 homes available without cost for the units. My office, with UIA funds, paid for transit from the Pennsylvania flood areas to port. FEMA also prepared the mobiles for ocean transport, tying down movable equipment and taping up windows and doors.

As the homes were on wheels, a major trucking company agreed, for $650.00 per unit, to tow them to Port Holabird in Baltimore Harbor for shipment to Israel.

In Hadassah's name, I chartered a medium-size container ship, the *Caribbean Princess.* Transport of the mobile homes to Baltimore was accomplished with a minimum of crises. When the ship arrived in Baltimore, all the units were on the dock ready to be loaded.

During the two days of loading I spent an afternoon observing the operation. Each unit was towed to the dock alongside the vessel, then hoisted up by a crane and placed in the ship's hold. As the crane was designed to lift sea-going containers, not mobile homes, the lifting tackle was a jerry-rigged arrangement. It worked for all but two mobiles, which slipped out of their harnesses and fell into Baltimore Harbor. Everything else went well. The *Princess* pulled out on schedule, but with only 123 units.

While the ship was making the passage from Baltimore to Haifa, the Agency was developing five different mobile home sites for the units near Israeli cities where employment opportunities existed. This involved laying concrete pads, installing facilities for water, electric service, and waste disposal.

Israel uses the European system of 50 cycle, 220 volts. The homes had been built in the U.S. for U.S. use and were wired with 60 cycle, 115 volt electrical systems. It would have been expensive to change the wiring. The solution turned out to be simple and inexpensive. For sixty dollars each transformers were bought to convert the Israeli current to the American electric system.

When the *Princess* reached Haifa, the mobile homes were unloaded. Heavy-duty tractors towed them to the various permanent installation sites, though only 121 of the 123 units actually found Agency platforms. They were hooked up to their utility pads ready to receive the Russian occupants. The Israel Defense Force requisitioned two of the units for special service in the Negev.

THE RUSSIANS REFUSED TO MOVE IN!

Even though the mobile homes offered better, and in many cases, more luxurious quarters than the Soviet refugees were used to in Russia, they refused to move in. Their perception was that caravans were poor peoples' homes, or okay for short vacation trips, but not what people lived in. Convincing them that their perceptions were erroneous called for a PR job.

Photo companies were retained to make movies of several mobile home trailer parks in California and Florida. The movies were shown to the Russians, who saw TV antennas, and Buicks, Fords, and Cadillacs parked beside the homes. They saw individual gardens next to the units and "rich" Americans living in them.

They moved in gladly.

Years later, on one of my frequent trips to Israel, I saw many of these homes, well worn, still being used by Ethiopian immigrants, and some are still in use today.

FIGURE 14: As part of the author's efforts on behalf of Hadassah
he would introduce Hadassah leaders to government officials.
Here they are greeted by Vice President Fritz Mondale.

H A D A S S A H

THE WOMEN'S ZIONIST ORGANIZATION OF AMERICA, Inc.
EIGHTEEN HUNDRED NINETEEN BROADWAY, NEW YORK 23, N. Y.

September 18, 1950

Mr. Maurice Atkin
213 E. Franklin Avenue
Silver Spring, Maryland

Dear Mr. Atkin:

Thank you very much for your message of good wishes which
I deeply appreciate. I warmly reciprocate your good wishes,
and extend hearty New Year's greeting to you and your family.

I want also to extend to you officially our warm thanks for
your wonderful and effective cooperation with Hadassah
in sending food supplies to Israel. We know that in the
complicated and difficult negotiations involved, your
assistance has been invaluable, and we do want you to know
how grateful we are.

With all good wishes,

Cordially yours,

Rose L. Halprin

Mrs. Samuel W. Halprin
National President

FIGURE 15: A letter which the author has treasured over the years

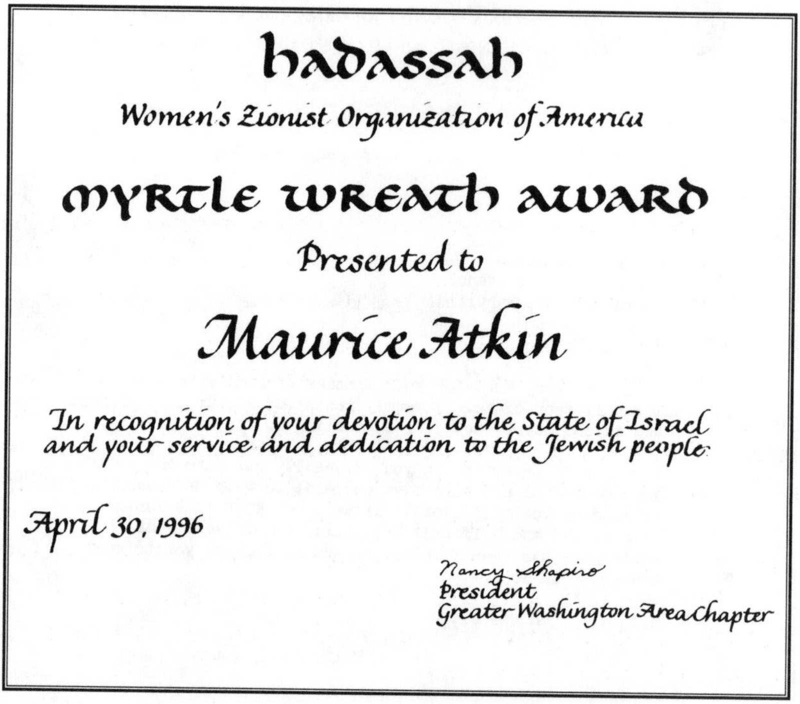

hadassah

Women's Zionist Organization of America

MYRTLE WREATH AWARD

Presented to

Maurice Atkin

In recognition of your devotion to the State of Israel
and your service and dedication to the Jewish people

April 30, 1996

Nancy Shapiro
President
Greater Washington Area Chapter

FIGURE 16:   The author was honored to receive the
Myrtle Wreath Award from Hadassah.

7

Surprise! VIP Guests
of the Israeli Government

NINETEEN FIFTY-ONE! WHAT a totally unexpected surprise to receive an invitation to visit Israel "As Guests of the Government of Israel." The invitation was accompanied by open first class round trip tickets for Flora and myself.

To visit Israel, particularly under VIP conditions, was an exciting prospect. But there were problems, personal and professional. Our three children, Joseph, Jonathan, and Barrie were very much in the recuperative stage of their battle with polio. Joseph was five years old, and Jonathan and Barrie not quite two. All needed considerable help and attention. Who would be responsible for this not easy task? And could I professionally afford to take time from a relatively new job? And when could we make the trip, for how long, and still feel comfortable eight thousand miles away?

With tremendous support from Flora's parents, and my mother, as well as from my office associates, we decided to go for it. So on April 15, 1951, we boarded the Pan Am Stratocruiser at New York's Idlewilde Airport (later renamed John F. Kennedy) for the start of one of the most momentous trips of our lives.

It had been just about a year since I had resigned from the Embassy of Israel staff and joined Robert R. Nathan Associates, Inc, economic consultants, as a senior associate. The PL 480 surplus food program that I had established just prior to leaving the embassy, was working well, and I had enlarged my list of Israeli clients.

FIGURE 17: Atkin family, 1949. Joseph, Flora, Jonathan, Maury and Barrie

The invitation came from Minister of Agriculture Pinchas Lavon. I later learned that Michael Palgi, director of the ministry's meat section, with whom I had worked closely was the instigator. We were sent first class tickets, including a cabin with a full-sized bed, aboard Pan Am's Stratocruiser.

From Idlewilde to New Brunswick, for refueling, then to Heathrow Airport, London. With a few hours before transferring to an El Al flight, Flora was able to take advantage of the British medical system and get her second typhoid shot. There had not been time enough in our hurried departure from Washington for this. An hour after leaving London we were in Paris. Next stop, Athens, Greece, and finally, 48 hours after leaving Idlewilde, we touched down at Lod Airport (later named Ben Gurion), Israel.

During the last leg of the flight, Captain Hoffman invited me to take the copilot's seat, which I did for two exciting hours. Under his close direction, I flew the propeller plane for about three hundred miles, bringing it down from cruising altitude to about four thousand feet. While quite a thrill, I felt as if I had had the wheel of a big truck in my hands.

The arrival at Lod Airport was filled with emotion and excitement. Despite the stewardesses' pleas, there was no way that the several dozen bearded chassids, members of an ultra religious orthodox sect, approaching the holy land, were going to stay in their seats, and not

FIGURE 18: A special visa for the Atkin family's VIP trip to Israel

excitedly congregate in the aisle. Most were coming to spend their remaining days on the sacred soil of Eretz Yisroel. These were the days when tourism to Israel was practically unknown. Flora and I were probably the youngest persons on board. The excitement and noise built even as we landed and the chassids could pour down the ramp and kiss the ground in Israel.

We were met on the tarmac by a delegation from the ministries of Agriculture, and Trade and Industry. We were especially pleased to find Dr. Eliezer Samuel and his wife, Mira, in the delegation. Haim Raday was also there. I ignored him. Whisked quickly through customs and immigration, Flora and I accepted the Samuel's invitation to be their guests for our first nights in Israel. So, In Eliezer's Pontiac sedan, a large car for Israel, we enjoyed a guided trip to Rehovot while catching up on family events of the past year.

Later, Raday came to our hotel in Tel Aviv, the Pension Shalva, and begged me to talk to him. I agreed.

"Why did you ignore me at the airport?" Raday asked.

I reminded him that despite the fact that I had done an outstanding job at the embassy, he had cut my salary below anything I could possibly live on. "Moshe," he replied. "I did you the biggest favor of your life."

I looked at him for a long moment. "You son-of-a-bitch, I guess you did. But that wasn't what you intended."

We shook hands and became friends after that.

During the entire time we were in Israel, April 17 to May 3, we received celebrity attention, almost embarrassingly so. The ministries of Finance, Agriculture, and Trade and Industry went out of their way to make our visit comfortable and memorable. Arrangements were made for us to experience all of the tourist sites that we could handle, to visit many agricultural and industrial facilities, to participate in meetings with government officials, and, of course, to visit immigration absorption centers and see firsthand how the surplus food program was being handled.

In each major city—Tel Aviv, Haifa, and Jerusalem—handpicked families were "assigned" to be our hosts and guides. These families were non-government professionals who spoke English and, as we discovered, several other languages. In Tel Aviv, Gershon Kaddar, an agricultural economist with the Anglo-Palestine Bank, and later a vice president of Bank Leumi, and his wife, Yael, were our hosts. In Haifa, James Sassower, a prominent freight forwarder and his wife, Leni, made our time in the north exciting, and in Jerusalem, we of course were introduced to that city by our old friends from embassy days, Uriel and Shoshana Heyd. These turned out to be wonderful selections. Even today, they and the children of those who have passed remain close friends.

The Finance Ministry also extended itself by supplying us with a more than adequate amount of ration coupons, and enough Israeli currency so that we should not have had to spend our American dollars while there, although we did, and gave back most of the

Israeli currency. The Jewish Agency and Hadassah were most gracious offering numerous courtesies that made us feel most welcome and special.

Our first experiences with Israeli life style were interesting enough to relate here in some detail, particularly in contrast with life in Israel in later years. Taking a page, literally, from Flora's diary "From Dan to Be'ersheva, 1951."

After the usual customs simplified by Maury's passport stating "par l'invitation of the Israeli government," we drove to Rehoboth (population, 18,000) with the Samuels to their home. En route we saw many bomb holes and much damage. We had seen the same in London. We drove through the colorful Yemenite area, past the temporary camps for the Iraqi refugees—in tents and tin huts, refugees who were dressed as they landed—many who looked like pajamas with a western business coat on top. Later we were to realize that this was a style of dress native to the Iraqis and that underwear is worn underneath. The loud striped so called pajamas are not just for sleeping.

The roads were not bad, but not marked (military precautions). Settlements stuck up here and there and in the middle of nowhere. The surroundings looked very tropical, much like British colonies in the West Indies—colorful; donkeys and carts, every kind of person, abundance of flowers, poppies and daisies growing wild along the road, many adult men in khaki shorts.

We had lunch with the Samuels and they were thrilled to receive our gifts—the salami and corn starch in particular. The white wrapping paper on the salami was most welcome in this paper scarce country. The Samuels have a flat in a two family house which has suffered heavy bomb damage. Small rooms, large windows, beautiful gardens, high ceilings, sparse severe furniture, amazingly old fashioned plumbing. WC in a separate room. A good idea. Kitchen equipment included a primus stove, and only one spigot, cold.

We had lebenia for the first time at lunch. It is a cross between yogurt and sour cream and made from dried milk. And the base for everything eaten in Israel. We also had sheep cheese. Plenty

of good bread. The Samuels shared their sparse coffee and sugar with us. (But later we went to the tourist bureau, got ration
cards, and more than repaid them.) Also oranges, home made
strudel and little olives.

Their house, like all others, made of cement, tile floors, blinds
on the outside, and no basement. Part of the second floor was
boarded up from bomb damage. Sandy unpaved roads.

After lunch a shower. Water heated in a kerosene heater, and
a good nap.

People tend to forget or don't want to remember what conditions
were like during the *tzenna* or scarcity period of early statehood.

The tiny hole-in-the-wall stores with almost bare shelves, no
fresh meat, a bit of smoked fish, some sickly green vegetables, lots of
second rate canned vegetables (never given to children) bread, cheese
and lebenia, along with an abundance of dried eggs, dried milk,
butter, and canned meats were a distant cry from today's modern
Israeli supermarkets with fully stocked shelves and computerized
checkouts.

The dried eggs, dried milk, butter, and canned meats were mostly
from the "surplus" food program. All foods, other than bread, were
rationed. Being just before the Pesach (Passover) holiday a larger than
usual allotment of fresh eggs was given. However, we were surprised
that not a single Pesach product was visible in the grocery stores we
visited. We learned that matzohs had been distributed earlier. Milk
was delivered to the housewife from a large vat on a donkey cart. The
watery milk, non-homogenized, was dipped out of the vat with a ladle
and placed in a pot or other receptacle supplied by the housewife.
The early customers received the cream. Kerosene was similarly sold
and delivered to the households.

Again, referring to Flora's diary:

> . . . we went to Givat Brenner, a kibbutz, near Rehovoth. It is
> about 22 years old and fairly prosperous. The buildings remind-
> ed us of a children's summer camp. It is on top of a hill from
> which the views were exquisite. Bougainvillea plants, cedars,
> lots of sabra (cactus), A delicious odor from orange blossoms

permeated the air. The children's house was very well appointed, and the children looked healthy. The children were now living in their quarters, although the swing is away from this system.

After several days in the Tel Aviv-Jaffa area, meeting various dignitaries, such as Dr. Hoofien, president of the Anglo-Israel Bank, the predecessor of Bank Leumi, and Gershon Kaddar, our guide and mentor during our later visit in the Tel Aviv-Jaffa area, we left for Jerusalem, in Dr. Samuel's Pontiac. Replacement car parts were extremely difficult to obtain, particularly for the rare large American car. Any breakdown meant that the vehicle could be out of commission for days if not weeks. It was considered an act of either great love or lunacy to let some one else drive one's car. I was invited to drive. I accepted.

The road to Jerusalem was a narrow two lane, curvy road running through forests of pine, eucalyptus, and cedars. Much of the road was directly along what would be the 1967 truce line, delineated by small white concrete markers. Many wrecked and burnt-out military vehicles were on the side of the road. It was crowded with trucks, cars, military vehicles, and an occasional donkey drawn dray. A slow process. But the views of the countryside from the roadside overlooks were magnificent, enhanced by spreads of blooming wild flowers. We also drove by and through small Jewish settlements, and more ancient Arab villages. More were visible on the distant hilltops.

Jerusalem

Entering Jerusalem was a scenic and emotional experience. One of the most ancient and pivotal cities of the modern world, the point of origin of three great religions, and holy to all three, the place where Jews world-wide had been praying for 2000 years, "Next Year in Jerusalem."

Banks of red, blue, white, and purple blossoms marked the entrance road. The houses, almost all built with the famed golden tinted Jerusalem stone, stood as sentinels to the ages. The roads were narrow and crowded, but there was a serenity and dignity that was absent from the hustle and bustle of Tel Aviv.

Jerusalem was quiet and seemingly laid back, except for the open vegetable and poultry market off Jaffa Road. There shouts of the market people extolling their wares were heard far away. In contrast to Tel Aviv the street dress was also much different: many ultra-religious Jews, the men in their black mid-calf coats with hats designed to reflect their individual religious communities, women in long full sleeved dresses, with *shaytls* (wigs), and many children in tow.

What a thrill it was to pass the many legendary buildings and sites: the campus of the Hebrew University, the YMCA Tower, the King David Hotel, the Hadassah Hospital, and of course, the most famous of all, the old city walls of biblical Jerusalem. A once in a lifetime emotional experience! And despite the strangeness of it all, we felt 'at home.'

As a courtesy, we made a stop at the Ministry of Agriculture office to pay our respects to Michael Palgi, now the food controller. This was in a former Arab hotel that the British had taken over for offices. Parts of the outside walls had suffered moderate bomb damage that even now, three years later, had not been repaired.

Eliezer directed us through the city to the home of our friends, the Heyds. The reunion with Uriel, Shoshana, and the boys, Michael and David, evoked many wonderful memories of their service in Washington. Their home, in the Talbieh section of Jerusalem, was in the lower half of a large rambling two story former Arab mansion built with Jerusalem stone with thick walls, recessed windows, high vaulted ceilings, tiled floors with a geometric printed design. Off the large entrance foyer, used as a dining area, a patio led to two bedrooms, and two other large rooms, a library and living room. To the rear another large foyer, used for clothes storage, led to the kitchen and pantry. Off a hall in the rear were two more large bedrooms and a bathroom. A side door opened to a lovely garden. Bathroom plumbing and kitchen equipment were antiquated, but in good condition. The upper floor was occupied by a Martin Buber library. The house exuded solidity and dignity, sparsely but tastefully decorated, with many shelves of books, magazines, and artifacts from Shoshana and Uriel's travels. There was no bomb damage.

After a quick visit with the Heyds, who insisted that we stay with them, Uriel, Flora, and I returned to the Ministry of Agriculture to meet Minister Pinchas Lavon. We were greeted with great warmth and welcome. After several minutes of pleasantries Uriel and Flora left. I was asked to stay for a private talk with Lavon about Israel's food situation. From that chat I was just beginning to get an idea of the importance to Israel of the food programs that I had initiated and developed.

It was a humble but proud sensation, as if all of my past training and background had been for this moment and these activities.

During a three hour walk in Jerusalem with Uriel, his intimate knowledge of this ageless city was priceless. We visited Mt. Zion, and went as close to the walls of the Old City as possible. It was easy to see armed British trained Arab soldiers patrolling the walls. With the Wailing (Western) Wall unavailable, the orthodox prayed and were buried on Mt. Zion. The Mt. of Olives was also unavailable to Israelis. But from Mt. Zion the view of the old city and of Mt. of Olives was spectacular. Land mines and barbed wire were strewn around in abundance in the marked areas that was no-man's-land between the Jewish and Arab sectors. We had to walk with great care.

The oldest Jewish section outside the city walls, built in 1860 by the Montefiore family, consisted of two sections of row houses, and a windmill. It was now a slum area with no plumbing and great poverty. (After the 1967 war the area would be renovated into an upscale apartment and artist colony.)

Pesach seder in Jerusalem with the Heyds was a never-to-be forgotten experience. How Shoshana managed to prepare a feast for ten people, using a two burner kerosene stove was an Israeli miracle. Following the usual seder rituals, including some lusty singing, Shoshana served soup with matzoh balls, chicken, potatoes and gravy, string beans, and ice cream. It was not made easier by the shortage of basic foodstuffs as well as specialty items. Our abundant ration cards, plus the availability of the American foodstuffs alleviated the food problem somewhat. A sabotaged water line created a real problem of water for cooking and cleaning.

Utilizing our abundant ration coupons, as well as the delicacies we had brought from the states along with some specialties that Shoshana's brother had sent from Detroit, all our meals were tasty, more than adequate, and nourishing. Except for the coffee. It was generally terrible. We had brought a supply of jars of Nescafe Instant Coffee as gifts for our hosts. This was unknown in Israel and heartily welcomed. The term 'Nescafe' was derived from the Nestle Company's name. Coincidentally, the word *nes* in Hebrew means miracle. To our hosts, Nescafe was a miracle.

Following the seder, Uriel invited me to take a midnight walk. From his house, in the light of a full moon, we walked to the Old City walls—no man's land. With armed Arab sentries directly above us, razor wire in pockets around us, we picked our way through narrow streets to the Meir Shearim, sector of the new city. As we walked we heard beautiful songs and chants from the open windows of various homes and yeshivas. They were in Hebrew and Yiddish, as well as every language of the countries where Jews had lived.

Here I was in Jerusalem. The goal, wish, and hope expressed in the final words of the Pesach seder, "Next Year In Jerusalem" had become a reality. I could not help but think of my grandfather chanting those words at our family seders back home, of my father's Zionist work before his premature death, and of my mother's work in the Pioneer Women's organization. How much they would have loved to have been in this place at this time. Would I ever come back? Would I ever get a chance to get inside these ancient walls? All of this and more raced through my mind as prickles raced up and down my spine. It was indeed a very emotional moment and experience.

The first day of Pesach was also Shabat (the Sabbath). Jerusalem had a holiday atmosphere. No cars, trucks or busses moved. The streets were full of walkers. No one smoked. People were dressed in their Shabat best, particularly the children. The quiet in the streets, a welcome relief from week day noises, was almost spiritual.

Among the walkers going to and from synagogue services, or just strolling, one could spot a checked or plaid jacket—very non Israeli. This was usually a gift from an overseas relative. It seemed that everyone had a relative in St. Louis, or Pittsburgh, or New York. "Do you know my cousin in Milwaukee?" was not an infrequent question, with the town varying. We actually knew some relatives in Washington of total strangers, who stopped us and asked the usual question. On the other hand, during our stay in Israel, we frequently bumped into people we knew from other places, visitors, consultants, government officials. It was almost a small town atmosphere in this respect.

We walked and walked in the clear crisp April air. We climbed the steps of the 172 foot tall YMCA tower, then the tallest structure in Israel, went through the historic King David Hotel and its gardens, and to the poorer and more colorful part of Jerusalem. We observed Yemenites with their traditional robes and shawls over long pantaloons, Polish yeshiva *bochers* (religious students) dancing to the Wall, bearded ultra orthodox Jews in knee length striped coats, curling *payess* (sidelocks), large black hats, often fur trimmed, and many handsome, frequently blond, small children with long payess.

Incident: Two Boukarian boys admonishing Uriel for bringing Americans to see their part of Jerusalem. "It is not pretty. Have they come here to laugh at us?"

After more walking and visits to two Yemenite synagogues, listening to beautiful chants, we returned to Heyd's home to wash and prepare to go to two parties that night. But, there was a power outage. This meant no water for washing or drinking. Uriel and I went to a pump nearby to get water for the toilet.

Beryl Locker, vice president of the Jewish Agency in Israel was our host at party number one. Other guests were mostly foreign diplomats stationed in Israel. Lots of food and drink. The guests probably used as much sugar as a year's ration for many Israelis. I had guilt feelings.

The second affair was at Supreme Court Judge Halevy's home in a much more relaxed atmosphere. Most of the attendees were academic types. At both parties we found that we knew some of the guests as well as had mutual acquaintances back home with others. In those busy, exciting Jerusalem days we realized that the people had many other hardships than just food, water, paper, and a scarcity of consumer goods.

Transportation and Communication Problems

Car and truck tires were in very short supply. Too many large trucks were running on dangerously thin tires. Trains between Tel-Aviv,

Jerusalem and Haifa were normally jammed with passengers. Busses were even more crowded.

Almost all taxis were Mercedes-Benz cars, imported to the Middle East by a Jordanian dealer before 1948. Taxi drivers might be *sabras* (native born Israelis), recent immigrants, or Arabs. It was not unusual for Jewish drivers to have their radios tuned to classical music or news in English from Jordan or Egypt. Arab drivers usually listened to Arab music or news in Arabic from Jordan or Egypt. Unlike American cabbies, tipping was frowned upon by the Israeli Jewish drivers. This attitude would change in time.

No family was permitted more than one car. Replacement parts took weeks to obtain from abroad. Large family or official cars were so few that everyone knew whose car it was.

Much, and most efficiently, inter city travel was by *sherutim* (jitney service). These were large, always black, retreads from U.S. limousine fleets. They were also always seven passenger Chryslers or Dodges with two fold-down extra seats. To use the service one bought a relatively inexpensive ticket for a reservation for one of six seats for a fixed time and destination. We used this service frequently, and thoroughly enjoyed meeting most of the strangers with whom we rode.

Telephone service was almost nonexistent. The Ministry of Agriculture, with hundreds of employees had only two trunk lines to the outside. To place a long distance call from home, office, or hotel it was necessary to get a reservation from the post office. It could take hours before a connection was established. Later, in Haifa, at an exclusive hotel, we had a phone in the room, but most of the time it was not working. Transferring a call from one place to another was an impossibility. Wires and cables had to be sent from the post office which was always crowded. On one occasion we stood in line for over an hour to send a wire from Jerusalem to Tel Aviv. It arrived two days later.

⋰

Despite shortages of food and often water, lack of modern household conveniences, up-to-date office and communication equipment, and problems with unfriendly neighbors, there was a wonderful spirit of idealism evident at all levels and all classes of the population. Volunteerism and a can-do atmosphere was pervasive. Sharing what one had with others was the norm, not the exception.

More discussions with officials of the ministries of Agriculture and Trade and Industry, additional sightseeing at Herzl's tomb and Hadassah installations, wound up our all too brief stay in Jerusalem prior to heading back to Tel Aviv and Rehovoth.

To Tel Aviv

After four memorable days in Jerusalem, we bid adieu to our hosts, the Heyds, and from the government taxi stand in Jerusalem took a sherut to Beit Dagon in the Hakirya[5], Tel Aviv, where Eliezer Samuel was waiting to take us back to Rehovoth and a most welcome hot shower. The Samuels complained about the *chamsin* (hot winds), but to us they felt delightful.

Following a night with the wonderful hospitality of the Samuels we headed for Tel Aviv. En route we stopped at Richon to meet Eliezer's two talented sisters. One made dolls and miniatures from spent bullets, the other had an art ceramic factory. Their work was beautiful.

The government tourist office planned to house us in Tel Aviv's most posh hotel. I demurred and requested that we stay at a 'pension' in the heart of the city, named "Shalva." This appealed to me as it was the name of my parents' cottage at Herald Harbor, Md., on the Severn River.

And wonder of wonders, the Shalva had hot running water. Mrs. Ben Schlomo, the owner, was extremely gracious and helpful to us. After settling in, Flora went on her own to visit relatives of friends back home, while I attended one of many meetings at the Hakirya.

Gershon Kaddar, our designated host in Tel Aviv, met us at the pension to take us to midday dinner at a seaside tourist restaurant. Assisted by our abundant ration coupons, the meal was ample, but plain. No complaint. As Gershon was our host, he needed a receipt for the meal. This lead to an interesting, but not unusual scene. Gershon asked *Adon* (waiter or Sir) for a receipt. The waiter suddenly had to add and re-add the bill, subtract and change the bill for whatever bureaucratic purpose Gershon needed it. When the waiter was asked to sign or initial the bill, he renewed his mathematical forays on the poor bill all over again. Finally on the fifth try he seemed to get it right, and initialed it.

And now our education in immigrant absorption began. As an agricultural economist I was very interested in seeing the unique settlements in Israel about which I had heard so much. Gershon Kaddar had intimate knowledge about them.

There were various types of agricultural settlements. Within each type there were diverse political and religious groups—from the most radical to the most liberal.

Roughly grouped they were:

- Kibbutz—predominantly a socialist agricultural structure, but of necessity, often with some small industry. Initially and idealistically, no hired labor was permitted. Family life was subservient to the community. All property was communally owned and worked. Communal dining room with food prepared by assigned cooks. No money wages. Earnings used to buy supplies, including clothes that were distributed to members as needed.
- Moshav ovdim and moshav shitufi—Workers' cooperative small holders settlements. Each family had its own house and land to cultivate and animals to raise. Product marketing was cooperative. Earnings distributed in cash. Some communally owned land and infrastructure. The moshav shitufi had many of the characteristics of a kibbutz; collective ownership and economy, but each family had its own house, and was responsible for its own cooking, laundry, etc.
- Cooperative village—like a simple village, but with central marketing and purchasing units.
- Moshav—ordinary village, often grew into a town or city.
- Ma'abara—new immigrant settlement, frequently temporary, established by The Jewish Agency. Members were employed in government and Agency projects, but encouraged to work their own allotted land.

First we stopped at a ma'abara near Rehovoth. Here only tents were used for housing, although at other ma'abarot there were tin huts and even wooden or cement houses with corrugated iron roofs, very hot in the summer, and equally cold in the winter. Some ma'abarot had been in existence for some time. The residents of these had added gardens, fences and decorations to their 'temporary' houses. New immigrants were pouring in at more than one thousand a day from Europe, North Africa, Yemen, India and a smattering from the western hemisphere. They were coming into a country that had barely enough resources to feed, house, and clothe its existing population. But resources available were shared with the newcomers.

Visiting these temporary settlements and reception centers, I realized the importance from a subsistence standpoint of the thousands of tons of surplus foodstuffs.

The newest immigrants, just arrived from Atlit, a reception camp near Haifa, where they had spent their first four or five days in Israel, were all Iraqis. Their 'pajamas' reminded me of the clothes worn by Jews in the European concentration camps. In contrast, the women's long dark dresses and babushka type head coverings, often included beautiful embroidery across the front. Some of the newest immigrant groups lacked the basic elements of hygiene. Young children were without diapers or panties. One man walked out of his tent and urinated right in front of it. Trash cans around the camp were ignored. Trash, and orange peels were simply thrown on the ground like chewing gum wrappers in the United States at the time. We observed a social worker, while giving a lecture on sanitation, demonstrating to the men how to put on and wear underwear.

I was anxious to see how U.S. surplus foods were being doled out for relief. To my surprise, I learned that no food was distributed at this ma'abara. Everyone was expected to go to work right away. Each immigrant family was given a little money advance with which to buy food and tools. Each worker was expected to buy his own tools. Hard experience taught administrators that giving out tools taught no respect for them. Work was available in nearby kibbutzim, in the cities, on the roads, and on various public works projects. Social workers recognized that many mistakes were made as they coped and learned, often by sad experience, how best to handle the flood of new citizens.

Due to housing and job shortages families often remained in a ma'abara for several years. If they had relatives elsewhere, new immigrants frequently joined them. It was also not unusual for new immigrants to move into evacuated Arab quarters—generally illegally.

Our guide in the ma'abara had been an accountant in Czechoslovakia. In Israel, he was a farmer. He took us to his home and farm in Aquir, a moshav ovdim. In the beginning the Jewish Agency built the roads, the basic house and gave each family a cow, a barn, and a utility shed. They were also allotted about twenty dunim, five acres for agricultural uses. The Ministry of Agriculture guaranteed support prices for their vegetables the first year. Many residents had made substantial improvements to their units, others had not. Some had added rooms, gardens and attractive decor. Others had done nothing. The contrasts were often startling.

From Aquir, we went to Dr. Moshe Witkon's home for tea. Witkon had only recently returned from Washington where he had served in the Israel Embassy as Financial Counselor. In Germany he had been a banker and lawyer. The outside of his three-room flat was representative of the ubiquitous grey concrete Tel Aviv architecture. The inside however, reflected upscale European taste. The furniture, designed by the Witkons, had been brought from Germany when they left that country. Included were sectional bookcases with recessed lighting, elegant dining room cabinets, and luxurious sofa beds. Mr. and Mrs. Witkon slept in the adjoining living dining room area. Their teenage daughter and son shared a small bedroom. When Rya, the daughter entertained, the Witkons could not go to bed.

Returning to Israel after their tour of duty in America was quite an adjustment. This was, she explained, no time to start in housekeeping. They had given away many staples of housekeeping that were not easily replaceable in the tzenna years of scarcity. Not even bottles were available to get kerosene, milk, or catsup at a store.

By this time, Montezuma's revenge, touristitis, or as known in Israel, *shilshul*, had caught up with me—but good. Back at Pension Shalva, Mrs. Ben Schlomo fixed special foods for me using a combination of our ration coupons plus American packaged dried soups and Jello that we had brought with us. Flora was able to luxuriate with hot water in the shower and sink, and do a needed laundry job. No soap was provided. But fortunately we had brought our own. The toilet paper was similar to Halloween crepe paper, and our supply of peelable disposable diapers, thanks to my shilshul, was running low.

Shortly after my in-room breakfast of American (surplus) cheddar cheese[6], matzoh, sour orange marmalade, American (surplus) butter, soft cooked egg—thanks to our ration points—and tzenna coffee, a pre-state immigrant from Russia named Moshe Atkin called. He had read in the paper that I was in Israel, and he wanted to try to trace ancestry. We were unable to find a connection, alas. "Did he need anything?" "Oh, no, we have all we need."

I found out after he left that he was one of the founding members of the Egged Bus Cooperative—and was well off.

After I recovered from shilshul and under the knowledgeable direction and care of Gershon Kaddar we set out to learn about the Negev[7]. In his tiny Czechoslovakian Skoda, Gershon, and his wife, Yael, a school teacher, Flora and I were off to visit some settlements. The bumpy, jolting, rock and roll ride made us appreciate the smooth ride of Samuel's American Pontiac. Being in the back seat, Flora suffered the most. I noticed that Gershon kept a loaded pistol in the car.

First stop was Kfar Warburg, a ten year old moshav ovdim, of about 100 farms, and relatively prosperous. Homes there were quite spacious, with a concrete porch, electricity, an electric stove—but a kerosene primus unit for use during the frequent outages—and a piano. And of course, many books and art works.

The farmer, originally from Poland, had been given two cows. He now had many more. On his 20 dunim he grew 20 tons of turnips, and managed to get five cuttings of green fodder per year. In Israel the feed/fodder was brought to the cows, rather than the cows browsing in a pasture. The practice was three milkings a day. He planned to buy a refrigerator and a milking machine as soon as he could afford them.

Leaving Kfar Warburg, we passed a former British police station, a deserted Taggart house, named after the British colonel who developed this particularly offensive institution to the Jews. In May '48, when the Brits left Palestine they turned these small fortresses over to the Arabs. During the War of Independence elements of the invading Egyptian army occupied and operated out of this particular

Taggart house. With just a few defenders, kibbutz Negba, about 400 yards away, held out against the Egyptians, and routed them. This was a turning point in the war.

A stunning change of pace was a stop at a Bedouin tent village. The inhabitants, particularly the children, were filthy. The goat hair tents reeked. Animals and humans lived together. Here we had our first experience riding a camel. The driver was dissatisfied with the tip, and requested more—a sharp contrast from practices in Jewish Israel at that time.

Next stop, a few hundred feet away from the Bedouin camp, and in great contrast to it, was kibbutz Shoval, started in 1946 under the Jewish Agency program "Operation Negev." While predominantly agricultural, Shoval also produced prefabricated huts for the Jewish Agency, and Swedish styled furniture. Its defense system included a two story fortress building with mounted machine guns on the roof. The second floor was a well equipped library. The first floor was the armory. Each floor had sniper slots.

The average age of the kibbutz members was 26, so the children were still nursery school age. The school was a must on the visitor list. Excellent equipment, all scaled to children's size, very healthy clean looking kids, many blondes. The immaculate cribs, and nurses in white seemed strange in the desert. They were even stranger in the bomb shelter beneath the children's house. In those days, in all socialist kibbutzim, the children lived in the children's house, not with their parents.

The communal dining room, where we enjoyed lunch was decorated by a kibbutz artist, who was then in Paris studying art underwritten by the kibbutz. The food was good, and, European style, the soup came after the main course. Adults, except those on guard duty or otherwise required to be away, ate together. The children ate in the children's house. Kibbutz table manners left much to be desired. No napkins, all cutlery in a common bowl. The same plastic bowl was used for the main course and for the soup. Each table had a *kolbol*, the garbage depository. Lunch, the big meal of the day, included spaghetti and gravy, pickled vegetables, meat loaves, an excellent soup, bread and matzoh, and orange-raisin-banana compote.

It was also at this kibbutz that we had our first experience with a Turkish toilet, a hole in a wooden floor over which the user had to squat, hoping to aim straight, with no paper provided. The members must have been adept at using this facility, as it was extremely clean.

After lunch the secretary of the kibbutz invited us to return with him to the Bedouin camp to meet its chief, Sheik Saloman. The Sheik, about 70 years old had accumulated 36 wives, seventy six sons, the youngest fourteen years old, and uncounted daughters. The story was told about a day that he was walking through his fields and saw a lovely young girl working. He told her that he wanted her for his wife. She replied that she would have to speak to her father. "And who is your father?"

"Sheik Saloman," was the answer.

However, we did not get to meet the famous Sheik Saloman for he had driven for the day to Be'ersheva in his Buick, a gift from the government of Israel.

We were received, however, by his eldest son.

The Sheik had a simple cinder block building as his office and receiving room. On one wall were crossed Israeli flags, surrounded by framed pictures of Herzl, Ben-Gurion, and Weizmann. The area had experienced a damaging drought and food stuffs were short. I asked the eldest son what his people would do about food to offset shortages. He shrugged his shoulders, and said, "The government will provide." I did not think he was wrong.

Flora and Yael were honored by an invitation to visit the Sheik's harem which they accepted. About ten women, they later reported, were seated on the ground around a fire in the courtyard of a stone building. Children, filthy and diseased around the eyes, were running around, amid the swarming flies. A baby in a cradle was being licked by a dog. The women were all bedecked with jewelry, flowing robes, and black tattoo designs over their faces. Every woman had a large silver piece of jewelry fastened to one side of her nose. The son's wife was nursing a baby as was the Sheik's youngest wife. Pictures were not permitted—but Flora's movie camera held against her body just happened to be turned on.

Next stop, south to Be'ersheba, a desert town that would have been at home in a Hollywood western film. Thinly populated, it showed no signs of the modern city it has become. Its central feature was a mosque and minaret.

Then on to Kibbutz Revivim, with a previously issued military pass allowing Sgan Aluf (Colonel) Atkin and party to travel south. We left the impossible roads and drove through the desert sands. Despite all windows being closed and no air-conditioning, the sand and dust infiltrated the car.

Revivim was an agricultural settlement experimenting in partial salt water irrigation. Date, olive, and pomegranate trees seemed to flourish in the briny brew from the salty wells. Revivim also produced wheelbarrows and steel cots. The average age of the sixty members was twenty-one. The kibbutz was particularly important as a military outpost, being only fifteen miles from the Egyptian border.

A full day!

Headed North

The next day after a morning of meetings in the Hakirya involving immigrant absorption matters and paying visits to several food processing plants with the Kaddars as our guides, we drove north along the Mediterranean coast to Kfar Vitkin and Kibbutz Herut.

Yael had been raised at Vitkin, originally a kibbutz, but now a prosperous village with plenty of cows and chickens. We enjoyed tea with Yael's parents. Then we crossed the highway to Herut, a well established moshav shitufi, an American colony. One of the prominent families was the Allentucks, from Washington D.C. Carl and Blossom Allentuck. During our teenage days they had been members of our Young Judea group, which met every Sunday afternoon at the Jewish Community Center in Washington. Carl and Blossom had put their money where their mouth's were and made early aliyah to Israel.

The Allentucks operated a very modern and apparently successful silk screen printing plant at Herut making painted tiles, greeting cards, children's puzzles, and wooden dolls. They lived in a charming rambler well equipped with American appliances. Even then in Israel, with dollars, one could have everything. They also had an abundance of food, all sent from America. It was good to spend some time with this family.

It was time to go to Haifa, Israel's third largest city and industrial center. Back in the Samuel's comfortable Pontiac the next day we headed through Zikhron Ya'aqov, Mishmar-Ha-Emek, Nazareth, Kfar Hittim, Tiberias, Afikim and then to Haifa; like going to Boston from Washington by way of Chicago, but fascinating.

At Mishmar-Ha-Emek we caught a thrilling sight of the snow covered Mount Hermon, on the Syrian/Israel border. Its ski slopes were avidly used by former western European Israelis. A scenic drive, with many hairpin turns and magnificent views of the fertile Emek valley, alone made the trip worth while.

The mountain climb brought us to the ancient Biblical city of Nazareth. Its Arabic architecture fit beautifully into the mountainous slopes. Arab men in their white headgear sat and smoked in the open-air coffee shops. Some women toted rectangular oil cans on their heads to be filled at the nearby Well of Nazareth. Others similarly carried earthenware jugs as depicted in historical paintings. Old churches and landmarks denoted where Christ did this and that. We took the time to visit a few of them. My passport with the magic Government Invitation worked wonders at the military checkpoints. While in Nazareth, we picked up a French woman eye doctor hitchhiking to Tiberias. She had missed her bus.

Kfar Hittim, a moshav shitufi, merited a short stop. In addition to agriculture, it had a textile plant. Our guide there, from Bulgaria, spoke French and Hebrew. Our French lady doctor came in handy as a translator, and Flora had an opportunity to practice her French.

Our next stop was Tiberias where our Frenchie left us. Tiberias, on the western shore of the Kinneret, or Sea of Galilee was a busy picturesque tourist and fishing town. The promenade along the shore was lined with restaurants featuring fried St Peter's fish, otherwise commercially known as *tilapia*. Seasonally, tourists could, on the same day, ski on nearby Mt. Hermon, and later swim in the sea. Across the Kinneret, the ground rose steeply to the Syrian Golan Heights. There Syrian gunners in concrete pillboxes, overlooked a major agricultural and industrial part of Israel. And they let the Israelis know it by too often shooting into the villages and farms of Israel. Hotels were crowded with Passover guests. Unable to find lodging for the night we proceeded to Afikim, one of the oldest and most prosperous kibbutzim in Israel. This turned out to be a delightful unique experience. A long time member of the kibbutz, a friend of the Samuels, graciously and with extreme hospitality took us in. Afikim has new modern apartments for its older members.

A good supper in the kibbutz adult dining room was a one plate meal with plenty of tasty food—cheese, fresh sour cream, tomatoes, fish, potato salad, bread! (It was still Pesach), matzo cake dessert, and something that passed for coffee—no sign of a food shortage. After supper a symphony orchestra composed of members of several kibbutzim gave a concert including Haydn, Mozart, and Handel. The dining room did double duty as a concert hall. The walls of the dining room were decorated with murals painted by our host's brother, who was then in Paris studying art at kibbutz expense.

While Afikim had an agricultural base, its prosperity was due to a modern plywood plant—with logs imported from South America. Unlike most kibbutzim, some workers at the plant were hired employees and not kibbutz members. The factory's general manager, formerly a Chicago CPA, was our guide around the plant.

After leaving Afikim the Samuels dropped us off in Tiberias and they returned to Rehoboth. We stayed overnight in a most unsatisfactory pension where the beds had obviously not been changed since the previous occupants.

Haifa

A taxi to Haifa and the luxurious Megiddo Hotel on the slopes of Mt. Carmel was our compensation for the previous night in Tiberias. To us the Megiddo was like an oasis must have been to a merchant caravan after days of traveling the desert; clean, spacious, good beds, plenty of hot water, working telephones, and good food. All this and a beautiful scenic view of the Mediterranean coast from the balcony to our room.

Haifa, situated on the picturesque slopes of Mt. Carmel, was a bustling business and commercial city. Many of its buildings were bullet marked, and in many places war related structural damage had not been repaired. The city's economy seemed dominated by a motivated population of highly educated German Jews who had come to Palestine early in the Hitler period. Many had advanced degrees from some of Germany's most prestigious universities.

Haifa had also experienced attacks from nearby Arab villages, particularly Acco just across the bay. Everyone had war stories to tell, not with a sense of braggadocio, but about protecting their homes and hearths during the Arab uprisings.

Shortly after our arrival in Haifa, we were introduced to James and Helena (Leni) Sassower, our hosts and guides. James' freight forwarding firm, Sassower, Inc. was responsible for the customs clearance of much of the surplus food shipments from the U.S. Both James and Leni had come to Palestine as newly weds from Hamburg, Germany.

One early evening James and I were on the way to the docks. I wanted to see how the shipments were being handled. By pure accident we found Flora downtown waiting for a bus to take her back to the hotel. She joined us. We were stopped on entering the docks as women were not allowed in the area after dark. James, a member of the Port Authority, took care of that problem.

The port seemed to me to be much too small and crowded for the volume of commercial imports, exports, and the movement of new immigrants. Compared to other docks that I have seen, it appeared to be quite disorganized and chaotic. Broken cases, barrels and drums, with their contents spilled on the dock sides attested to poor packing or poor handling, or both. Commodities spilled included surplus dried milk and dried eggs, Rokeach soups, Czechoslovakian tiles, and kotex.

A ride on a tender, courtesy of the harbor police, provided us with a magnificent view of Haifa by night and Acco across the bay. This unexpected but most enjoyable treat was followed by dinner at the Sassower's very modern home high in the Carmel. The house would have been at home in any American upscale community.

The following morning a representative from the Ministry of Agriculture, Mr. Mazur, met us at the hotel. While Flora luxuriated at the Megiddo (oasis) catching up on personal and household duties, Mr. Mazur and I spent the morning visiting various food processing facilities. The Tnuva Creamery was repackaging the thirty to sixty pound cases of U.S. surplus butter to smaller sized units for distribution. The president of the company was our guide. The Shemen factory using vegetable oils from peanuts, sunflowers, olives and soybeans produced both food and non-food commodities, including cooking oils, soaps, shampoos, shaving creams, cosmetics, and detergents. Dr. Friedland, CEO of Shemen, proudly made sure that we had a complete tour of his facility. The Blue Band Margarine plant, a subsidiary of the Lever Brothers, a British firm, used vegetable oils for margarine. Mr. Ernst Teltsh, the general manager, seemed delighted to show us his well-run factory.

The next day I spent an exciting morning at Atlit, an immigrant reception center on the seacoast south of Haifa. Dressed in khakis like many of the new arrivals, but with a movie camera hidden in a rucksack, accompanied by a Jewish Agency social worker who was also my translator and also dressed as an immigrant, I went through the reception process (did not get the shots given to the new arrivals),and observed the distribution of foodstuffs, clothing, and cash for immediate needs. Iraqi women were squatting on the ground washing clothes in small wash basins. When tables were brought in, the basins were placed on the tables so the women would not have to squat. The women climbed onto the tables and then squatted by the basins. The Jewish Agency social workers obviously had much to do.

Much of the foodstuffs distributed came from the U.S. surplus stocks. These new arrivals were not used to these foods. Their diet had been principally rice, lamb, potatoes and some salads. They were given *lebenia*, a sort of yogurt made from dried skim milk, cottage cheese also made from dried skim milk, and American cheddar cheese. In many cases, trying these strange foods, their stomachs revolted visually. All of this I surreptitiously filmed.

May Day, on to Safad

May Day, a special holiday in socialist Israel, we were guests of the Sassowers on a motor trip to Safad. The roads were jammed with trucks of singing kibbutzniks: Mapai groups waving red flags, Mapam groups waving red flags with the hammer and sickle design. The Sassower's car was a seven passenger much used Chrysler limousine. Like most of the sherutim in the country it had been imported from

Detroit. James' car did not join the celebration and broke down near Kiryat Bialek. Although this was a fairly large settlement just outside Haifa, no phones were available, and James had to walk some distance to locate and bring back a mechanic. An hour later we were again on our way.

At a brief stop we viewed the Arabesque architecture of the fortress of Acco, and walked along the seaside walls that Napoleon had failed to breach. The gentle waves of the beautiful blue Mediterranean lapped at our feet.

Prior to reaching Safad, our destination, we came across a sight out of a thousand years ago. From a slight rise in the midst of Arab farmland, and as far as we could see in any direction, our car and ourselves were the only evidence that would have been inappropriate centuries ago. The center of the scene was an elaborate Arab water well. It was built on several levels. A large wooden foot-powered treadwheel pumped the water. On the top level, groups of turbaned men, seemingly in emotional discussions or arguments, oversaw their women working in the nearby and distant fields. The field workers, all women, walked slowly and gracefully up to the second level of the well with their ceramic jugs or oil cans balanced on their heads, filled their containers, replaced them on their heads, and gracefully walked back into the fields. Donkeys, horses, droves of cows and sheep were led to drink at the lowest level. A bit further away were water buffaloes, pulling plows and camels grazing. The entire panorama was a treat for the eye and mind.

Leaving this Biblical scene, we climbed the Swiss-like mountains to a view of the Kinneret, and then on to Safad, quaint, old Arabic, and steeped in history and religious lore. A noontime chicken dinner—our coupons—in a picturesque Arab building with a high vaulted ceiling, thick walls, and a tile staircase to a second level balcony provided a great view of the area. We did not have enough time to explore Safad's religious and arts center on this trip, but would enjoy it many times in later years.

Having a 5:00 PM appointment in Haifa we hurried back, except for another look at the still busy well scene. Ernst Teltsh, from Blue Band Margarine, and his wife Chava, had invited us for an evening trip to Kibbutz Ein Harod to see the Israeli Ballet in a new production. The kibbutz, politically leftist, had twelve hundred residents. Unlike other kibbutzim we had visited, it had a hostel for guests, a Hollywood style swimming pool, large fish (carp), ponds, and a printing operation. It seemed quite prosperous.

May Day activities were still going strong, as they had all day. Watching the crowds of people was a show in itself. Most had been trucked in for the performance from nearby kibbutzim and ma'abarot. There were also a large number of motorcycles, private cars, some busses, as well as a few horse drawn carts.

The Teltsh's apologized for locking their car, considered an insult to the kibbutz. However, they said that with all the new immigrants, and car parts almost impossible to replace, locking was an act of prudence.

The ballet, which did not start until 9:00 PM, was disappointing, but not the theater of the audience. Sabras, Iraqi Jews, German Jews, Russian Jews, farm types, city residents, in varied costumes and dress, young and old, created a dramatic Babel of languages. After the performance the press of people and vehicles of every description trying to reach the highway completed the ballet drama.

The next two days consisted of wrap-up meetings in Tel Aviv and Jerusalem with several government committees and planning sessions with the Jewish Agency and Hadassah for ongoing programs. Then the inevitable farewells and goodbyes to so many wonderful people, particularly the Heyds, Palgis, Kaddars, Sassowers, and Samuels, who did so much to make our trip memorable.

My special passport cleared us easily through departure rites at LOD airport for our trip home via Paris. Two days in Paris was such a psychological shift that, before we went to the Paris airport, we stocked up with packages of bon bons and pastries. After all, who knew what we would find in the United States!

8

Seas of Sheets
Israel—June, 1967

ON JUNE 5, 1967, the Israeli air force eliminated the Egyptian air force of almost 500 planes, losing 26 of its own. The next day, Jordanian, Syrian, and Iraqi planes took to the air, believing Egyptian President Nasser's personally telephoned lies, that his troops were half way to Tel Aviv and his air force was victorious. All three of these air forces were badly mauled. In six days, the war was over. Israel was now in control of the Golan Heights, the entire Sinai peninsula, the old walled city in Jerusalem and the total west bank of the Jordan river.

Background

Following Israel's War of Independence in 1948, not a single Arab state accepted Israel's existence in the Middle East. Plots and counter plots, threats and boycotts were the diplomatic and political currency of the day. A constant stream of UN Resolutions instigated by Arab states kept the pot boiling.

Yasser Arafat, who took control of the Palestine Liberation Organization (PLO) in 1965, initiated scheme after scheme to encourage every Arab state to mobilize on Israel's borders and simultaneously wipe out the stain to Arab arms and dignity of 1948. Syria and Egypt, encouraged by the Soviets, were responsive to these schemes.

From positions on the Golan Heights, Syrian troops shot and shelled the Israeli farms below, shot at Israeli fishermen on the Sea of Galilee, and entered into a program of harassment along the frontier.

Syria also developed plans to change the course of the Jordan River in order to deprive Israel of its main water source.

At the same time Egypt was saber rattling at the UN, Nasser forced UN Secretary General U Thant to withdraw the small UN force that for ten years had acted as a buffer between the two countries. Simultaneously, he threatened closure of the Strait of Tiran at the south end of the Gulf of Elat, Israel's sea gate to the Far East.

Israel had earlier declared that any diversion of the Jordan or closure of the Strait of Tiran would be considered an act of war. A few artillery shells from Israel to the diversion area took care of that threat. Syria realized that to continue would mean a full scale war for which it was not prepared. Nasser continued his daily belligerent rantings.

War

Nasser, on May 22, 1967, closed the Strait of Tiran. He massed troops and tanks along the Egyptian/Israeli borders. As a demonstration of strength he marched his 250,000 troops through Cairo on the way to the front.

King Hussein, warned by Israel to stay out of any hostilities that might evolve, made the mistake of believing Egyptian propaganda about battlefield and aerial victories and turned his Jordan Legion over to Egyptian command.

✍

"Maury, when will you be back in Washington?" asked the long distance caller.

Flora and I were in St. Louis for our son Joseph's wedding to Carol Friedman. It was a joyous occasion. The date was June 15, 1967. The caller was Israel's ambassador to Washington, Abe Harman. I had worked very closely with Abe on a variety of projects even after I had left the embassy, and we were close personal friends as well.

A few days later we met in his office. He briefed me on the Arab civilian situation in the new administrative areas, and some of the problems expected to be encountered. He also briefed me on damage to Israel's farms and cities from enemy shelling and attacks. Could I go to Israel promptly and join a team whose mission was to review the situation and make recommendations? Immigration and absorption were then the responsibility of the Jewish Agency for Israel. Also the Agency was expected to fund costs of war damage repair to the civilian economy.

On June 23, I arrived in Israel, joined the team, traveled extensively throughout the enlarged geography of Israel, conferred with Israeli and Arab officials, and yes, we wrote a report.

Sheets

White sheets, white flags, white undershirts were everywhere. That is, everywhere where Arabs lived. There were seas of sheets, particularly in Arab sections of Jaffa, Haifa, Nazareth, Beer Sheva, Accra, and of course Jerusalem.

There were even larger seas of sheets in towns and villages of former Arab territories. Bethlehem, Jenin, Gaza, Hebron, Jericho, and Nablus. Also hundreds of small villages had their white laundry flying.

About Soldier Friends

As soon as I checked into the Hotel Samuel in Tel Aviv, I made phone calls to all of our friends who had sons or daughters in the army. I was tremendously relieved to learn, with one very sad exception, all had come through safely, although they had been in the midst of some of the worst fire fights of the Six Day War. The one exception was Tommy Porat, son of Judith and Karl Porat. A tank commander, he was critically burned in a command car in which Life photographer Paul Shuster was killed. Tommy, an extraordinarily capable young man, an honor student at Columbia University, was the apple of Karl's eye. Despite heroic medical efforts, he succumbed to his injuries. This put a pall on much of my trip.

A senior parachute officer, Giora Kaddar, son of our friends Gershon and Yael Kaddar, had been helicoptered into El Arish in the Sinai, and later into Syria, He had many war stories to tell. His unit drove the Palestine Liberation Army from its headquarters in Gaza. He reported that the building, a very big, heavily built structure, could have withstood an assault for many hours. It had hundreds of soldiers in it, thousands of guns, and tens of thousands of rounds of ammunition. The PLA, despite their militant oratory, never fired a shot and surrendered. The generals attempted to flee in their underwear, having ditched their uniforms and shoes. Giora personally captured one of the generals. His unit also captured a Russian tank expert who, worried about his own hide, was glad to explain to the Israel Defense Force (IDF) officers the intricacies of the Soviet tanks. After two hours, said Giora, the Russian stated that the Israelis had learned more in two hours than he had been able to teach the Egyptians in two years.

Heading North and to the "Territories"

My traveling and working companions were Gott Hammer, Isador Lubin, formerly U.S. Commissioner of Labor Statistics, a confidante of Presidents Roosevelt and Truman, and now a statistical and financial adviser to the Jewish Agency; Lou Horowitz, American Joint Distribution Committee representative; and Col. Benny Kaplan, brother of Eliezer Kaplan, Israel's minister of finance. We also had available Israeli social, economic, and financial experts.

June 25, the team headed north to the Hula region, Safad, and the captured Golan Heights. The roads were crowded with military trucks loaded with unopened boxes of ammunition lettered in Russian and Chinese, and tank carriers with captured Syrian and Jordanian tanks. Most were Russian built. Some of the Jordanian tanks were American Pattons. Lines of flat-bed trucks loaded with anti-aircraft guns, boxes of rifles, and light and heavy artillery pieces made for slow traveling: all captured war booty supplied to Syria by Russia and China. These scenes were repeated over and over again during our travels, reflecting the vast quantities of armament supplied to the Arab armies. While some of the captured arms showed signs of service, for the most part they were new and unused.

From the hills of Safad the Sea of Galilee shimmered in the brilliant sunlight. Between us and the sea were beautiful rolling hills ablaze with wild flower blossoms. A gorgeous tranquil sight. It was hard to imagine that just a few weeks earlier a bitter bloody battle had been fought here.

From Safad to Banyas, by way of Rosh Pina and Gadot, vistas offered great beauty, but flatlands were covered with unbelievable amounts of captured military booty. IDF officers were much impressed with the high quality and finish of the Russian and Czech made equipment. It was an object lesson indicating where and how the Soviets directed their economic priorities and budgets.

These towns, as well as almost all others, showed ample evidence of war damage: windowless, roofless buildings, extensive shell, bullet and shrapnel damage, burnt fields and orchards, destroyed school buildings, dead cows, and wrecked industrial and agricultural equipment. Happily enough there were few civilian casualties. The credit for this must be attributed to a disciplined population, many of whom spent almost six full days and nights in the prepared bomb shelters.

It was reported to us that the young men and women from the town of Gadot, an agricultural settlement in the Hula valley, were called up to their reserve units. This left a few older men and women to protect Gadot. A small Syrian unit made a thrust at the town. To the amazement of the defenders when home guard shot at the attackers, the Syrians broke and ran. Had the Syrians come with a larger force, or better officers, they could have easily driven right through the Galilee and opened the entire north of Israel to the enemy.

Continuing to the area of Banyas, we crossed the Jordan on a hastily constructed temporary "Bailey" bridge into former Syrian territory. The original bridge had been destroyed. Our climb up the steep hills of northern Golan Heights via a constantly curving dirt road, mined on both sides, through tracks filled with six to eight inches of loose dust like dirt was a trial and a tribute to our vehicles and the drivers. At one point it was necessary for all but the drivers to leave the vehicles and walk. We were sternly warned not to step off the so-called road. The many Syrian planted mines alongside could be unforgiving.

The crests of the Syrian hills were covered with well-constructed pill boxes with heavy artillery overlooking the areas we had just left. It was a frightening sight to see the massive Arab fire power concentrated here. The removal of this military threat made possible the establishment of additional settlements in the Israeli sector of the Jordan valley and the cultivation of land previously unavailable.

Banyas, with a postcard view of snow-capped Mt. Hermon, was

the headwater of the Jordan River, and received its water from Mt. Hermon runoff. The mountain stands at a point where Lebanon, Syria, and Israel lay claims to strategic parts of it.

At one point our car, a Chevrolet, became stuck on a small hump on a side road to the fresh water Banyas Springs. It could not, would not, move. Fortunately an Israeli army truck approached. The troopers just picked up the car and deposited it back on a drivable road. Could the AAA have done better?

Near the Springs there was a large man-made gorge. The Syrians had planned to divert the Jordan River through this gulch, thus denying Israeli agriculture access to its water. The gorge was part of the diversion channel. Syria got the message when a few artillery shells destroyed the working equipment!

The waters of the Banyas Springs gush out of the sides of surrounding hillsides, into a large pool of about twenty acres, then disappear into another hill, emerging later as part of the Jordan.

Hard by the foothills of Mt. Hermon was the Druze village of Ashielya, (Tower of the Sun). Its population of 5,000, which had no love for the Syrian government, remained in the village during the fighting. There was much greeting and shouts of 'shalom' by both children and adults as our little group drove through the town. Their stores were well stocked.

Although Israelis were theoretically prohibited by their government from making purchases or spending pounds in the Arab stores, the troops here were buying cloths, textiles, fruit, and canned goods. Who could pass up the bargains of much lower prices than in Israel?

From the Druze village of Ashielya, our survey took us through Mas'ada and Kuneitra, both Syrian Arab villages. Mas'ada displayed white sheets everywhere. The only immediate evidence of destruction was a dead cow lying on a bridge. Closer inspection indicated considerable damage to many buildings in the village. The town was deserted. Next to the village was a large permanent Syrian army camp. It too was deserted. The parade ground was covered with new and hardly used paraphernalia of war. Israeli trucks loaded with all manner of equipment were moving everything from these newly conquered areas into Israel.

Kuneitra, basically a Syrian military town with a prewar population of about 30,000 people, seemed totally deserted. The military told us that there were 300 to 500 people still there. Store fronts were non-existent, having been blown out by aerial bombing. Sheets billowed in the breeze. The streets were littered with food, clothing, and household goods from stores of every description. Apparently, looting was restricted by the presence of Israeli soldiers. If the soldiers participated in looting they faced stiff prison terms. Some of the Russian-made equipment had the legend "From Russia, with Love" painted on their sides in Hebrew and English.

The roads to and from Kuneitra were littered with wrecked, burnt trucks, tanks, artillery pieces and other detritus of war. These were graphic indications of one of the hardest fought and bloody sectors of the ground war. The infantry and tank battles were fierce and costly to both sides. Although out-gunned and out-manned, the more highly motivated Israelis were able to force a Syrian rout. It was fortunate for the IDF that the Syrians, who generally fought well, had decided to cut and run.

False Egyptian reports of great victories and Syrian lies about bombed-out Tel Aviv led to much confusion for the 95,000 Syrian civilian residents of the Golan. The confusion was compounded, when on June 5, despite victory claims, civilians were ordered by the Syrian government to evacuate the area. Evacuation was mostly on foot, and to Jordan.

After Kuneitra, we had a brief view of Mevi Hamma, a large Jordanian military base, totally bombed-out. To see the extent of this base's destruction, we climbed over blown-out slabs of concrete. This was made unpleasant by the lingering odor of burnt flesh.

The entire area was sated with hundreds of well-constructed pill boxes and bunkers containing both light and heavy artillery. They provided a well engineered defense system. Had the Syrians been better trained and motivated, Israeli casualties probably would have been much larger. Spending time on the Golan convinced us that without a solid, dependable peace agreement this area could not be given back to Syria. Given the saber rattling in the Soviet and Arab media, such an agreement seemed far off.

The drive down a narrow, twisting dirt road into what had been Jordanian controlled land on the west bank of the Jordan River took us into 'liberated' territory east of Jerusalem and west of the Jordan River.

Unlike the Syrian Golan areas where we saw very few civilians, in the former Jordanian areas many people were working the fields and harvesting crops. Almost all were women whose colorful dress against the brown of the grain, was most picturesque. Unlike the Druze, the people here just stared as we passed by. Although the land was very fertile, there was a noticeable lack of agricultural machinery. Almost all of the work was done by hand with primitive hand tools, a sharp contrast to Israeli farming methods. The land here did not contain too many stones and rocks. The crops were abundant. Labor was cheap. There was little or no irrigation. Due to cheap labor and very fertile soil, production costs were lower than those in Israel.

This raised a question as to where the produce of the land would be sold. If sold in Israel, because of lower costs of production and resultant lower prices for farm products, there would be short term agricultural and economic dislocations. Also what currency would be legal, Israeli pounds or Jordanian dinars? And what would be the exchange rate between the two currencies?

Unlike Israel where small European cars prevail, autos in Jordan were either full size American ones, or Mercedes. All taxis were Mercedes. Petrol stations did not know what prices to charge—all problems for the incoming military government.

Jenin, a large Arab city on the west bank of the Jordan River, did not seem to have experienced much damage, although the central mosque did have a shell hole through the top of the minaret. Almost every building had a white sheet hanging. As we stopped to take pictures, the people stared at us. There was no unfriendliness, nor did there seem to be a great deal of animosity. They just stared.

The open shops were well stocked with food stuffs, textiles, hardware and all the normal goods of the retail trade. There seemed to be little business being transacted. This may well have been the result of uncertainty of the price and currency situation. Little or no evidence of IDF personnel, although I suspected that it was present—quietly. As Jordan had television, there were many TV antennas. Israel had not yet invested in TV. Signs were in Arabic, with some in English. Of course, no Hebrew.

Because Jenin was known to be a dangerous village for Jews, with many guerrillas, we only stayed in the town for a short while, and during that time stayed reasonably close together and near our cars. We were also each armed with M-1 pistols. Fortunately these never had to come out of their holsters.

As we drove from Jenin toward Nablus we noticed a large roadside billboard which faced away from us. The guessing was that it simply named the next town we would come to. I said, "Oh hell, it is probably a Pepsi-Cola ad." To everyone's surprise, mostly my own, it was.

The road to Nablus showed evidence of fierce fighting. About twenty shot-up tanks, half tracks, ambulances, and other military gear, Jordanian and Israeli, lay strewn along the road as was much personal gear such as shaving equipment, jerry cans, uniform parts, shoes, and helmets. All of the Jordanian tanks were American Pattons.

Nablus, with a population of about 60,000 persons, had some very beautiful houses. White sheets again were everywhere. The town itself was clean and well ordered. Terraced hillsides of olive and fruit trees, neat and well kept, imparted a sense of prosperity.

It was widely reported that between 1,000 to 20,000 civilian refugees a day fled from the Jordan River's west bank to the east. Fearing loss of remittances, families of thousands of men working in the oil fields of Kuwait and Saudi Arabia fled the west bank. Arab government policies stimulated this movement. These families were dependent upon the remittances being sent back to them by their men in the oil fields. Arab governments would not permit people to receive remittances if they were in Israel or Israeli occupied areas. Another refugee group consisted of Jordanian government officials and their families. Pensioners also would have been prohibited from getting their monthly allotments if they had stayed in Israeli occupied areas. And, of course, there were people who refugeed out of fear.

In Ramala, a pretty and obviously prosperous town, formerly Jordanian controlled and administered, the stores were well stocked with goods from Britain, Red China, Germany, and the United States. Business was brisk, particularly by Israeli soldiers. Israeli pounds were readily accepted. Their main concern seemed to be "How are we going to restock when this merchandise is sold?"

Along with white sheets from most of the houses, there were forests of television antennas on the roofs. Occasionally a house showed heavy bullet damage, reportedly occupied by snipers. The IDF did not deal gently with snipers.

Hebron, population, 50,000, an ancient city sacred to Jews and Moslems, was not on our official itinerary. However, I was anxious to visit the Machpelah mosque, the tomb of Abraham, Isaac and Jacob, as well as Sarah and Leah. For nineteen years following the 1948 War of Independence, Hebron had been barred to Jews. Prior to 1948 Jews could visit the shrine, but could only go up the first seven steps of the building, never inside. The Six Day War changed that. Accompanied only by a Jewish Agency guide and Yori Sassower, son of our friends in Haifa, I made a side trip to Hebron. The sacred shrine, a large structure, had high vaulted arches. The actual sacred tombs were many feet underground. Elaborate Arabic inscriptions covered the walls. The floors of the mosque were covered with beautiful, expensive oriental rugs. Protective polyethylene sheets had been stretched over the rugs. It was a strange and eerie sensation to realize that I, thanks to my military pass, was one of the first Jews, in nineteen years, to visit this tomb of our ancestors and even many more years to be allowed inside the building.

Hebron's stores and cafes seemed to be enjoying a brisk business. Urchins and young men, in abundance, peddled postcards, Arabic newspapers, LUX soap, pencils, mastique (chewing gum), clay urns, flashlights and cheap ceramic drums. The parking lot was crowded with many Israeli tourist busses. The Arab populace exhibited curiosity about the Israelis, not hostility. Food did not seem to be a problem. Stores were well stocked. Land around Hebron was lush with bumper crops.

The Allenby Crossing

Returning to Jerusalem, we drove through Bethlehem. A large crowd, Israelis and Arabs, gathered in the square in front of the church where Christ was reputed to have been born, watched new Patton tanks being loaded on tank retrievers. I was allowed to examine them more closely. Each of their odometers showed 45 miles, the distance from the Jordanian port of Aqaba to Bethlehem. The unopened operating manuals were wrapped in clear plastic. These American supplied tanks delivered to Aqaba, under a U.S./Jordan military aid program, had been off-loaded in that port, and driven directly to Bethlehem, 45 miles, before they became the captured property of the IDF.

A dramatic example of Jordanian religious insensitivity, despite the 1948 truce terms, was demonstrated to us by the wide, two lane Jerusalem-Amman Highway. This road ran straight through the most sacred Jewish cemetery in the world, the Mt. of Olives. Headstones from the cemetery were used for sidewalks and buildings.

Driving to Jericho one had to wonder why King Hussein succumbed to Nasser's lies and entered the war. He had nothing to gain and much to lose—and did. Jericho, located in a fertile, very productive oasis, had one of the largest refugee camps from the 1948 war. Arab countries stubbornly refused to recognize that the 1948 refugees resulted from their own miscalculations and refused to absorb the people into their economies. Arab authorities preferred to keep hundreds of thousands of people in miserable conditions in camps, mostly unemployed and social wards of the United Nations.

The Jericho refugee camp itself was spread over a huge acreage of no trees, no agriculture, no vegetation, no industry, and no hope. With the Six Day War, almost the entire population of the camp became refugees again—rushing east, across the river, to Jordan. Red Cross representatives begged and urged the people to stay at the camp. No one listened.

Trucks, cars, even donkey-drawn carts were piled high with mattresses, pots and pans, suitcases, string and rope-wrapped bundles. Frequently a bicycle would top the pile. These were the world possessions of the hundreds of families lined up to cross the Jordan River. Mostly it was old men, women and children. Many of the younger men were in the oil fields of Kuwait and Saudi Arabia.

It was a heartrending sight, more tragic as the famed Allenby Bridge connecting the West and East Banks of the Jordan River had been dynamited. To cross the river, about 40 feet wide at this point, the refugees had to climb or slide down a steep embankment, cross on unsteady scraps of lumber, carrying what they could, most often just one or two crying children, then climb the embankment on the other side. This exercise was not only arduous, it was humiliating, and devoid of any dignity. And to what and where? No one had answers.

Israeli soldiers helped where they could, passing out packaged C-rations and water. The temperature was in the high nineties F. For the refugees to get all their possessions across the makeshift bridge, multiple trips had to be made. That or jettison their belongings. Once they reached the east bank they expected trucks, busses, or taxis to be available to take them to Amman or other parts of Jordan. Unfortunately for them, the Jordanian government prohibited trucks and taxis from going to the crossing. The result was that there were stacks of household items covering a large acreage.

Of course, the scene was a picnic for the many TV crews and reporters. It was a made-for-TV situation. And they were there from all over the world. That night, back in Jerusalem I described this scene to Mayor Teddy Kollek. The next day, I was informed, a proper temporary bridge was installed that materially eased the situation at the river. However, there was nothing the Israelis could do to arrange transport from the west end of the bridge into Jordan.

Old Jerusalem after Nineteen Years

The Old City of Jerusalem was that portion of the modern city surrounded by ancient walls and containing special areas and structures sacred to Jews, Moslems, and Christians. Held by Jordan, Jews had not been able to visit their sacred Western Wall since 1948. Prior to the Six Day War, from 1948 to 1967, there was only a ten foot wide clearing in front of the Wall.

This narrow area was widened considerably after the Six Day War, so that more than an acre of land was now available for the daily crowds coming to pray at the most holy, and precious of Jewish structures. Mistakenly called the Wailing Wall, the Kotel (Western Wall), was the one remaining part of the retaining wall built by Herod to support the temple mount platform. On this mesa Herod built the Second Temple, later destroyed by the Romans. The platform now is the site of the Dome of the Rock.

Gott Hammer and I were anxious to visit the Old City. We had not been able to visit this most holy symbol of Judaism previously—to see and feel it up close. Accompanied only by our driver, Yitzhak, we entered the Old City via the Damascus Gate. It was a market day. As in Hebron, there were throngs of Arab men and boys in the narrow streets selling foods and a wide variety of cheap trinkets from red China. It was a strange and eerie feeling walking through the streets of this sacred city where Jews had been blocked from entering for nineteen years. We were without side arms or guards, and there were no soldiers in sight. Just a few weeks ago this had been enemy territory. Certainly the crowds of people did not love us As we walked by we received many stares, some hostile, most curious, and occasionally cautiously friendly, but not too.

Apparently we had entered by the wrong gate. To get to the Western Wall we had to climb over barbed wire and lots of rubble to reach the cleared area. Several hundred people were at the Wall praying. There were probably an equal number of media members observing and reporting. The sharp, mournful sounds of a *shofar*, a ram's horn, being blown, rose above the prayers. Normally the *shofar* is sounded only on the high holidays. To these praying Jews the return to the Wall was a high holiday. Two thirds of the wall space was reserved for men, the balance for women supplicants.

In 1948, tall concrete three foot thick walls had been erected in several sections between the Old City and the newer parts of Jerusalem to protect the newer, Jewish occupied, section from sniper fire from the Jordan Legion troops. On June 29, 1967 these walls were torn down, and all gates separating the old and new sectors of Jerusalem thrown open. I had been invited by Teddy Kollek to join him to watch the dynamiting of the walls in the Ma'ale Shalom area.

Israelis, joyous, often tearful, rushed to revisit the old almost destroyed Jewish sector and observed the rubble of ancient synagogues, roamed the various sections of the Old City, often taking advantage of the bargain prices for TV sets, radios, other household appliances, foods, jewelry, or just a meal, and the opportunity to pray at the Kotel. Many of the Arab stores in the Old City already had signs in Hebrew. For the most part the price differences between those in the new and old cities reflected Israeli taxes that had not yet been applied on merchandise in the former areas ruled by Jordan.

This was also the first time in nineteen years that non-Israeli Arabs could visit Israeli Jerusalem. Many of the Arab women wore crosses. Hundreds of west bank Arabs, many in picturesque garb, wandered in awe in the streets of the new city, marveling at the wonder of traffic lights, at the new hotels, at the economic vibrancy evident on every hand; and they also revisited former Arab residential areas. Hundreds of Arab kids, with an entrepreneurial bent, were busily peddling cheap Chinese parasols, pencils, and 'mastic' (chewing gum) The entire scene was awesome, one never to be forgotten.

Tough Problems

While there had been lots of interesting sightseeing of war areas, there also had been many substantive meetings regarding economic, social, civil, and industrial aspects and problems arising out of the expansion of Israeli territorial and population responsibilities. Arab resettlement and development was a frequent topic of discussion. The Jewish Agency was prepared to provide significant assistance in these areas. Arab leaders outside of Israel announced that any Arab accepting Jewish help would be considered an enemy, an infidel, and a target for killing. Simultaneously, Arab authorities made it clear that they were not going to lift a finger to help, or accept, the hundreds of thousands of refugees now in camps in their countries.

The government of Israel, too, was not much help, floundering in various directions. It was clear to our team that nobody had any real plans. Possibly our trip had been a week or two too early. Economic problems of considerable magnitude were developing rapidly. These included wage rate differentials between Israeli workers and Arab workers in the territories, how to handle the bumper agricultural crops of the west bank now that their normal markets, other Arab states, were closed to west bank farmers. The sheer volume of these bumper crops and their significantly lower prices would wreak havoc with the kibbutz economies if dumped on the Israel market.

The Israeli economy could not absorb lower cost produce without substantially damaging the economic well-being of the politically powerful kibbutz movement which enjoyed a much higher wage rate than Arab economies. Wage rate differentials were also a problem in hotels and restaurants. For example, hotel workers in East Jerusalem earned $28 to $30 a month. Similar workers in Jewish Jerusalem earned $150 to $250 a month. Increasing the Arab rate would not increase productivity, and under no stretch of the imagination could there be two wage scales for the same work.

Some of these problems were discussed by our team at the American Embassy in Tel Aviv with Ambassador Barbour and Economic Counselor Dick Breithut. Unfortunately, there was no outpouring of brilliant, practical, proposals from these and other meetings.

The Gaza Strip

One of the major problems that Israel inherited from the war was the Gaza strip. In ancient times, Gaza had been an important junction of the trade route between Egypt, Arabia, and Palestine. It was in Gaza that Samson lost his hair to Delilah and later destroyed the temple of Dagon. More recently it had comprised an inhospitable strip of land, about 24 miles long and 8 miles wide, given to Egypt when Palestine was divided in 1947. The 1958 population of Gaza was about 100,000. By June '67, with the influx of war refugees, the strip had about 300,000 persons.

Accompanied by armed security personnel, the team made its first visit to Gaza on July 1, 1967. Prior to the war the strip was Egyptian territory. The northern part had some rain-dependent fertile soil. The south was an absolute desert. Residents in a small village on the road to Gaza City, not refugees, seemed to be living in more wretched conditions than the refugees we had seen in Hebron or Jericho. This, we learned, was rather representative of the total strip. Egypt wanted no responsibility. Israel had no use for it. Viability to support prewar existing population was questionable. Support of a refugee-enhanced population was impossible.

Prior to 1967, Nasser, as part of his saber rattling, demanded that UN Secretary General U Thant remove the UN peace keeping force from the border of Israel and the strip. If a member of the UN group wanted to visit Israel, two yards away, it was a long trip. It was necessary, under the rules imposed by Egypt, that the trooper go to Alexander, take a plane or boat to Cyprus and take a plane or boat from there to Israel. From Israel, he could return directly to his unit, two yards inside the border. The UNEF complained that it could not get fresh milk from the Egyptians. Egypt's regulations required that there be no personal contact with the Israelis. Kibbutzim, which had plenty of milk, solved this problem by tying bottles of milk to dogs or donkeys and sending them across the line. The UN group was composed of units from different countries. Each had its own camp. There was no operational or living integration.

The road to Gaza showed many signs of heavy fighting; bullet pocked walls, shrapnel shredded trees, wrecked and burnt vehicles, and other pieces of discarded equipment. All along the road hundreds of children waved, and smiled what appeared to be greeting, as they called out one word in Arabic: *khubiz* (bread). The fertility rate must have been very high. We did not see many young men. They apparently were working in Kuwait or Saudi Arabia. However, their ration cards, which entitled them to food at the UN depots were never turned in. No one ever dies according to ration card lists. When there was little else for residents to do, they created children, with a vengeance.

The fighting had been heavy and bloody. The Egyptian regulars had put up a real fight, with heavy losses to the IDF. Very little of it had been done by the Palestine Liberation Army which surrendered without a fight, although it was exceedingly well armed with Chinese equipment.

From Gaza City, where the usual white sheets waved in the sea breeze, we drove to El Arish. Our intention was to go as far south in the strip as possible in order to get a broad view of the situation. We also wanted to be out of the strip before nightfall.

While we were looking across a battlefield where one of the most intense and bloody battles had occurred, just south of Gaza City, a young Arab came walking down the road with a golf club in one hand, and some gold balls in the other. Naturally, we were curious about this. He told us that the Gaza airfield was a short distance away, and that there was an eighteen-hole course there. Asked what was his interest in golf he remarked, "I am the pro, but there haven't been many people playing lately."

About half way to El Arish the road took us through the town of Rafiah. Twelve Arabs had been killed in a food riot that morning.

They had tried to force open the door of an UNRRA food storage. Someone shot off a percussion cap. The guards panicked and fired on the crowd. A nearby store bore a sign "Victory Trading Post." Here too there was a large amount of wrecked, burnt, heavy duty equipment. Next we came to a marshaling yard for captured equipment. In addition to much used material there were about thirty brand new Russian and Czech made antiaircraft guns. A few miles further we approached an area that had seen what was the largest tank battle in military history, including those of World War II. Wrecked Egyptian and Israeli tanks were scattered about as far as the eye could see. In addition, the desert sands were littered with shoes, helmets, bits of uniforms, boxes of small and large shells, hand grenades, machine guns and parts, field kitchens, broken down half tracks, and other detritus of war.

As bad as this was to see, worse was the odor of decomposing bodies. We did not see the bodies. They must have been buried in shallow trenches. It was in this area that the IDF took its worst losses. But for every Israeli tank there must have been ten Egyptian pieces of equipment. The fortifications, concrete bunkers, and tank traps must have extended at least ten miles on each side of the highway.

At El Arish, a major Egyptian military base, MIGS and an occasional torpedo bomber were lined up as if on parade. But no parade for these birds. Each had been surgically hit immediately behind the cockpit by a missile that destroyed the plane so that there was no part that could be used except as a photo backdrop.

We left the Gaza strip before nightfall.

June '67 taught me much about postwar problems faced by victors and losers. There were many human, civil and social concerns that had to be addressed. Physical reconstruction of direct war damage would require a huge amount of non-existent funds. A terrible financial and physical price had yet to be paid for care of the wounded, physically and mentally. And with these as well as other concerns there was no assurance of a meaningful peace.

9

Alligators in Israel
...and Parrots Too

MOSAICS UNCOVERED IN archeological digs indicate that in Biblical times there were crocodiles in the marshes of the Holy Land. However, for many years they have been non-existent.

About 1978, I began hearing stories from the U.S. Department of Interior Fish & Wildlife Service (F&W) officers, not about crocs, but about an exhibit of American alligators at Hamat Gader Hot Springs Park, a tourist resort in Israel. Export of live American alligators was strictly prohibited, the species was not found in other countries, and the export ban was strictly enforced. So how could there be a live exhibit of American gators at Hamat Gader?

This tourist resort, just south of the Golan Heights, is on a bluff overlooking a point where Israel, Syria, and Jordan meet. Looking down from the bluff, one has a magnificent view of the bombed-out railroad track of the famed Orient Express trunk line that ran from Cairo to Damascus, and a tributary of the Jordan River. It is a short drive from Tiberias.

Several years earlier, a fast-talking director of the Hamat Gader Park, seeking new and interesting features to draw tourists, had persuaded U.S. Department of Interior officials despite F&W objections, to sell the Park 120 baby alligators. They were to be housed in a specially constructed exhibit to provide an opportunity for tourists and school children to see and become acquainted with an exotic part of nature. The agreement between the Department of Interior and the Hamat Gader Park provided that except for the exhibit there could be no commercial use of the animals. Neither they nor their offspring or products could be exported from Israel or sold commercially in Israel.

Gators being gators, male and female, matured. They began having their own baby gators. Soon the exhibit was awash in brown and yellow wiggly babies as well as three and four foot mature reptiles.

Not being able to dispose of them commercially, nor expand their exhibits in other sites around Israel, the Park faced a real problem. Appeals for relief to the F&W, which had objected to the original export to Israel, were fruitless.

Eventually, the surplus gators were air freighted to the United States and sold by the U.S. government to breeders. The considerable expense for this reverse export was borne by Hamat Gader.

The gators continued to propagate. On one of my frequent trips to Israel, about 1983, at the suggestion of the Israeli Ministry of Agriculture, I paid my first visit to Hamat Gader and listened to its problem. I indicated that I thought I could help. The director of the Park remarked that he did not need my assistance adding, "I know how to handle the Americans."

Two years later, I received a phone call in my Washington office from Yolanda Schohory, Agricultural Attaché, Israel Embassy, Washington. I had met and worked with Yolanda on many occasions. I liked and respected her ideas and competence. She also knew of my work in the U.S. regarding alligators, and of my previous experience at Hamat Gader.

Yolanda reminded me of the Hamat Gader problem, and said that they needed my help.

"Forget it," I said. "They think they know how to handle the Americans, and did not want to listen to my advice. I want no part of that group."

"Please," she said. "As a personal favor to me, come over and talk to their new director. He is in my office and wants to talk with you. The man you met in Israel has been fired and is no longer connected with the Park."

At the Embassy, I met Ronnie Lotan. Ronnie was a large, jovial man with a Santa Claus white beard, sparkling blue eyes, and a most friendly demeanor. Within thirty seconds I knew that Ronnie and I could be a team. After talking for a while about the proliferation of alligators and the financial hardship of having to ship the extras back to the states, I agreed to give him a proposal to solve Hamat Gader's alligator problem. That afternoon I sent it to him. It would cover basic time input at a minimum rate, out-of-pockets costs, and hefty contingency fee for success. In addition to a dollar payment for success, the proposal included one full cost paid trip to Israel for Flora and me for each of the next three years.

He will never accept this, I thought. Within the hour I received the accepted, signed proposal with a retainer check. I was pleased and surprised. I knew from my own sources that Ronnie had visited the Fish & Wildlife Service that morning, pleading for relief, and had been turned down cold.

The next week, I spent hours at the Department of Interior discussing the situation faced by Hamat Gader with anyone who would talk to me. I determined that the restrictions placed on Hamat Gader need not be ironclad, provided that it could be demonstrated that modifications were beneficial to the American alligator producers, or that the restrictions were unfairly extreme. I also found out that the objection to change was the work of one single official. I knew him, and had never developed a high opinion of his hard nosed approach in general to the alligator industry in the United States. If it had been up to him, state or federal regulations on alligator hunting and marketing would never have been modified from the then status whereby almost any trade in alligator products was illegal.

After a few weeks of gathering information, I prepared an economic brief titled "Relief for Hamat Gader." In this brief I gave the history of the original purchase and the history of the existing exhibit. It stated that any exports of alligator skins or products from Israel would be such a small fraction of total U.S. present and potential sales that the impact would be diminimus. When worldwide crocodile sales were included, Israel's percent of total sales would require several zeros after the decimal point. The brief also stated that Hamat Gader would agree to a restriction prohibiting the export of live alligators from Israel and that the government of Israel would enforce this restriction. This would prevent competitive sources for American alligators being developed in other countries, one of the concerns of F&W.

Also, I argued that export sales from Israel were relatively much more important to its balance of trade than alligator product sales from America were to the U.S. balance of trade. Given this fact, Israel would be expected to make a greater effort to develop new markets for alligator skins. Such new markets would also be available to the American gator industry.

When I first showed this brief to a few of F&W officials, I received encouragement to proceed. Knowing where the major roadblock would be I decided to get some Congressional backing. Accordingly, with a copy of my brief in hand, I visited Congressman Sidney Yates of Chicago. I had known and worked with Sid from day one of my Israel Embassy association. He was throughout his congressional career of over fifty years an ardent champion of the State of Israel. It also did not hurt that he was also chairman of the Congressional Sub-Committee responsible for the Interior Department's annual appropriation.

He was most sympathetic to Hamat Gader's problem, and gave me some valuable insights about the Department of Interior. However, he said that he could not get directly involved in the matter, and wished me success. But, as it turned out, this veteran legislator knew how to insert his oar discretely.

Three days later, I received a call from an Interior official asking me to come to his office for a discussion. I was met in the reception room. Strangely, he took me to his office by a roundabout way. At one office, Mr. X's, he said, "Look in." I did. At the desk sat an almost life size gorilla doll, body hair and all. My companion, in response to my puzzled look, said, "Mr. X was fired. Your appeal has been approved." *Wow.*

This was an interesting situation where I developed a new client despite a stubborn Israeli, and was able to perform for that client despite a stubborn American. Is there a moral in there somewhere?

Later when I was shown the official approval, I noticed a letter in the file from Congressman Yates to the Secretary of the Interior in which the Congressman requested that he be kept informed regarding a decision on the application for relief. Nothing else. No recommendation or statement of support. But it was enough.

With this start, and with financing from Gordon-Choisy, several more alligator farms were established in Israel. The raw hides went to France. The meat, mostly from the tail, went to Japan. Costume jewelry made from claws, teeth, and scales were sold in Israeli gift stores.

Ted Johanen, director of the Rockefeller Game Refuge in Grand Chenier, Louisiana, at my request, arranged to train Paul Rappaport, assistant manager of Hamat Gader, in the proper technique of killing, skinning, and packing gators for market. He was also most helpful with gator husbandry suggestions.

After a series of alligator farms were successfully started, several groups tried to import and raise African crocs. As these animals are harder to raise and more difficult to breed than alligators, their efforts were not successful. The farms lost a great deal of money in the experiment.

Ronnie Lotan fully and most graciously carried out his obligations to me under our agreement. In the years that followed, Flora and I enjoyed his visits to our home in Chevy Chase, Maryland and to our winter retreat in Marco Island, Florida. We also enjoyed the Lotan family's hospitality at Hamat Gader and at their kibbutz on the Golan.

A few years after the alligator problem was solved, Ronnie, in order to develop an additional tourist exhibit, came to Florida and arranged to buy several trained parrots from Parrot Jungle, near West Palm Beach. These birds, trained to roller skate, drive small trucks and do other tricks, cost about fifty thousand dollars each. Hamat Gader was erecting a special pavilion in which these birds would perform. Ronnie wanted them in Israel before the start of the tourist season.

However, since parrots were on a special CITES (Conference of International Treaties for Endangered Species) list with special export regulations, it was necessary to have veterinary health certificates, proof that these particular birds were hatched and raised in the United States, and export permits from the F&W.

Ronnie arranged to get the first two items in a timely fashion. The export certificates were troublesome. The F&W official responsible for this simple task had excuse after excuse about the delay. Finally, Ronnie called me about the problem.

After talking to the F&W officer responsible for parrot export regulations, I realized that he had some kind of personal problem about issuing a license for export to Israel. He was deliberately holding up signing off on the export permit application—even though he was aware of the time factor. Our deadline was only a few weeks away if we were to get the birds to Israel and acclimated in time for the tourist season.

I had to break the papers loose soon.

I called the office of one of Maryland's senators, Paul Sarbanes, and briefly described the problem to his secretary. Within a half hour I received a phone call suggesting that I visit Ms. Rebecca Wagner, the senator's constituent representative, in her office in Silver Spring, Maryland. I met Ms. Wagner the next day. In my presence she made one phone call to the Department of Interior. The necessary papers were ready the following morning. Ah, the value of knowing where the buttons are and how and when to push them.

On our next trip to Israel and to Hamat Gader, Flora and I were treated to a special and private trained parrot show.

PART III

Expanded Horizons

10

Chilewich Sons & Co.
"I Want To Be Able To Sleep at Night"

ONE MORNING, BOB Nathan called me on the inter-com and said there were people in his office whom I should meet. A few minutes later, I was introduced to Aaron Chilewich and Peter Ronald of Chilewich Sons and Co., one of the three leading cattle hide dealers in the United States.

Aaron was the senior partner and CEO. Peter was a vice president. The partnership's interests extended far beyond cattle hides. In addition to domestic and international trade in cattle hides, I soon learned that the company's interests included coal and oil, timber and pulp wood, turnkey industrial plants, and sales of capital equipment. Its operations were worldwide. Export of cattle hides to Europe was the foundation of the firm's business. The Soviet Union was a major buyer of its services and commodities.

Peter had come to the firm from the Bear-Stearns brokerage company. His main responsibilities had to do with Chilewich's widespread investment activities. Active in the New York chapter of Americans for Democratic Action (ADA) Peter knew of Bob's national involvement in ADA, and of his generally excellent reputation as a Washington personality.

The discussion in Bob's office centered around Chilewich's expanding commercial interests in many parts of the world—with an emphasis on cattle hide imports and exports, the core business. The Chilewich company felt that it needed a Washington presence which could keep the principal partners of Chilewich abreast of government rules, regulations, and programs that affected its commercial operations. After several hours of discussion, we agreed upon a trial period for Nathan Associates to be its Washington consultant for six months.

As Aaron and Peter were leaving the office, Aaron turned to me and said, "Maury, your job is to see that our firm complies with all government requirements. We don't even want to be close to the line. I want to be able to sleep at night."

During the eighteen years that Chilewich was a client of Nathan Associates it became abundantly clear that Aaron meant every word of that statement. It was a wonderful, often challenging, satisfactory client/consultant relationship. The associates of the company involved me in all of the company's areas of interest.

Like other leading cattle-hide merchants in the United States, the Chilewich company had started in Poland. Political, economic, and military unrest drove them out of Europe. In New York the firm prospered and built an international business.

Aaron and his brother, Michael, were the principals of the firm. Aaron was dominant, but by no means a domineering brother. Aaron treated his brother, who years earlier had experienced some psychological problems, as an equal partner and always brought Michael into discussions of all major and often minor company matters.

Aaron Chilewich was one of a kind, a scrupulously honest businessman, philanthropically generous but shying away from public acclaim of his generosity. Always gracious, he never to my knowledge ever showed a temper. He demonstrated old world culture and refinement. His close friends and social associates were artists, writers, musicians, politicians, academics and theatrical personages—including Isaac Stern and Elie Weisel. In all circumstances he treated me as a close and valuable member of the firm, and Flora and me as members of his extended family.

We visited and socialized with Aaron and his first wife Bronia, until her sudden and unexpected death. Several years later Aaron married Nussia, a cousin of Bronia's, in many respects very much like Bronia. We thoroughly enjoyed the social evenings at Aaron's apartment overlooking Gracie Mansion, the New York mayor's home, as well as visits to his Southampton, Long Island estate. On several occasions Aaron and Nussia were my most gracious hosts in Paris and Jerusalem.

Aaron would frequently phone to invite me to a meeting in New York to get my ideas about some venture or other. It was not unusual for these 'talks' to be around the lunch table in the office, with all the major associates of the firm present. Although most of these meetings were business related, it was not unusual, however, to have a one or two hour session on events in Israel, a subject very close to Aaron's and Michael's hearts. It was also of considerable importance to others in the firm, such as Herman Elbin, a hide trader, who, upon retirement, made aliyah to Israel.

To say that I was highly flattered by his wanting my opinion—after he had discussed the project with his other associates—would be a massive understatement. His main concern with my advice, was not how profitable the project might be, but how it would appear to the U.S. government authorities, such as the Departments of Commerce, Agriculture and/or State. If I turned my nose up at the idea, Aaron would simply say, "Let's drop it." And that was that.

Michael, the younger brother, had an encyclopedic knowledge of the Bible, Jewish history and traditions. One of the pleasures of my frequent visits to the Chilewich office in New York was to listen to some of his Biblical stories and how they related to current events. He was always courteous and considerate, and almost always in good humor. Flora and I occasionally socialized with Michael and his wife Bracha, and enjoyed their company.

Aaron and Bronia had two children, Simon, an executive in the family company, and Edith who had her own career in the arts.

Simon, born in Europe, was fluent in Polish, Russian, and French in addition to English. During World War II he had been an OSS operative who was dropped and worked behind enemy lines. His specialty in the firm was in the growing and profitable trading business with the Soviet Union. It was not unusual for Simon to make two or three trips to Russia in a month. He developed an extremely valuable expertise in bilateral and trilateral trade, and used this expertise effectively.

In contrast to his father's seemingly relaxed, genteel personality, Simon, a chain smoker of strong French Gaulois cigarettes, was tense, and always seemed to be in movement although he could be suave and persuasive in a negotiation. He was a free spender to secure a contract, or make a sale, or even to pave the way for a possible sale in the future. He entertained business clients and government officials lavishly and frequently. To watch him operate, as I did in Russia, was straight theater. And for the most part he was successful.

Dealing with the Russians was not an easy business. It took incredible patience and protracted negotiation, particularly since the Russian negotiators rarely had the authority to make a final decision. Every discussion point had to be referred back to some central body for a yes, no, or even a maybe. Often the business could be done only with a three, and occasionally, a four-way trade.

However, Simon made some terrible mistakes, most particularly after Aaron's death, and most particularly in a long odds oil venture that ultimately wrecked a prosperous firm. In Simon's favor, it must be said that he made sure that none of his Chilewich investors, including myself, got hurt financially. But his risk-taking, which Aaron, while alive, had been able to curb, ruined a good and ongoing business.

Peter Ronald, another member of the Chilewich firm, brought Nathan Associates and Chilewich together. He was one of my frequent contacts, both in person and by phone. It was not unusual for Peter to call several times a week and spend a full hour on the phone discussing and analyzing a current situation or problem. Given the Chilewich interests in different parts of the world, these discussions could encompass a wide range of subjects.

Peter's wife, Anita, was a competent pianist. One of her close musical friends in Great Neck, Long Island, where they lived, was Rita Relson, a friend and sorority sister of Flora's. We also visited each other in our homes.

About a year after the Atkin/Chilewich relationship began, our daughter Barrie, Flora, and I were vacationing in the Grand Tetons in Colorado. By pure coincidence, Peter and Anita were also there. This was the first time he had met our daughter, who was about 12 years old. Peter was dazzled by her knowledge of biochemistry as she asked questions and explained things to Peter about a book he was reading.

Once when Peter and Anita were weekend guests on our yacht, *Serenade,* we cruised up the South River from Selby Bay Yacht Club to a waterside restaurant. It was after ten o'clock at night when we headed down river to the club. The Route 2 bridge over the South River, which we had to pass, had a maximum vertical clearance of about fifteen feet. Our vessel needed eighteen. In theory, a bridge tender would open for boats requiring greater clearance.

As we approached the closed bridge I gave the requisite horn signals requesting an opening. No response. I tried the radio. No response. These procedures were tried several times. No responses.

Finally, I pulled the *Serenade* alongside the bridge. Peter and I climbed up a ladder to the bridge tender's cabin. He was there—dead drunk. A call to the Ann Arundel County police, just down the road, finally solved our problem. The bridge was opened. We got back to the yacht club after midnight.

Whether on a boat, in the Tetons, or in their home, the Ronald's were not only good business acquaintances, but good and stimulating personal friends.

The Hide Embargo Case

Sometime in the mid-sixties, Massachusetts shoe manufacturers complained bitterly to the U.S. Department of Commerce, and to Senator Ted Kennedy, that the export of cattle hides was making it difficult to buy hides at a price that let them produce competitively priced shoes. They also wrapped themselves in the flag by claiming that they could not produce shoes for the military—then engaged in Korea—at prices demanded by the military.

To appease the senator, as well as other legislators from the north east, The Department of Commerce instituted a total embargo on the export of American cattle hides. This action could have been a disaster for Chilewich and other exporters.

With no foreign markets the domestic price of hides dropped, reflecting the decrease in market demand. Those hurt the most were farmers and cattlemen throughout the United States. Wholesale prices offered dropped rapidly as surplus stocks of raw or salted hides quickly built up.

Yet, prices of American-made shoes changed little if at all in response to cheaper hides. But farmers and cattlemen were hurting, as were hide exporters.

Aaron asked me to meet in New York with his senior people and Mathew Ross, the firm's outside lawyer. The embargo was a Washington action, and Washington was my area of 'expertise.'

Following a lengthy discussion about the impact of the embargo on Chilewich, other hide exporters, cattlemen, and the domestic market, it was decided to file an appeal with the Department of Commerce protesting the embargo and requesting a repeal. If repeal was not possible, we would request an export quota system that would allow American exporters to maintain part of their customer base rather than lose it to South and Latin American hide dealers. A quota system would also provide some market relief to the American cattle industry.

It became my responsibility to prepare the economic background and recommend a strategy for the appeal. A little analysis demonstrated that prices of raw or salted cattle hides had almost no impact on the price of a finished pair of shoes. If the price of raw hides dropped or rose by 50 percent the changes in the final cost of producing shoes would be negligible. Capital investment, labor, costs of tanning, and other factors of production had a much greater price impact than the cost of the raw or salted hides.

Raw hides are a by-product of the slaughter of cattle for food. No one raises cattle just for the value of the hide. However, the loss of the hide income to the cattle industry could be disastrous. This was particularly true during periods of drought, dried up pastures, and higher than usual feed costs. At these times, farmers, unable to afford to feed their herds, were forced to dump cattle on the market at great loss to themselves. To also lose the value of the stripped hides was adding insult to injury. High beef consumption and low feed prices would also result in more hides becoming available. On the other hand, a dietary shift to less beef with lower cattle prices could influence farmers to hold back on marketing and/or produce fewer calves, resulting in fewer hides being available.

Knowing that we would need all the muscle we could muster, given the political interest in the embargo, I went to the Washington office of the American Cattle Association. I received excellent cooperation. I also met frequently with Department of Commerce and Department of Agriculture officials. For the next several weeks I worked on this case night and day, collecting data, writing analytical position papers, meeting with lawyers, both Chilewich's and those of the cattle association.

A hearing was held at the Department of Commerce before an administrative law judge. It lasted all day. Matt Ross testified, I testified, and a representative from the cattlemen's association testified, as did officials of the Department and representatives of the shoe industry.

The final result was a recommendation by the judge that the embargo be lifted promptly and in its entirety. It was.

After I had gotten some rest and recovered my breath, I prepared a bill for services rendered. It was based entirely on my time input as well as that of other members of Nathan Associates staff. There was no "extra" for success. The fee billed was about $8,000, not an insignificant fee then.

Several days later Aaron called me. He said he had my bill and wanted to talk about it. My stomach did a flip. I knew that the bill was fair and was not padded. I had worked damned hard for several weeks, and for Chilewich to complain about a bill was most unusual.

I explained to Aaron that the bill was based on real time worked, and that we felt it was very much in order.

Aaron took my breath away with his next statement. As well as I can remember it, he said, "No, it was not in order. It should have been much higher. Please send me a new bill."

This had never happened to me before—nor since.

Anyhow, I suggested to Aaron that it would be difficult for me to send another bill that he and we might consider fair. He agreed and said that he would take care of it. He did.

He sent us a check for $42,000. That was Aaron Chilewich.

I do believe that Aaron never lost a minute's sleep because of our work on behalf of his firm. And neither did I.

Russian Encounters: "Bring Boots"

Among Chilewich's Russian activities was the sale of agricultural equipment and entire operating food production plants on a turn key basis.[8]

In the 1960s, a Russian team came to the United States to 'study' American feed-lot operations. Simon Chilewich arranged for the team to visit a very efficient and successful operation just outside of Sterling, Colorado. I was invited to join the group.

When Simon called, he said, "And bring a pair of boots."

The only footwear I had that might qualify as boots, was a pair of galoshes. He was horrified when I showed up in my eastern galoshes. I was embarrassed. Simon had already arranged for each member of the Russian team to have a pair of cowboy boots—the appropriate attire in the cattle country.

We postponed that morning's planned session at the feed lot while Simon rushed me to a local boot maker with instructions to have a handmade pair of elephant skin boots ready for me the next morning. They were and they were beautiful.

Getting my feet into them was another story. They hurt like hell. I was told that this was normal and that in three or four days they would be fine. Much of those three or four days was torture. They did loosen up and felt pretty good. I was later told that when one of the ranchers gets a new pair of boots he lets one of his Mexican ranch hands wear them for the first week. I did not have that luxury.

The boots turned out to be most appropriate wear as we trudged through the feed lot almost daily. At the end of each day we simply took a hose and sloshed off the accumulated cattle manure. The boots came through as good as new. Later when I wore the boots to a meeting at the State Department, one of the government participants commented on the boots. I announced "These are my bullshit boots, and I wear them when appropriate." The meeting was efficient and successful.

A feed lot takes young cattle from surrounding ranches, uses computer controlled feeding over a fixed period of time to increase their weight and meat content. At the end of a specified time the cattle, in practice, have put on substantial weight. In theory, the market value of the additional poundage is more than the cost of adding the additional weight, taking into account capital investment, feed, and operating costs. The fattened beef are then moved to nearby abattoirs for slaughter, packaging and shipment to markets.

The Russian team was impressed with the plant and its operation. The Soviet delegation decided that Russia needed a plant identical to the one it was visiting—identical even to the Dodge trucks, and GE light bulbs.

A contract was signed for Chilewich to furnish a twin plant in Kharkov, Russia. Chilewich agreed to supply the equipment, build the plant, provide American staff for six months to operate the plant and teach the local workers how to operate it. The equipment for the plant was assembled and shipped to Russia. It was built in the image of the Sterling facility.

For the six months that the American trainers from Colorado were on scene, the plant worked well, almost at production levels equivalent to those in Sterling. After the Americans left, the facility managed to struggle along for another six months before it shut down altogether, not an unusual experience in the Soviet system.

The raw material—young cattle—was available. There was no problem with adequate supplies of feed. The computer settings depended upon simple computation. The equipment performed as expected. The Russian staff lacked management supervision, maintenance ability, and most importantly, incentive. And the Russians would not ask for help. That would have admitted incompetence.

The Wheat Team in Washington

During the Kennedy years, 1961–1963, the USSR had experienced a wheat crop failure for two years in a row. The U.S. had huge surpluses. The USSR and the United States entered into an agreement whereby the U.S. would sell wheat to the Soviets under favorable terms for the Russians.

Chilewich Sons & Company negotiated part of the wheat sale to the Soviet purchasing mission that had been sent here. I was a member of the Chilewich team. The Russian team consisted of the Director of Rossno-Import, the Soviet government grain importing authority, two technical wheat experts, and a 'lawyer.' It quickly became evident that the 'lawyer' had functions other than legal questions.

The Soviet team was headquartered at the then most expensive hotel in Washington, The Madison, on the corner of 17th and M Streets., N.W., a location convenient to the Soviet Embassy on 16th Street.

The Russians were tough negotiators. They knew prices and qualities. They also knew that the U.S. had large surpluses, as did Canada. We had many sessions at the Madison Hotel and at the Russian Embassy. We also had many social gatherings, as well as brief visits to see some of the sights of Washington.

One night Simon Chilewich would host a dinner for both teams. The next night the Russians would be the hosts. The meals were heavy with steak or lobster, of course with copious quantities of vodka and caviar.

Before each such meal, Simon assembled his people in his hotel room for 'strategy sessions.' Part of the strategy was to coat saltines heavily with butter and eat several of these crackers. This was supposed to be helpful to prevent being hit too hard by the vodka. It worked.

When the Soviets were hosts, the drinking got rather heavy with frequent toasts. However, if one said he didn't drink, the Russians honored this and didn't push. But if one took the first drink, it was expected that all other toasts would be matched drink for drink—and no sipping. I cheated, I sipped.

Most of the toasts were after dinner and became more expansive and laudatory as the vodka levels in the bottles diminished. Soon, we noticed that some of the participants were absent. Actually, they were there, but under the table. Passed out dead drunk. Some of the others seemed to be getting a bit boisterous. I can truthfully say that the Chilewich group was fine—thanks to the buttered saltines.

About midnight, at the end of a particularly gregarious dinner, the Soviet mission chief said he would like to see the Lincoln Memorial. So everybody still awake, piled into Soviet Embassy limos and off to the Memorial we went. A full moon night, the Memorial was gorgeous. Its beauty and solemnity seemed to make a deep impression on our guests. It was surprising to me how much these foreigners knew about Abe Lincoln. The Mission head recited most of the Gettysburg Address by heart. The Park Service guard on duty was not the least bit surprised at being descended upon by this group. In fact he seemed to enjoy the opportunity to tell the Russians even more about Mr. Lincoln than they already knew.

Armistice Day Boat Trip

Early in the month when the Soviet wheat purchasing team was in Washington, I invited the two technical people to join Flora and me for a short cruise on our power boat on the Chesapeake Bay. They were enthusiastic about the idea. But it took some arranging.

State Department regulations for visiting Soviets did not permit them to travel more than 25 miles from the capitol without special authorization. To my surprise permission was readily granted. When I informed State that my boat was near Annapolis, about 35 miles from D.C., I was told that the *USNS Alexander Hamilton*, a nuclear submarine, was in the Annapolis Harbor. The control officer suggested that I take my guests to see this sub, but not to get closer than 100 yards.

The two technicians were anxious to make the planned trip, but said that it would be necessary to bring the 'lawyer' along. It was his ostensible responsibility to make sure that there would not be too much fraternization with Americans by his people. I interpreted this to mean that he would make certain that the techies did not express adverse opinions about their homeland. He was in fact a KGB agent. I had no choice but to agree to include him, but I wasn't happy. The technicians did not seem too happy to have him in the party either.

Armistice Day, November 11, symbolically, was the day set for the trip. The day started out bright and sunny, and for November, rather balmy.

Flora and I arrived at the Madison Hotel promptly at 9:00 AM. I phoned the technician with whom I had been dealing. He apologized and said, they had a problem, namely that the 'lawyer' was sick and could not go. When I said that that was too bad, but couldn't they go without him. They would like to, but had to get clearance from the mission head. Fortunately, they were able to get a green light and soon were in the car headed for our yacht club. It became apparent that they were not unhappy that the 'lawyer' was not with us. Incidentally, their English was quite good.

On the way we passed Logan Circle. Once an elegant area with many large three and four story homes, it was at that time rather seedy, with rental units frequently having four or five persons to a room. Certain houses were used by the numerous local hookers.

As we drove around the circle, one of our guests said, "This must be where the capitalists live." I assured him that there were few, if any, capitalists living in the area. We proceeded out Route 50 toward Annapolis. As we were passing the cookie-cutter town of Bowie, Maryland, with its several hundred postwar Levitt built homes, some with small boats on trailers in the driveways, and every house with a car, our guests again asked if this was where the capitalists lived. They did not believe me when I told them that the residents were government workers, small store merchants, teachers, policemen and firemen—definitely not capitalists. I suggested that they pick out two or three houses and that we would visit the occupants. The first house they picked out had a car and a small trailered boat in the driveway. The owner was cleaning them.

We stopped, made introductions all around. The resident said he was a Washington fireman, and invited us inside his house. Our guests were amazed. We did the same thing at two other houses that they selected. Same results. No capitalists. The Soviets were convinced, and the home owners were excellent ambassadors for American democracy.

We had a delightful time on the boat, and did cruise around the *USNS Hamilton*. The Soviets, not being military men might or might not have been impressed—but they enjoyed the day and the lunch that Flora had packed.

On the way home, I told them that I would show them what might be considered homes of capitalists. Needless to say they were impressed by the drive through parts of Chevy Chase and Kenwood, Maryland, suburbs of Washington. They saw big homes on large well manicured lots, many with tennis courts and swimming pools.

They were in no hurry to get back to the *Madison*. When we

reached our home, Flora threw together a delightful supper. Now, it was the Russians' turn to relax, and they did. The talk about living conditions in Russia and the United States was stimulating and revealing, particularly their descriptions of Russian housing and living conditions. I showed them my work room, the power equipment that I had, including a bench saw. One of our guests blurted out, "Of everything I have seen, this bench saw I would like to be able to own." Surprised, I replied, "Not a car, not a boat, not a house?"

"No," he said. "Those things would be impossible. This would be possible."

When we showed them our eleven-year-old son Jonathan's room with his electric train set-up, their eyes bulged. Not for the train, but because of the 15 by 18 foot size of the room. "All this for one little boy? In Russia enough room for three families."

Considerably later they left our home after gifting us with records of Russian music, and a beautiful carved walrus tusk. This scrimshaw depicted, in color, a seal hunt on one side and an Eskimo village, complete with igloos and reindeer pulling sleds, on the other. It had been a beautiful day.

"To Moscow, with Love"

In June, 1968, the U.S. government again agreed to sell large quantities of wheat to the USSR. Previous sales had been made during the Lend-Lease days of World War II, as well as postwar sales during the Kennedy years, as mentioned earlier.

Simon Chilewich was determined to use his contacts in Russia to secure some of this potentially profitable business. He put together a negotiating team which included some of the Chilewich executives from South America, France, and the United States and myself. I was the 'authority' on U.S. government regulations that might have an impact on the sale.

Simon and I flew to Moscow on the June 1968 inaugural flight of Pan American Airways' new non-stop New York/Moscow service. Of course, we flew first class.

Upon arrival at Moscow's Sheremetyevo Airport, we cleared customs rapidly as Simon distributed ballpoint pens and Kennedy half dollars liberally to the customs and visa clearance officers. Simon, who almost commuted to Moscow from New York, was clearly known to the airport personnel. Shortly after collecting our baggage we were on our way to the Hotel National in Moscow. The ride into the city was an overdose of Soviet propaganda. Many huge billboards lined both sides of the highway from airport to city. These extolled Soviet Russian achievements, glory of the army, glory of the worker, and, of course, glory to Stalin. It was impossible to avoid such glorification.

The Hotel National, a major establishment right on Red Square, had a tourist view of the Kremlin, Lenin's Tomb, and the famous onion shaped St. Basil church domes. And for those with dollars, the Gum Department store was a short walk. At the end of each hallway on every floor, near the ancient, creaky elevator, sat the omnipresent "babushka" (old woman) with her rack of keys, and ever-hot samovar of tea. She cast a gimlet eye on whoever went in or out of the rooms. Simon and I each had what passed for a suite overlooking Red Square. A major problem with my 'suite' was that the toilet was firmly affixed halfway under the sink in the bathroom. This made for certain inconveniences to say the least.

In the morning I looked out my window to see the domes of the Kremlin with their windvane five-pointed stars just a few hundred feet away. Sweeping the street with crude looking brooms were many babushkas wearing rubber boots and the traditional head scarves over their heads and tied under their chins.

Thirty-two years later, while Flora and I were in Moscow on vacation, I made a short visit to the Hotel National. Except for the exterior walls it had been completely renovated as a first class five star hotel, with prices to match.

Each member of the Chilewich team was assigned a Moskova car and driver and an InTourist guide. Whenever the guide was not around, my driver complained about the quality and performance of the car, and several times said, "Oh how I wish I could have a Ford." After three days in that car, I also wished he had a Ford.

The business meetings, typically Soviet style, were revealing. If our group had four people in attendance the Soviets had four. If we had five, they would have five. Discussion was in Russian with translation—even if everyone at the meeting was fluent in English. We early on found that the Russian negotiators, like those we encountered in the Kennedy period wheat sales, were market wise. They knew world prices and stock levels. They frequently offered barter deals in butter or other commodities such as poor quality industrial goods. Some of these were interesting to Simon who felt that he had possible markets for them in Latin America.

While the Americans had authority to sign and seal a deal, every time there was a decision agreed upon, the Russians had to get it approved by some one higher up, but someone never at the meetings. This could be cumbersome and annoying. However, to work in the Soviet milieu one had to accept this and work around it. It also required extra meetings. Also just as frequently, Mr. Higher Up would find some trifling, unimportant point to criticize and demand a change. It was hard to know when the negotiation was finished.

Almost every night we had a social or cultural function. At one of the big dinners, with lots of vodka, caviar, bad borscht, and songs, Simon began taking pictures with a Polaroid Camera he had brought from home. This was a new and wonderful gadget to the Russians. Have your picture taken, and in a few seconds get the print!

One of our hosts was a Mr. Balin. He was the number two man in one of the Soviet trading companies. Almost always, it appeared, the number two man was Jewish, but never the number one man. I suspected that Balin was Jewish, but he parried every hint or suggestion that I made to him about this.

It was time for Simon to take a picture of Balin and me alone. As we posed for the shot, with no one but Simon within ten feet of us, Balin leaned over me and in his Russian-accented English, said, "Maury, tell me, is *Fiddler on the Roof* still playing in New York?" I said that it was. "Oh, how I would love to see it." Period. Nothing more. But I got the message.

InTourist Guide

In 1968, every visitor to the USSR had to have a specific itinerary approved by InTourist. That government agency controlled the movements of visitors, almost with an iron hand. In addition, an InTourist Guide was assigned to each visitor to make sure that there was no deviation from the approved itinerary.

During this visit to the USSR I had two such guides, one in Moscow and one in Leningrad, now again St. Petersburg. Both were young women, and that is where the similarity ended.

My Moscow guide, Natasha, was twenty-three to twenty-five years old. Her English was quite good. She was neatly dressed in a blue two piece suit—every day the same suit or its sister. But always neat and clean.

She was determined to prove that I, as a 'capitalist'—her word— had to exploit my workers and particularly my secretary, to enjoy a decent life. From the first ten minutes she started with the propaganda and party line. If it weren't the sweat shops, it was the brutal tactics used to break up the unions—methods true early in the 20th century. She had the entire catalogue of Soviet anti-American propaganda. I tried to avoid the subject, particularly her recitals of the economic wrongs we Americans were doing to our 'poor struggling workers.' I agreed with her that in the United States everything was not perfect. But I also pointed out that most of her criticisms were very much outdated.

Finally, fed up with these harangues, on the third morning, as we got into our Moskova, I asked the driver to take us first to the American Embassy before going to another negotiating meeting. This request upset Natasha, and she told me that we were 'not authorized' to go there. I told her I needed a document for the meeting. The driver who had imperfect English, and early on made it clear to me that he didn't buy Natasha's propaganda, paid her no heed and made the short trip to the Embassy.

With Natasha's protests ringing in my ears, I went in the Embassy, showed the Marine guard my credentials, and asked him to get me any recent copy of *The New York Times*. He did.

Back in the car with the newspaper, I asked Natasha how many pairs of shoes she had. "Three," she said. I asked her how long she had to work to buy a pair of shoes. "About a month" was the answer.

I repeated this question and answer line with reference to her dress her TV, and other items that the average American secretary would own.

Turning to the help wanted columns of *The Times* and the many ads for secretaries. I pointed out the salaries being offered. Having established some base line salary levels, I turned to the many retail ads for shoes, dresses, TVs, cameras, and sports equipment. A comparison of these prices to the salaries offered quickly demonstrated even to this hardcore communist that my secretary could buy shoes or dresses or even a TV or a camera for considerably less than a month's income. Showing her the ads for automobiles, and telling her that my 'exploited' secretary had her own car ended her daily propaganda stint.

At this point, the driver repeated his manta "Oh, how I wish I had a Ford." Later, when Natasha was not in the car, I asked him what was wrong with the car he was driving. "Needs to go in shop almost every week for repair. No good." My undiplomatic activity with reference to *The Times* was undoubtedly reported to the proper authorities.

Moscow to Leningrad.

After the negotiations ended, I took a few days to visit Leningrad. Having heard of the superior Red Arrow Train which ran overnight between the two cities, and not wanting to fly in Russian planes, I booked a first class sleeper accommodation. I was looking forward to the experience as well as to seeing the Russian countryside. That night before the midnight train time, my stomach revolted from the heavy greasy Russian food. I canceled my reservations. I was ill.

Feeling better the next morning, and still wanting to see Leningrad, and to inquire about an address I had in that city for my late father's family, I had my driver take me to the airport. To my surprise, I had no trouble buying a ticket to Leningrad. I was pleased that the flight was uneventful. The stewardesses were attentive—but huge. There were no seat belts, and the service, in contrast to what American and European aircraft offered at that time, consisted of hot tea, and a hard cracker.

Arrival at the Leningrad airport was another experience.

Leningrad

Upon entering the arrival terminal, I was accosted by a uniformed officer. Police, customs, army? I didn't know. But his English was good enough for me to understand him when he said, "You have no authorization to come by air. You have to go back to Moscow."

What a welcome! I, of course argued. I stated that going back was ridiculous; that I had a hotel reservation etc. etc. "No, you must go back." He said, "Your luggage did not come. Go back."

I pointed to my B-2 flight bag—a popular type of travel luggage—sitting in a corner of the next room, and told him that that was my luggage. It was also clear to me that the luggage had been opened and examined. I had nothing to hide, so I was not concerned.

As Mr. Uniform continued to insist that I take the plane back to Moscow, I finally said, "I will go to Finland. I will go to Paris. I will go to Copenhagen. But I am not going back to Moscow." Mr. Uniform walked out of the room. Another man came in, this man in civilian clothes. (Bad cop-good cop routine). He gave me his name and offered his handshake. He said, " I am also Jewish. I want to help you." My being Jewish had not previously come up.

He made some small talk, but at the same time let me know that I had violated one of the travel rules of the USSR, and that I could be in big trouble if I did not go back to Moscow. Again, I repeated my litany of where I would go, but not Moscow. I had not mentioned the official capacity of my trip to Russia, as I did not want to get our team in trouble. My 'proteczia' was my ace in the hole. After further discussion, I told him that the best way he could help was to get me the taxi, or car, that I had ordered.

After about five minutes that seemed like an hour, he left the room, making it clear that I was not to leave without permission. Not much later, he returned and said that there was a taxi for me. I picked up my baggage—yes it was mine, and it had been opened—and had no trouble getting to the Hotel Astoria, the best hotel in Leningrad. By American standards it was comfortable, but certainly not a first-rate hotel. Yes, a babushka, with her omnipresent samovar, was on every floor. The elevators were open cages that creaked as they slowly moved from floor to floor. I was not comfortable. I found myself imagining all kinds of scenarios that might happen before I left the people's paradise. I didn't sleep much that night, expecting a knock on the door by uniformed men. With every sound I heard in the hall of the hotel I was sure that they were coming. Nothing happened.

After I had been released from the troublesome detention at the Leningrad airport and had checked into the hotel, I met Maria, my

Leningrad InTourist guide. I was not prepared for the total difference between Maria and Natasha.

Maria, my assigned InTourist guide was a charming, wholesomely attractive young lady of about eighteen or nineteen, whose English was absolutely perfect with a flat American Midwest accent.

While we walked and saw some of the sights of the city, she told me an amazing story. It was somewhat chilling, particularly given the cat and mouse games that the KGB and the CIA played with each other.

From the time she was three years old, she had been educated in a special school that concentrated on English as spoken in the United States—in her case—in Ohio. She knew more about the history, geography, economy, and culture of Ohio and its principal cities than most Ohio residents. She knew a great deal about the baseball teams, the players, the universities, and the political leaders.

This was her training from age three through high school. She was frank to say that she had been trained to be put into Ohio as part of the USSR spy system. But somewhere along the line, she messed up on her Sovietology, and was de-selected for work outside of the USSR.

Was her story legitimate? Was it even believable? Why did she tell me these things? Was she a 'plant?' I don't know. She was a damn good guide. However, following my airport experience, and being fearful of some kind of a trap, I made sure that we were never alone. I have often wondered what became of her. I will never know.

The next morning Maria and I were off to the sights of Leningrad; the Hermitage, with its art riches, the Winter Palace, where the Tzars spent much of their winters in French style pleasure and ambiance, and the naval vessel *Aurora*, moored in the harbor as a permanent exhibit. The 1917 revolution had been started by the mutinous crew of this vessel. We also roamed along the banks of the Nepa River, fascinated by the many rapid commuter vessels. Unlike today, where every tourist site has long lines waiting to enter, in 1968 there were few if any tourists and entrance was immediate

Late in the afternoon, and still a free man, I dismissed my guide and found my way to the Leningrad synagogue. Although somewhat run down, it was still an imposing building. There were a few elderly

men sitting in the pews. As far as I could tell, they were just schmooz-
ing, not praying. Two of them spoke a little English, but all spoke
Yiddish. It was amazing, how after a few minutes, *mamalochen* (Yiddish) came back to me and we were able to have a somewhat stilted
conversation.

I showed them the envelope I had brought with me with a Leningrad address. It had come with a letter from Sima Mazo, a niece of
my father. The letter was dated April, 1946, twenty two years earlier.
There had been no communication with the family since that letter. One of the old men said that he knew where that address was
and would take me there. We made an appointment to meet the next
morning at the synagogue.

Later, walking from the synagogue toward my hotel I became
aware that someone was walking beside me, pace for pace. Without looking at me, he said, in Yiddish, "Don't believe him. Don't
go with him. He is an informer." And then my walking companion
disappeared.

When I showed the envelope to other people, I was told that the
address did not exist, that the area had been heavily damaged during
the war and had been rebuilt with different names. Since the letter
had been sent after the war, there was something strange. In any case,
I understood that it was not a good idea, for my safety as well as that
of my relatives, to pursue the inquiry. This was confirmed by a call
to the American Consulate. The paranoia and fear of contact with
foreigners was thick enough to cut with a knife.

I did not meet my would-be volunteer synagogue guide. At that
point I had had enough of Russia.

The next day I left for Paris, via Finland.

⁂

In 2000, Flora and I were in Leningrad while on a Russian River
Cruise. We visited the Hotel Astoria. It had been completely rebuilt
on the inside. Definitely to five star standards and prices.

In 2001, I did locate my father's niece, Sima, in Moscow. Accompanied by my son Joseph, daughter Barrie, and niece Jani Barquist,
I went to Moscow and St. Petersburg (Leningrad) and enjoyed an
emotional reunion with the remnants of my father's family.

11

Gordon-Choisy
Pierre Grawitz
I Become an Alligator Maven

S HORTLY AFTER THE Chilewich hide embargo case was settled in 1964, a handsome athletically built man, with close cropped gray hair, and a heavy, but delightful French accent visited the offices of Nathan Associates.

Pierre Grawitz introduced himself as president of the French Federation of Reptile Tanners, and managing director of Gordon-Choisy (G-S), a large French tanner of exotic skins.[9] He said that RRNA had been recommended to him by Aaron Chilewich to help solve problems with the American customs authorities and the U.S. Fish and Wildlife Service of the U.S. Department of Interior.

To control the movement and use of exotics, many of which were in danger of extinction, the International Conference on Endangered Species (CITES) established rules and regulations regarding the "taking and marketing" of animal, plant, and bird species worldwide. The United States, through the Department of Interior, was a major participant in CITES.

After we had spent a few minutes together, I remarked that I knew nothing about producing or marketing alligator, crocodile, or snake skins. I also said that I knew nothing about the background or legislation and rules governing 'endangered' species.

Pierre's answer was straight to the point. "I assumed that was the case. Take thirty days, with the clock running, and learn as much as you can about exotic skin marketing and the regulations. Then let's talk." This sounded like an ideal situation to learn something about a new, to me, marketing subject, get paid for it, and have an interesting client at the same time.

About two weeks later I had exhausted the printed literature that I could find, had interviewed Fish and Wildlife officials about endangered species legislation, rules and regulations, and had talked to U.S. Customs officials. I had also studied the American regulations governing endangered species. I found the world of producing and marketing exotic leathers a complicated realm with its own interest groups of environmentalists and herpetologists, the fashion world, and agriculturalists. 'States' rights questions, political positions, and many international facets also had to be considered.

I also tried to find out as much as I could about the firm of Gordon-Choisy and its principals.

Gordon-Choisy was one of the largest exotic skin tanneries in Europe, specializing in tanning and marketing high quality reptile skins for boot, shoe, and leather goods manufacturers such as Judith Leiber (purses) and Tony Lama (cowboy boots) in the United States. G-S was the supplier of choice to numerous up-scale fashion houses throughout Europe and Japan. In addition skins of lizard, ostrich, frog, and shark were tanned and marketed by Gordon-Choisy.

Leon Gordon and Pierre Grawitz were the directors of the firm. Mr. Gordon, a French Jew with a Catholic wife, was one of the firm's founders. Pierre, about thirty years younger than Gordon was from a southern French Catholic agricultural family. After getting his doctorate in chemistry in England, Pierre came into the business through some family connections on the Choisy side. An astute businessman, fluent in several languages and a very good salesman, he rapidly rose to be the one who called most of the shots, subject to Leon Gordon's approval—which in my experience he always had.

Pierre and his wife, Christine, tall, attractive, and from a French royalist family, had three charming daughters, Sylvie, Rosalyne, and Carole. Flora and I became fast friends of the family, visiting in each other's homes. Rosalyne was a guest in our home for one summer while interning at the International Monetary Fund. We attended the weddings in Paris of two of the girls.

Leon Gordon and his wife had no children. But, Patrice Mathieu, a nephew of his wife came into the business and was being groomed for subsequent leadership in the firm and the industry.

Patrice's main responsibility was to travel extensively into Africa, South America, and Asia to buy raw skins for shipment to France for tanning and finishing. After Mr. Gordon's death in his late eighties, Patrice became a director. The chemistry between Pierre and Patrice was not always harmonious.

My initial responsibility for G-C was to study the regulations of the U.S. Fish and Wildlife Service affecting imported exotic skins. I was then expected to advise G-C as to the impact of such rules and orders on their activities and markets.

The World of Exotic Skins

There was a whole new world out there that bore little or no resemblance to what I had learned through my Chilewich experiences about cattle hides and their production and marketing. With rare exceptions, all exotic skins destined for the shoe and fashion markets came from the wild, the product of hunters in Africa, South America, South East Asia, and for the really big crocodiles, the South Pacific Islands. Today, a growing percentage of raw exotic skins is produced on farms developed for the purpose. This is especially true for alligator, snake, and ostrich skins.

Endangered Species regulations were a complicated group of rules, citations and decisions intended to control the hunting or taking of animal, plant, and bird species in danger of becoming extinct. The International Conference on Endangered Species (CITES) was the loadstone of the various laws and regulations. Each member country of CITES had its own laws and regulations regarding hunting, exportation, importation and trade regarding endangered or species under threat of becoming endangered. A considerable, and for the most part successful, effort was made to standardize these regulations under the CITES umbrella.

A certain species of reptile in one country, for example, might be plentiful and not on a restricted list, while the same species from another country might be listed. Accordingly, some market countries prohibited the importation of any reptiles. Other countries permitted importation provided that official CITES documents were available as to a legal (not restricted) point of origin. It is easy to imagine the machinations that went on, and still do, in many areas of the undeveloped world (and often in the developed world) where administration of CITES regulations was less than a developed science or where the regulations were observed more in lack of implementation than otherwise.

World-wide, the principal exotic leather demand was for crocodile skins. These were found in Africa, Southeast Asia, and the South Pacific. Caiman, a croc cousin, was generally abundant in Central and South America.

The hunting, killing, and marketing of skins from American alligators, a close cousin of the crocodile, was strictly prohibited. Nevertheless, poaching was endemic, and threatened the existence in this country of this prehistoric animal. The fresh waters of Louisiana, Alabama, Texas, Georgia, Mississippi, and Florida were the gators' principal habitat. Alligators not being legally available as a cash crop, there was an incentive for land owners to drain marsh land and convert acreage to sugar, rice, or beef feeding operations, diminishing the habitat for alligator populations and thus further reducing such populations.

In Africa there were two major croc species—the niloticus-niloticus and the crocodylus-crocodylus. Populations of the former had been seriously depleted. Accordingly they were on most countries' restricted lists, and definitely prohibited in the United States. On the other hand the crocodylus were more plentiful, and under certain controls, skins of this species were permitted into this country. However, often it was extremely difficult to tell the species of one tanned and colored skin from another—particularly where there had been cross breeding in the wild. On several occasions I have seen 'expert' witnesses identify skins as one species one day, and several days later identify the same skin differently.

Caiman, a much smaller reptile, but looking much like a small crocodile and highly desired for men's 'alligator shoes' and for trim on up-scale ladies footwear, was plentiful in several South American countries, but scarce in neighboring countries. This led to much cross border smuggling and trade using false documentation.

My Function in This Wild Industry

Gordon-Choisy, as a major tanner and exporter of exotics to the United States, needed to know, on an almost daily basis, what changes were occurring or proposed in the exotic leather industry, in both state and federal regulations as well as in the market. Not infrequently, there were problems with import documents which would include point of origin papers, and questions of species identification. In such cases the Fish and Wildlife Service was judge and jury, and could (and did) levy heavy, often unfair fines for violations—willful and otherwise. While the F&W performed a needed function, in many cases I found its officials and agents were often down right unfair, particularly if they had a grudge against a particular firm. The "expert witnesses," mostly zoo herpetologists, seemed to have a built in bias against any one who "looked at an alligator cross-eyed."

Specifically, my job was to keep Gordon-Choisy advised about current and proposed U.S. and CITES regulations; to prepare documentation and argue cases when accused of import or CITES violations; to be aware of the American market and changes therein for tanned skins; to work with several of their major customers when they encountered regulation problems; and to study the possibility of getting the American alligator off the endangered species list.

A full plate, but a challenging and exciting one!

Many officials of the Fish and Wildlife Division of the U.S. Department of Interior with whom I had frequent discussions, often had a totally negative attitude about marketing alligator skins. Some, however, were interested in studying gator demographics and possible economic benefits to farmers, land owners, hunters and the fashion industry. It would be necessary to demonstrate that the wild populations had reached a sustainable level, and that the illegal trade in skins could be controlled.

Poached skins were being sold by the hunters for about six dollars a linear foot. Whether the landowner received part of this price is problematic. As mentioned earlier, the return was not enough to keep landowners from clearing and draining large tracts of marshland, eliminating the alligators, and turning to farming cattle, rice and sugar cane to improve the economic return on the land.

Grand Chenier

The Rockefeller Game Refuge and Experimental Station in Grand Chenier covered 88,000 acres of Louisiana marsh and delta land. In the process of gathering information, I spent some time with Ted Johanson, probably the most knowledgeable man in the United States on gator husbandry. He was the director of the station and was a fountain of information and ideas.

Although there had been some small movement in developing farm raised alligators, which would not have been subject to the same restrictions as those in the wild, this husbandry was still in its infancy. On the Rockefeller Game Refuge, there were many experiments being conducted on methods to enhance the breeding of gators, and to reduce costs at the same time. It was clear that if there were any chance of getting the Mississippi alligator off the endangered species list we would have to prove to the bureaucrats in Washington that the wild population was adequate to support a controlled and limited legal sale of wild skins.

To do this, arrangements were made for local watermen in Louisiana to count nests in the spring. The Louisiana Department of Fisheries and Wildlife agreed to have its agents fly over nesting areas to supplement the count information from the Cajun watermen.[10]

I was able to fly on one of these surveys. The plane was a small two seater, piloted by the assistant chief of the Louisiana Fisheries Bureau. We flew at slightly above tree-top level as slowly as was safe. We were looking for newly made gator nests, and trying to count them.

Initially I had considerable difficulty spotting the nests, even when the pilot pointed them out to me. Finally, probably in desperation at the inability of this city guy to see a nest in plain sight (his idea of plain sight) at about fifty feet over a sandy break in the marsh grass, he banked the plane sharply to the right so that the wing was almost perpendicular to the ground and I was between him and the ground. In this position he circled tightly, while pointing to new nests on the sand below. At last, I did manage to see the nests and learned for what I should be looking. We then flew for quite a while over marsh area. I found that I became proficient in nest counting. We did this all the way from Grand Chenier to New Orleans. I was glad to get back on the ground.

After three years of gator counting by state officials, plus information from production records of the farms, I put together my economic analysis proposing a limited legal hunt for wild gators in one parish of Louisiana. One of my big arguments was that keeping the gators on the prohibited list meant they were of no economic value to land owners. If it were the policy of the U.S. government and environmental groups to preserve these animals for future generations, it was necessary that they become an economic asset instead of a liability.

In 1972, the U.S. Fish and Wildlife people reluctantly agreed to allow a limited hunt in Cameron Parish, Louisiana. State game tags were allocated to local hunters. Each tag permitted the taking of one animal and had to be attached to the animal's jaw when taken, and to the salted raw skin when marketed. The limit that year would be 4,500 skins. Each had to be six linear feet or more. To insure that no poached skins or those out of freezers were included, each hide also had to include the skin from the front left leg, not a normal industry practice. This latter requirement was announced only a few hours before the hunt began. Since poached hides, already in cold storage, could not possibly have had this extra skin attached, and since each skin offered at the subsequent auction would have a state issued tag, the state wildlife officials had a fairly fool proof method of making sure that the raw hides offered were all legal.

The first auction was big news in Louisiana, and indeed throughout the American fashion industry. Whereas poached skins could only bring about $6.00 per foot, the first auction brought prices of up to $75 per foot.

There was now a legal market for gators. Dealers with legal skins could openly offer them for sale. Everybody was ecstatic. Well, everybody but the U.S. Fish and Wildlife Service. But it came around, so that the following year the experiment was increased to three parishes. Later to the entire state.

To insure that only legal skins were included in the now annual auctions, in addition to the state tags, the hunt provisions required that the hide include skin from a different announced part of the animal. Where this extra skin would come from was changed each year.

Several years later the American alligator was taken off the endangered species list. Today, between wild animals and those being raised on farms, alligator areas are 'up to their hips in gators.'

The flip side is that there are now so many gators that prices have plummeted below the cost of production and many farmers face bankruptcy.

Ted Johansen

For years, Ted Johansen, director of the game refuge, had been experimenting with different methods of raising gators from eggs. He tested different feeding ratios, varying light, humidity and temperature combinations. For example, he discovered that eggs exposed in incubators to one temperature and humidity combination would give more female young than eggs exposed to a different temperature and humidity combination. He also had wire pens with gators of various ages and sizes. In these he conducted experiments with regard to methods of egg production from captive animals, as compared to those in the wild. Experiments with different feeding programs were useful in determining what feeding programs would result in more rapid growth. Ted, a tall, handsome, soft spoken biologist could easily have been the model for Mark Trail of the comic strip.

At the Refuge Station, he had various types of tanks in which the young were raised, exploring for the most efficient method of gator husbandry, studying questions of the effect on growth of light and noise.

It was impossible to visit the Refuge and not learn something. And I would not think of going to Louisiana without a visit with Ted.

John Paul Crain

In my work in Louisiana I had the pleasure of meeting many fascinating people; hunters, alligator farmers, biologists, bankers, politicians, graduate students, exotic skin dealers, and state and federal wildlife officials.

Few, if any, however were as colorful as John Paul Crain, a local land owner, alligator breeder, and operator of a prosperous oil well supply firm. He was also a farmer, fishing camp operator, and community leader. He had a big home in Grand Chenier, and was generally recognized as the pre-eminent citizen of the town. Politically, he had all the right connections in Baton Rouge. This seemingly "ol' boy" Cajun was also extremely helpful to Pierre Grawitz and me.

John Paul was the managing director of Crain Brothers Co., one of the largest independent oil field supply operations in the delta. Also, John Paul owned and managed over 5,000 acres of alligator and nutria rich marsh land in addition to a large acreage of sugar cane. He also had several fishing and hunting camps in Johnson's Bayou, Louisiana. This acreage was bounded by the Gulf of Mexico and the Sabine River, separating Texas from Louisiana. It too was rich in marine wildlife and ducks.

Scotch, straight, was his favorite drink. He could and did consume a half a bottle in several hours, and not seem to show it—even driving a car afterwards. But it sure scared me riding with him at the wheel. The effects did catch up to him and he died in his early sixties.

John Paul had a fascination with big Lincoln Town Cars. During the Vietnam war when automobiles were being substantially downsized to make them more fuel efficient, and Lincoln announced that the big cars were not going to be produced anymore, John Paul bought five new ones. They were stored in one of the Crain Brothers garages. On one occasion, Pierre and I went bream fishing with Mrs. Crain in one of the nearby canals. She was an ardent light rod fisher woman. For transportation she used one of the new Lincolns.

When it started to rain Pierre and I thought we would be going back to the house. "No way," said Mrs. Crain. "Fishing in the rain is good fishing."

Moving the car to a bridge spanning the canal, she showed us how to fish from this brand new vehicle, through the windows. And it was raining. Yes, we caught a lot of fish, but didn't bring them into the car. One of the Mexican workers protected from the rain by a poncho, was outside to take the catch off the hooks. It was a strange experience.

Each January, for about ten years, Pierre Grawitz and I were guests of the State of Louisiana and John Paul for a week of duck hunting and fishing; usually duck hunting in the morning, and Gulf of Mexico fishing near the oil rigs in the afternoon.

Becoming a Duck Hunter

Pierre was a crack shot. I was a novice wannabee. On our first visit to the Johnson Bayou camp we were awakened about 4:30 A.M. by the smell of strong coffee, bacon and deep fat frying. Breakfast also included pancakes, waffles, grits, and hushpuppies.

It was pitch dark outside the warm and comfortable camp building. It was also raining buckets.

Not being enthusiastic about shooting ducks (actually I thought they were rather safe from me) and hoping to use my camera more than the shotgun supplied to me, I was pleased to see the heavy rain, believing that the shoot would be scrubbed. No such luck. The other hunters rejoiced in the weather. "Great for ducks" they said.

After breakfast, the local hunting guides having arrived, dressed in warm clothes, boots, and ponchos and carrying shotguns, we climbed aboard marsh buggies. They were converted World War II surplus command vehicles with specially constructed bodies and huge over-sized wheels. The chassis were built to clear three to four feet above the ground. The all-wheel-drive, guaranteed to propel these awesome looking monsters through any marsh or bog, reminded me of pictures that I have seen of soldiers going off in pouring rain to the front.

Wearing our ponchos we took off on a ten minute bouncy ride through the still dark morning, our headlights punching twin holes in the rain and the darkness. That short ride seemed like an hour. Thanks to the ponchos, we were not yet soaked through. After a few minutes' walk through the marsh grass, we came to our assigned duck blind. In front of it there was a small bay off the Sabine River. About twenty decoys had been set in the water in front of the blind.

I was introduced to our young Cajun guide, and the Labrador retriever that would go after any downed ducks.

In the blind, the guide asked me how often I went duck hunting. When I told him that this was my first, he paled. It is not uncommon for accidents to happen with gun-holding novices. He moved his seat much closer to me so that if I pivoted or swung while shooting, the muzzle of my gun could not come between us and accidentally blow his head off. He relaxed a bit when he heard that I had earned a marksman medal in the Marines.

In the marshes around us, nutria were making their distinctive calls, sounding like babies calling "maamaa." Nutria are swamp animals whose fur is used to produce 'sheared beaver' skins.

When the ducks started flying, Pierre demonstrated considerable skill as a hunter and had no difficulty getting his bag limit. I was surprised by the utter stupidity of the four or five ducks flying into my pellet spread. I also managed to get some good pictures.

Just outside of gun range, two alligators of four or five feet cruised the water. Any duck that fell near them became a gator's meal. The dog in retrieving each duck made sure that he did not get near the gators.

The whole camp ate delicious wild duck that night, being careful not to bite into a lead pellet.

A Fishing Experience

One morning John Paul arranged a special fishing trip for large-mouth bass in the bayou. Each of us—Pierre, John Paul, and I—had a guide and a marsh skiff. Off we went with instructions from John Paul to be back at the dock in three hours.

Using a small white plastic lure, at the guide's direction, I started casting. First cast, a three pound bass. Second cast nothing. Third cast, a one pound bass. And so it went. At the end of the three hours, my take was sixty-five fish ranging from a half pound to five pounds. I was exhausted.

Back at the dock, Pierre had the largest fish, six and a half pounds. He also had a goodly catch of smaller fish. John Paul came back with about thirty fish, and at least one, possibly more, empty scotch bottles.

Assessing the results he started mumbling "Gawd damn, Gawd damn, Gawd damn. Gawd damn Jew catches the most fish, Gawd damn 'frog' catches the biggest fish. What in hell is this Gawd damn Cajun doing—and on his own land." We broke up in laughter.

Paperwork Violations

All was not fun and games representing Gordon-Choisy. There was considerable work interpreting the complex F&W regulations to the G-S home office. This required a thorough knowledge of those regulations. Much time was spent in the offices of F&W trying to develop agreement between our client and F&W as to the intent and implementation of the regs. More often than not, we were successful.

Shipping exotic skins in international trade requires many documents for every shipment: certificates of origin, veterinary papers, Cites documents, customs forms, import/export declarations, certification of species, bills of lading, shipping manifests, and import/export certificates.

A slip-up in filling out these papers could result in delay or, worse, confiscation of the shipment if authorities had reason to believe that there was fraud or misrepresentation in the documentation.

Considering that many skins originated in extremely primitive areas of Asia, Africa, South and Latin America, where literacy was not a household talent, it was amazing that there were not more improperly prepared documents than there were. One of Nathan Associates functions was to receive the documents for a shipment by Gordon-Choisy before the goods were presented for clearance. We would then check the papers to make sure that they met the requirements of the various agencies concerned.

We, of course, could not independently check the points of origin of skins. For example at one time caiman skins from one South American country were not permitted into the United States. At the same time skins from a neighboring country were legal. No doubt there was cross-border movement of skins by local hunters and buyers. There was no way that we could check the accuracy of the certificates of origin. However, if the volume of skins shipped from the legal country increased substantially, there was the possibility that some of the skins were smuggled across the border.

There were several cases that we had to argue with Fish & Wildlife on behalf of Gordon-Choisy. In these instances, the F&W Service was prosecutor, judge, and jury. Often the fines F&W attempted to levy were unrealistically high with little reference to the severity of the alleged violation. For example, a $25,000 penalty where one or two skins might have been questionable out of a 20 skin shipment worth $8,500. In addition, the entire shipment could be confiscated.

One case I remember vividly. A shipment of South American caiman sides (used for women's shoes), worth several thousand dollars, was held up by the assertion that they were from a prohibited South American country. There was no way that Gordon-Choisy, probably the third or fourth unit in the market stream to handle the skins, could prove that they were not from the illicit country (no DNA then) and that the certificate of origin was genuine.

The F&W Service set a penalty of $20,000 plus confiscation. Sure, we could have taken it to court, but that would have cost many times more. Also, if we had won in court, it is certain that given the attitudes that existed at that time in the F&W Service, Gordon-Choisy would have been a marked firm, and its economic life in the U.S. would have been hell.

I made a trip, one of many, to Newton Center, Massachusetts, the headquarters of the enforcement division of F&W to discuss the case with the regional solicitor. My argument was that the fine plus confiscation was just unconscionable, considering the 'crime'; that Gordon-Choisy had acted in good faith having no reason to believe that the skins were not from an approved point of origin, and that the dealers from whom it had bought the skins had no record of illegal activities.

Well, I couldn't get the case killed, but I did get the fine reduced to $2000 and this was to be paid to the Sloan-Kettering Cancer Fund as a tax deductible charitable donation. This was readily acceptable to Gordon-Choisy. It was also an approach we used successfully on several other cases. This kind of a settlement lead to interesting unspoken conclusions about the validity of the government case.

Ostriches

One day in the early eighties Pierre telephoned from Paris and asked "What is the ostrich population in Israel?" This was the first time that I had had any indication that there were any ostriches in Israel.

Rapid inquiry developed that there was a South African Dutchman, Mike Van Grevenbrock, who had, about seven or eight years earlier, smuggled ten ostrich eggs out of South Africa, a serious offense. From these eggs he had developed a small flock of ostriches on a ranch near Ofakim in southern Israel, close to the Gaza border. Mike had also sold a few birds to a nearby moshav and it had a small flock. Another small flock existed at Kibbutz Ha'on, on the shore of the Kinneret, below the Golan.

Pierre indicated that he thought there might be 25,000 head of ostriches in Israel. As it turned out the actual number was considerably less, but the potential could be much higher.

A few months after I had submitted my report to Pierre, Patrice Mathieu of G-S and I were on our way to Israel to do an on-site study of the ostrich potential. G-C's interest was in a future source for supplies of ostrich skin.

Together with a representative from Israel's Ministry of Agriculture, we drove to Mike's farm. It was not easy to find as it was hidden from the road by a group of hillocks. There was no sign of the road to the farm. We found what looked like a cut through the roadside brush and tried it. This turned out to be the road, if one could call it that. I was glad that we were not in my car. Barely wide enough for one car, it consisted primarily of two parallel ruts through a stretch of rocks and boulders. After about a hundred yards of torture to car and passengers the 'road' did open out to a real road thru groups of low hills almost bare of vegetation. Finally around a bend we came upon the farm. It consisted of a fairly comfortable and pleasant planked wooden house which I was told had been designed and built by Mike. Small barns and utility buildings were in abundance. Nearby were a series of fenced plots of about two dunim (a half acre) square with a stable-like structure in each.

In addition to ostriches, Mike was experimenting with a hybrid cross between Nubian and Syrian goats. The offspring had long silky hair, and *no odor*. Working with the animal husbandry scientists of Ben Gurion University, he was also experimenting with camels for camel milk production and for breeding camels that would produce twins. There were other animal experiments going on, with poultry, with sheep, and of course, with ostriches.

Mike was a large, powerfully built man, with little or no fat on him.

He was also a gracious host, plying us with fruit, juices, cakes, and scotch, along with a continuing saga of his adventures in escaping from South Africa with ten eggs, and ending up in Israel where his love for an attractive sabra made him a settler in that very inhospitable part of Israel.

He, of course, was interested in the idea of developing the ostrich population to a viable commercial level. To do so there had to be prerequisites: farmers ready to breed and raise the birds; training in ostrich husbandry; training in the art of skinning an expensive skin so that there were no cuts and no spoilage causing fats in the raw leather; and financing for developing the industry. And, there had to be a market.

Patrice and I indicated that we could help on each aspect of the program, particularly the market. But the nub was financing to do all that was necessary. Here the Gordon-Choisy firm agreed to advance funds to increase the total ostrich population, with repayment over a period of time out of the shipment of raw skins to France.

Over the next several years, I was a frequent visitor at Mike's ranch. On one trip Flora learned more about ostriches than she cared to know. But she was entranced, as was I, to watch ostrich mating dances. The female would bow and scrape with wings spread around the male. Then he would do the same, but with his long neck expanded from about three inches thick to well over 12 inches, at the same time emitting loud throat whoops. We also collected many ostrich feathers and a few hollowed out ostrich eggs. The contents of an ostrich egg is equal to about three dozen chicken eggs.

Over time the ostrich population approached 25,000 with birds being raised throughout Israel. A breeding adult pair had a market value of almost $75,000. A four week old chick could bring $1,500, and a fertile egg, $500. With these values, there was little incentive to kill and skin live birds. In addition, the long, black or white glossy feathers of the male were in demand for fashion purposes. Israel became an exporter of birds and eggs. The cash advances made by G-S to growers were paid back, either in cash or in skins.

Ostrich meat, very low in cholesterol, tasting and looking like beef, started to appear in menus of up-scale restaurants. Most of the meat comes from the legs. Packaged, in the early days, it was selling for about $20 a pound. Because there are not three toes visible, the meat cannot qualify as kosher.

Ostrich feathers are unlike others. Most bird feathers are characterized by the feathery part (barb) being interlocked, forming a smooth surface along the vane or web. About two-thirds of the barb are on one side of the quill. The ostrich barb is evenly divided along the quill. However, the ostrich feather has no web as such and no interlocking. The feather is fluffy and loose. Also the fluff extending down both sides of the quill are of the same size. Accordingly, those feathers not used for fashion purposes find a ready market as feather dusters.

Many Arabs believe that ostrich feathers provide protection against bullets. Mike's farm was close to the Gaza strip and its large Arab population. Accordingly, he often had midnight visits from Arabs intending to steal ostrich feathers.

Market forces are a strong determinant as to how ostrich products will be marketed; feathers for fashion or dusters, skin for expensive leather, meat for human consumption, live birds—chicks or adults—for raising or breeding, or fertile eggs will be marketed. It was exciting for me, together with the Gordon-Choisy company, to open up and develop this potentially lucrative industry in Israel.

12

To the South Pacific

IT LOOKED LIKE a small brown postage stamp on an endless empty green sea. It was Wake Island. That was the view from the window of the Pan American Stratocruiser flying west across the Pacific from Honolulu to Guam on this beautiful May, 1965 day. For unexplained reasons we were going to make an unscheduled, but brief stop at Wake. From Guam I was headed for Saipan, Administrative Headquarters of the Trust Territories of the Pacific Islands.

Nathan Associates had a contract with the Trust Territory Administration of the U.S. Department of Interior (USDI) for a development program in the Trust Territory of the Pacific Islands. The area consisted of hundreds of islands spread over an ocean expanse greater than the size of mainland United States. Many of the islands had been the locale of fierce bloody battles during the war. Names familiar to me include Saipan, Tinian, Truk, Rota, Yap, Ponape, Kwajalien, and Palau.

After World War II, these islands had become a Trusteeship of the United Nations with the United States as administrator. In 1965, the population of the 97 inhabited islands and atolls numbered 81,000 persons. The land area covered about 700 square miles in an ocean area of approximately 3 million square miles. The American High Commissioner, M. W. Goding, had his headquarters on Saipan. I was heading there to work with the Trust Territory Government to prepare proposals for providing surface (ship) transportation within the Territory.

There was an existing contract between the USDI and the Pacific Micronesia Line, a subsidiary of San Francisco-based Pacific Far East

Line. Under a cost-plus contract, PMI operated two vessels owned by the Department of Interior among the Micronesia Islands (PMI), Guam and Japan. The operation, which was expected to show an annual profit, in fact, reported large losses each year. These losses were covered by the American taxpayers. My responsibility was to review the overall operation, examine costs and prepare new proposals for the USDI to solicit new bids to provide surface shipping.

En Route

From Washington en route to the Territories I stopped in San Francisco. It's always good to see old friends. This time is was Hugo Loewi, ZIM Israel Navigation Co. local representative who met me at the plane, and Gerson Levine, a former U.S. Department of Agriculture colleague then working for Merrill Lynch.

The next morning, I met with A.M. Pilgrim, president of PML. This meeting turned out to be quite important and illuminating, for items that were discussed but also for those that were not. According to Pilgrim, there were major differences between the Trust Territory Administration (TTA) and PML.

It seemed that Pilgrim felt that PML's parent company, Pacific Far East Line (PFEL) was subsidizing the TTA through its economies of scale for insurance, accounting, etc. While PML professed that it wanted to get out of the contract, it certainly fought hard to keep it.

In my report from my inquiries in San Francisco with Pilgrim and his colleagues, I had written:

> Pilgrim indicated that foreign flag lines could now come to Guam as often as they wanted to. There was no security problem anymore, but despite this PML felt it necessary for "policy reasons," to maintain the two senior officers on the Trust Territory vessels as American citizens. I could not get satisfactory information what the policy reasons were. I asked what he thought might be the feasibility of having a foreign flag line service to the islands from Yokohama and other places with the island vessels picking up at Guam for redistribution. He didn't think too much of this idea. He pointed out that there was no transshipment to Ponape

and Truk. These were directly served from Japan. He felt that this was more or less essential.

I wonder if a foreign flag line operating from Japan to Guam with transshipment on feeder vessels from Guam to Ponape, Truk, and other islands might not be more efficient. I don't know but it will take a little looking at.

The vessels operated by PML had very high repair and maintenance costs. I looked forward to an opportunity to compare their experience with those of two privately owned vessels in substantially the same trade.

Mr. Pilgrim also talked about PFE's patriotic interest in operating the lines and building the American position in the islands. He said that the long run economic development of the islands was to a great extent dependent upon the quality and volume of transportation available. I certainly don't argue this point. He also discussed Pacific Micronesia ideas for economic development. A publication *Final Proposal of Pacific Far East for the Commercial Operation of an Ocean Transportation Service in the Trust Territory* had much economic data. I don't know of what value.

Mr. Pilgrim, who is an impressive gentleman, took me through the PFE operation and introduced me to many people—the executives, the operating personnel in the offices as well as on the piers. All this, I imagine, is to impress me with the efficiency and operating capability of the company. Lunch was at the posh St. Francis Yacht Club with other PFE executives. From our table, we could look out at the top of the Golden Gate Bridge, but not the bottom, shrouded in fog. Through the fog would come various vessels—freighters, passengers, fishing boats and navy vessels. It was an imposing scene. As they came through the fog they blew their fog horns—suddenly breaking out into full sunshine. Awesome!

The 'treatment' included an invitation for a day's sail on the company's yacht on San Francisco Bay. "No thanks." I said.

A few hours later I was on my way to Hawaii, and from there to Guam and then on to the Trust Territory.

With exactly twenty-six hours in Honolulu before departure to
Guam, I took advantage of the beach and sun to review the many
documents I had been given in Washington and San Francisco. The
more documents I read, the more complicated this whole business
became. The magnitude of the distances, the sparse population, limitations of current cargoes, the Far East on one side, the U.S. on the
other with Honolulu between, coupled with security and naval interests, made the logistics of an efficient transportation system almost staggering. I must admit that I wondered at this point whether
I could handle it. Would I fall flat on my face? Would I embarrass
Nathan Associates?

As the flight from Honolulu-to-Guam was scheduled to take off
in the small hours of the morning, I had planned to have a light supper alone, and take a nap before going to the airport at 11:00 PM.
However, I received a phone call from Frank Midkiff, chairman of the
board of trustees of the Bishop Estate, and a former Trust Territory
high commissioner. The Bishop Estate owns all the land in Hawaii,
never sells any, but does extend 99-year leases. The immense cash
flow generated is used to fund schools for Hawaiians.

Mr. Midkiff told me about three men who had some ideas and
interest in a shipping operation between the Islands and Hawaii. He
asked if I could have dinner with them and listen to their ideas which
he thought had a lot of merit to them.

During an excellent meal at the Pacific Club, the oldest and most
exclusive in Hawaii, George Over, Jr., president of the Hawaiian
Freight Lines, Jacob Nebeling, vice president of Marine Chartering
Co., and Lester Clark, a local attorney, discussed their ideas with me.
Basically they wanted to establish a foreign flag service between the
Marshall Islands and Hawaii with modern fast 1,200 ton vessels. Protective congressional legislation prohibited foreign flag vessels from
operating directly between two American ports. Technically, however, the Marshall Islands was a UN territory in trust to the United
States. Accordingly, a court might decide that the ports of the Marshalls did not qualify as an American port. This would certainly be a
political hot potato.

They were not wrong claiming that copra production—the Marshall's principal export—was badly neglected because of the insuf-

ficiency of ship calls to the islands. Copra (dried coconut meat, the source of coconut oil) was picked up in a more-or-less haphazard schedule and taken to Guam to be held for transshipment to Japan where it was a low value item. They felt that the economy of the islands would be better served if the copra came to Honolulu. They further pointed out that presently wheat flour and other staples, including industrial and maintenance items, going to the Marshall Islands were shipped from Honolulu or even from California to Guam with the result that there was tremendous loss and waste. They also felt that the vessels currently in use were so old, obsolete, and inefficient, that no steamship line would want to operate them.

I was told that for a ship operator there were all kinds of side benefits such as agency fees and kick-backs from ship chandlers, port agents, stevedores and the Japanese ship yards. This was of great interest to me and gave me a clue for something to investigate, quietly, in Micronesia. I was later to find out that these 'side benefits' were endemic.

At 6:20 AM, May 14, I arrived at Guam. PML representatives, Captain Kerr and Mr. Sied, were at the airport to meet me. PML didn't miss a beat. A good shower, a little rest at the Micronesia Inn, the rest house for the Trust Territory, and I was ready to meet them for breakfast and a talk before leaving for Saipan a few hours later. The Micronesia Inn, a converted quonset hut, was located a short distance from the runway for B-52 bombers. And they were constantly taking off with a roar.

During breakfast, I learned about some of the technical shipping and documentation difficulties that lead to fuzzy records and lack of follow-up to cure problems. I felt that Kerr and Sied were honest and forthright with me. I also had the sense, without it being said, that they would be just as happy to continue what they were doing with any other operator. Visiting the piers and offices, we reviewed a lot of statistical and operational data that I was sure would be of use later.

Off to Saipan the same day aboard a Territory owned DC 4, operated by Pan Am! Arriving in Saipan I was met by Jim Cook, Territory transportation officer. Jim drove me up the hills to the TTA offices and residential area, formerly a CIA regional headquarters. It was apparent that the CIA took good care of itself insofar as comfort and accommodations were concerned. But surprisingly, there was no swimming pool.

I was assigned a car, a room, a desk, and a secretary. The car, a small Toyota pickup truck, had been made for the Japanese market. Everything in it was much smaller than Toyota cars later shipped to America. Definitely not automatic shift, it had both a clutch and a brake pedal. As they were so close together, it took some practice to keep from stepping on both pedals simultaneously. The room contained a shower stall, but no shower head—a replacement had not yet arrived. It also contained a 'hot-box.' This was a wooden box about two cubic feet square with a glass side door, and a 50 watt electric bulb. Each night all leather items, shoes, wallet etc. went into the 'hot-box.' This kept them from turning green with mildew during the night.

Wasting no time, the same day Cook and I started to discuss the transport situation. We had only begun to talk when a call came from the High Commissioner inviting me to come to his office. Cook, John Spivey, the Assistant Commissioner for Administration, and I joined Goding for a meeting that lasted an hour-and-a-half. Interestingly, there seemed to be agreement not to go into the past history of the PML operation in the TTA, not to indulge in personalities, and not to use my time as an arbitrator of what had happened in the past. The point was clearly made: I was to pursue the question, "Where do we go from here?"

This discussion sharpened my antenna. How does one prepare recommendations for the future without knowing what has happened in the past? It became obvious that there was much more of a story here than I knew.

The next day I realized that I did not remember much of what we discussed. I had been that tired. However, Cook told me that it had gone very well and that my ideas had been well received. I also learned that Cook and his wife, while stationed in Okinawa, had been next door neighbors of our Sierra Leone friends, Earl and Hope Diffenderfer. Small world!

The island transport system was a hodge-podge of privately owned and operated vessels and TTA owned and operated vessels. The TTA vessels had the dual responsibility of carrying commercial cargo as well as TTA officials among the islands. This was obviously an inefficient operation and a major headache to anyone who tried to establish a time schedule. The shipping mess was a strong disincentive for copra production increases and quality control. Producers could not depend on shipping dates for ready to move products. Often harvested copra sat around on docks or in storage waiting for shipment. The product would frequently dry out and spoil. It was clear that a complete separation of field trip (island-to-island) personnel movement and commercial cargo was needed. The two were totally incompatible.

To acquaint myself with the problems, I visited the docks and the ships, talked with the officers and often with the crews. Depending upon with whom I talked, I heard conflicting stories of how the operation was run by PFL. The TTA vessels seemed to be well maintained. With crews of almost 30 persons, including at least two, often three, American officers at American salary rates, they seemed to me to be overmanned. Maintenance was done in Japanese shipyards, and the few cost figures that I first obtained, appeared to me to be very excessive. However there was nothing that I could really prove at that point. In addition, given the number of vessels calling in the islands, the volume of cargo, and the limited passenger business, the shore-side staffs seemed to be much overstaffed.

I also flew, with Jim Cook at the controls of the two place TTA plane, to many of the producing islands in the Marshalls. These trips enabled me to get a firsthand sense of shore-side shipping facilities, cargo storage arrangements, and personnel adequacy. Yap, an island where the native money was stone wheels varying in size from two or three inches to over four feet in diameter, was extremely interesting. The natives wore a minimum of clothing, a 'g' string for the men, and little more for the women. They had an abundance of Japanese minibikes. Riders often rode holding a Sony radio to their ears. A fascinating combination of primitive and modern.

Flying into Rota, a smaller island, I noticed a large log in the middle of the runway as we were descending. Jim pulled up suddenly. The log, a huge crocodile, slowly moved away.

While driving on Saipan it was not unusual to come across the rusting remains of U.S. and Japanese World War II aircraft. The jungle, of course, was rapidly absorbing these relics. Finding huge lizards sunning themselves in the middle of the roads was also not unusual. And strangest of all, when we drove at night, the roads would be covered with hundreds if not thousands of big frogs. They were reputed to be the reincarnated souls of the 3500 Japanese soldiers who chose suicide by jumping off a cliff rather than surrender. This cliff had a sheer 500 foot drop to rocks below and was known locally as Suicide Cliff.

The Catholic priest serving the islands was an ardent fisherman. One day he took me tuna fishing in a native dugout canoe equipped with outriggers. The fishing lines, hand held, were made of locally spun twine. No rods or reels. Fortunately the tuna were only two feet long, and the sea was calm.

An evening at a retirement party at the Toppa Tappa Club on Saipan turned out to be a delightful cultural experience. Demonstrations of native dances were scheduled to be performed by groups from Palau and Truk. The Palauans were scheduled to perform first, but refused to. They insisted that the Trukese perform first, claiming that Palau was more important and they would not dance ahead of the Trukese. This created quite a back-stage brouhaha and almost wrecked the party.

The Trukese men did a stick dance, a fighting dance. The two main things they fight over, according to the announcer, are land and women. As the dance progressed it became increasingly more rapid and feverish. Occasionally one of the dancers received an unintended whack across the head.

The Paluan dance, which included both men and women, was more sinuous and willowy. The songs and movements were gentle, the music was a modified march, with the leader playing a harmonica.

One night, during a typical South Seas monsoon, as the winds raised the corrugated roof on my quarters, letting in gusts of horizontal water, there was a pounding on my door. I opened to find one of the TTA ship captains, carrying a cardboard box, urgently wanting to see me.

Captain X was grateful for a towel and a good drink of bourbon (Jack Daniels cost $2.30 an imperial quart). After partially drying off, he explained that he was leaving the islands the next day. He wanted me to have the contents of his box before he left. With no further word Captain X left my quarters, and I never saw him again. He never gave me his name, and I never asked.

The box contained a treasure trove of documents that vividly demonstrated why the current PML operation resulted in huge annual losses, but remained quite profitable to the mother firm, PFE.

Repairs and maintenance for the ships were done in Japan. Supplies, such as paint, spare parts, sandpaper, as well as general chandler supplies such as ropes, electrical and plumbing fittings, and small marine parts, were shipped from California. One particular San Francisco supplier seemed to have a monopoly on this business. They were shipped to Japan from California on PFE ships, of course, at full tariffs. The work in the Japanese yards, was done at high hourly rates. Kick-backs—probably. Even food for the crew was shipped from California.

According to the documents I had, the crews ate as well as on the best U.S. flag vessels in transatlantic or Pacific service. But in fact, the crews were fed a heavy low cost rice diet and saw little of the foods shipped to Japan and billed to the TTA accounts. And the PFE contract with TTA was on a cost-plus basis. No wonder PFE did not want to give up the contract.

With the help of an able secretary, cooperation from the TTA staff, and Jim Cook's expertise about shipping and the islands, I put together a draft proposal calling for bids from interested shipping companies. They would bid on a contract to operate the TTA vessels, including two new, more modern ones, offering cargo service within the islands, to and from Guam and to and from Japan. The contract would be based on a percentage of gross rather than net profits. Operating and supply costs would be subject to strict audit. The tariffs would be the same in effect as previously. Supplies and services would be bought from the lowest bidders, U.S. or foreign.

My draft proposal was accepted by the Department of Interior Trust Territory Administration. Although PFE was one of the bidders, the contract was awarded to another ship operator. After a year's operation under the new contract, the successful bidder was able to turn over almost one million dollars to the Department of Interior. This was in contrast to the huge annual losses previously carried by the U.S. taxpayer.

Did we make a difference?

Before I left Saipan, Jim Cook in his capacity of Transportation Officer, gave me an abbreviated ship master's test. He then awarded me Certificate No.1, as a Trust Territory ship master. A wonderful souvenir.

13

African Adventures

The Dark Continent

CHATTERING MONKEYS HIGH in the trees! Termite mounds eight feet tall! Swaying palm trees on snow white sand beaches! Traffic gridlock! Red laterite roads! Straight backed women balancing huge loads on their heads! Fishermen with sun flecked purple hued bodies pulling in their nets at sunset! Modern buildings next to native hovels! These were first impressions of West Africa, The Dark Continent.

My global horizons continued to expand. From 1964 through 1980, I visited/worked in Sierra Leone, Ghana, Nigeria, the Ivory Coast, and Liberia—all in West Africa, in addition to the Far East, Mideast, Europe, and Latin America.

Sierra Leone

In 1964, retained by the government of Sierra Leone, I flew to Freetown, its capital, for a short two week exploratory visit. Decidedly primitive by western standards, Sierra Leone had an interesting and in some respects exciting level of sophistication, particularly Freetown. The British expatriates[11] had done a comparatively good job in developing an educational structure, a competent civil service, and an appreciation for the arts, both African and European.

Freetown, a port city, enjoyed a magnificent stretch of beaches with sand almost as white and fine as confectionery sugar. Curving palm trees added to the beauty of the scene.

MISSION: U.S.-SIERRA LEONE, P.L. 480 AGREEMENT

My mission was to assist Sierra Leone to obtain a Public Law 480 agreement as I had done in Israel. Such an agreement would make U.S. agricultural products, surplus to U.S. domestic or international commercial markets, available to Sierra Leone under extremely favorable terms. Payment to the U.S. for the foodstuffs would be in 'soft' local currency which could then be used for local expenses of the U.S. embassy or other U.S. government agencies working in the country. Under the terms of the Cooley Amendment of PL 480, U.S. owned local currencies could also be lent to local entrepreneurs or overseas firms investing in approved capital developments in the host country. Actually, for the most part 'soft' currencies were lent for new start up or expansion purposes such as warehouses, production facilities, or port development, rather than for U.S. embassy needs.

This first visit to Sierra Leone allowed me to meet the players, spend some time explaining how the program worked, its advantages and disadvantages, the timing needed for preparation of the program application, the responsibilities of both governments, U.S. and Sierra Leone, under the program, and the limitations in the agreement. I also used this opportunity to collect statistical data that would be needed in preparing the agreement application. Israeli diplomats were responsible for my PL 480 expertise being known by Sierra Leone officials.

The chief player was the prime minister, Sir Albert Margui. A British trained barrister, Sir Albert cut a large handsome figure. While he often wore western attire, in native robes he was most imposing. When he went 'up-country' he always wore native garb. Generally, on 'up country' trips he flew in a small plane belonging to the Diamond Trust. But his favorite method of general transportation was a large black Rolls Royce sedan. He had two of them, in case one was not running. I was told that they were duplicates of the ones used by the Queen of England.

Sir Albert was clearly 'the man.' I felt he was genuinely interested in the welfare of the country and its people. He encouraged modern agricultural techniques to increase the quantity and variety of the domestic food supply. He brought Israeli agricultural experts to Sierra Leone to teach new techniques to his people. One joint Israeli/ Sierra Leone project was the development of modern chicken farms, for both eggs and meat. The United States Agency for International Development (AID) also supplied various agricultural experts. The Peace Corps had several teams in Sierra Leone. These teams worked directly with the people throughout the country to improve sanitary conditions, teach English, instruct in new irrigation and farming techniques, and help build small power dams, bridges, and feeder roads.

Sierra Leone's ambassador to the United States, Gershon Collier, a tall, dignified, articulate, London trained lawyer was always impeccably dressed in western attire as befitted a successful barrister. I never saw him in native garb. He was a published poet and authority on Shakespeare and had translated several Shakespearean plays and sonnets into Creole.

Sam Bangura, permanent secretary (PS) of the PM's office, was an intelligent, jovial civil servant who took his job and responsibilities very seriously. Basically, he was the PM's 'gofer', and performed that function very well.

Another participant in the office of the PM was his economic advisor, Dr. Frederick, (PhD) His doctorate was from George Washington University (GWU) in Washington, D.C. More on this later.

And not least, was Mr. Bill Greenwood, the British ex-pat advisor to the prime minister, a tall pleasant, very intelligent Scotsman. He was a holdover from the days when Sierra Leone was a British colony.

Whenever I indicated that I was unable to find needed statistics of production and/or imports of various commodities in government or World Bank reports, I was told, often by the PM himself, "We will get them for you." At such times I was sure that they were 'manufactured' that evening. An example: as cotton was one of the commodities that was to be included in the program request, I needed data on the volume of cotton goods imported into the country. These were not available in any published reports, yet we knew that there had to be substantial imports. The PM personally promised to get the data needed, and in my presence requested Dr. Frederick to have a table ready the next morning. The table was ready the next morning.

I doubt that any of the data in the table could be found in any official source. One of the reasons that data on this product were hard to find, is that most of the cotton was smuggled in by traders to avoid import duties. And some suspicion existed that various government officials might have been involved in the smuggling—by no means an unusual situation in newly independent African countries.

SECOND VISIT

In the winter of 1965 on my second visit to Sierra Leone, I brought the rough draft of the PL 480 application for review and discussion with local authorities, to tighten and edit it, make adjustments, and to initiate discussions with the American Embassy. Flora joined me this time.

LIFE IN FREETOWN

We were housed in the Paramount, the premier hotel in Freetown. Several interesting incidents happened in the hotel that in a small way describe or demonstrate the sophistication or lack thereof in this capital city.

On our first Sunday morning we came to breakfast a bit late. I ordered, along with juice and coffee, scrambled eggs. To my surprise the waiter said "Scrombled eggs gone. Would mon like boiled eggs or fried eggs?"

"No, we would like scrambled eggs." The maître d' came to our table and repeated the information that my choice of eggs "were gone" and offered the same choices as had the waiter. I suggested that we could wait a few minutes until they prepared an order of scrambled eggs. Well, the wait became quite long. I called the maître d' and asked about the problem with getting an order of scrambled eggs. "Oh," he explained, "Not enough people."

It seemed that the chef had learned to make scrambled eggs in batches of 24 eggs. He had no idea how to prepare an order of two eggs. And apparently, neither did the maître d'.

We had a somewhat similar experience when we ordered iced tea, a new concoction to the dining room staff. They had been trained by the British, who even drank their beer, or ale, warm. No one in the dining room or kitchen had any idea how to prepare such a barbaric beverage as iced tea.

I requested hot tea along with ice cubes and lemon or lime slices. I also asked for a wide mouth beer tumbler. When the hot tea came I put as many ice cubes as I could in the beer tumbler, poured the hot tea over it, added a bit of lemon juice and a slice or two of lemon. As the ice cubes melted, I added more, so that in a short time I had a reasonable facsimile of iced tea. As I went through these maneuvers, the entire wait staff stood around our table, observing every maneuver by this crazy American who was ruining perfectly good tea. Next time we ordered iced tea, we received iced tea.

One night we were awakened by the sounds of Scottish bagpipes in the courtyard below our window. Obviously we were dreaming. But both of us dreaming bagpipe music! No way.

We looked out. To our absolute amazement there were about thirty kilt-clad white Europeans playing bagpipes and dancing Scottish folk dances over and around crossed swords on the ground. It was strange but beautiful. The local chapter of the St. Andrew Society was holding its monthly meeting. At two o'clock in the morning the reels and jigs stopped. Why in the middle of the night? "Why obviously, Mon. It is too hot during the day to dance and play the pipes."

Usually in the dining room there were, perhaps, three of four Caucasian businessmen and government advisors. On Saturday the resident Europeans came out of the cracks in the walls. The dining room was jammed with Scots, Brits and Dutch who, with their families partook of the Indonesian curry meals, standard fare on Saturdays. And it was delicious.

Sam Bangura invited us to his home prior to an up-country drive. As we walked up the steps, several cute puppies came out from under the front porch. Flora started to pet them. The PS said "I don't think you should pet them. They have a little bit of rabies." So much for public health.

Although I was very busy during the day working on the proposed PL 480 agreement, we did take time to absorb the local culture—including the gorgeous white sand beach and the refreshing drinks of green coconut milk right out of the nut.

Freetown had a country club. To reciprocate invitations Flora and I had received from Sam Bangura we invited him to join us for dinner at the club.

"Oh no," he said. "The club is only for Europeans." I was shocked. Later that day I mentioned this to American Ambassador Correy. He too was surprised. He had never been there. He also found out that some of his staff were members. An order went out promptly putting a stop to staff membership in a segregated club. This created enough of a groundswell that this racist policy was changed.

The newly independent west African countries urgently needed to develop sources of government revenue. Accordingly, a brewery and a cigarette factory were top development priorities. Taxes on the beer and cigarettes provided quick, easily collectible funds to the governments.

In most of the west African countries the Heineken breweries of Holland were the partners. Two brands of beer were produced and sold: Star or Paramount and Heineken. Generally both were from the same vats and in taste were identical. But in marketing the local brand was always quite a bit cheaper than the Dutch label. It was not unusual to find the Europeans ordering the local brand while the natives ordered the Dutch label.

The locally made cigarettes competed with higher priced imported ones, usually Marlboro. Most of the tobacco for the cigarettes made in Sierra Leone came from the United States. We visited a cigarette factory. It so happened that while we were there mechanics were changing the cutters on the processing machines. The changing wrenches were laid out on a table with painted numbers showing the order of use. I asked the foreman, a Brit ex-pat, what would happen if the order of the wrenches on the table were changed slightly. In answer, he took two wrenches and switched their location without the mechanic seeing him do this. A few seconds later the mechanic came back to the table, picked up a wrench and climbed back on the machine. Of course that wrench was the wrong size for the operation in progress. The mechanic was absolutely stumped. Consternation. He became very excited, pointing and gesturing. At this point the foreman took the two wrenches and switched them to the proper order. This brought forth a huge grin. All was right with the world after all.

Some of the Europeans mentioned that the choir at the E. B. Evangelical United Brotherhood Church was extremely good and that the preacher, Dr. Renner, was famous for his sermons and their social content. We decided to find out. The next Sunday we went to church. The choir lived up to its reputation. The dress and the flamboyant hats of the women worshipers alone were worth the visit. After the service, the preacher of the day, Mr. Fitzjohn, a former Sierra Leone ambassador to the United States, introduced us to Dr Renner the pastor of the church. It was a memorable experience.

Word of our attendance at the service got back to the hotel before we did. The fallout was amazing. Suddenly, we were perceived in a different light and treated differently by the hotel staff. We were fawned upon, looked up to and given service above and beyond the usual—all because we had shown an interest in the local community.

One morning while driving down Freetown's main street we observed a jovial-looking, well-rounded Caucasian strolling along wearing a native costume. Aharon Gilshon, an Israeli on loan to the central bank of Sierra Leone as a technical advisor, was the first non-African we had seen in Freetown. We immediately established a friendly relationship which blossomed when we met later in Israel and the United States. In Israel he was a senior economist in the Bank of Israel and came to the U.S. as a consultant to the International Bank. Flora and I had very enjoyable times with Aharon and his wife, Naomi, a Hadassah nurse, and their children. We benefited by Aharon's knowledge of history on our joint vacations in Ireland, Turkey, Czech and Slovakia. We were saddened at their passing this past year.

BACK TO BUSINESS

The day came for presenting the proposed PL 480 program to the prime minister and his Economic Council. This occurred in a room adjoining the PM's office. About seven or eight persons attended: Sir Albert, Sam Bangura, Dr. Frederick, and Bill Greenwood, who was shortly leaving for home, plus an assortment of office bureaucrats.

I presented the gist of the program, outlining the advantages to Sierra Leone, as well as its disadvantages and responsibilities that the government of Sierra Leone would assume, and then asked for questions.

There was about a half hour of give and take questions, mostly on implementation procedures. As we were winding up, Dr. Frederick said that he had a question.

"Mr. Atkin, under the program we undertake to pay for certain expenses in dollars. We ship cocoa to Switzerland. We get Swiss francs. We ship high quality iron ore to Norway. We get kronen. We ship diamonds to Belgium. We are paid in Belgian francs. We ship cotton to England. We are paid in sterling. Where do we get the dollars to pay the U.S?"

I was shocked. Bill Greenwood put his hands to his head. No one else seemed to understand what the situation was. I knew that I could not embarrass the PM's economic advisor who had his doctorate from George Washington University in Washington. But I had to answer his question. He obviously did not understand that the currencies cited were all 'hard' currencies, and freely traded for dollars throughout the world.

After a few moments, I said "I am sure that the American authorities would be prepared to accept those other currencies in lieu of dollars." That ended the matter—at least until I arrived back home.

Back in Washington, I called Dr. Frederick's former faculty advisor at GWU, told him the story about the currency question, and asked how the University could grant a PhD in economics to Frederick.

"Yes, normally no degree would have been earned. Frederick comes from a very prominent family in Sierra Leone. At the time he was one of the best available. If we had flunked him he would have gone home embittered toward the United States and the University. So we adopted a double standard and gave him the degree. We understood that there were enough checks and balances that he would do no harm, and he went home as a friend." This was the answer. And it was not singular.

After much shifting and delays the PL480 program was signed several days after we left Sierra Leone. On our last day there, U.S. Ambassador Correy hosted a delightful luncheon with all of the members of the American and Sierra Leone teams as guests. I wish I could have taped the complimentary statements he made about me and my handling of the negotiations.

Ghana

In January, 1965, prior to leaving Sierra Leone, with the next stop scheduled to be Israel, I was asked by Zim Israel Navigation Co. to stop off in Accra, capital of Ghana, for some discussions with ZIM representatives there. Following ZIM's request, Flora and I arranged for a quick, three day visit to Accra. It was the first of several visits to Ghana, all fascinating.

In Ghana, as in the British Isles and in most former British colonies driving was on the opposite side of the road from what we in America are used to. Just two days before we arrived in Ghana, by public decree this was changed. The date for change-over had been set several months previously; public instruction programs were on TV and radio; special articles were carried in the newspapers; and many demonstration lectures were held. On the appointed day, at the appointed hour, the change-over took place. And it took place with almost no hitch, snags or problems whatsoever.

A pleasant two and a half hour BOAC flight to Ghana from Sierra Leone included an excellent lunch after which a good nap was most welcome. Emanuel Ron, an Israeli Foreign Office official, was on the flight. Naturally, we discovered we had many mutual friends and acquaintances. Through a communication slipup, there was no one to meet either Ron or Flora and me upon our arrival at Lumley airport in Accra. Ron made a phone call that promptly resulted in a car that took him and us to the government owned first class Ambassador Hotel, Accra's finest. The room rate of $25 per night, including breakfast, by African standards was expensive.

In 1965, Ghana was under a not so benign Soviet influence. Red Chinese and Russian "development" teams were everywhere. Hundreds of Ghanaian students were studying in Moscow; guests of the USSR. The streets of Accra were full of poor quality Russian-made Italian Fiats. Other products of Soviet factories, such as ceramic toilet bowls that did not fit the African piping systems and as such were useless caused much consumer grumbling.

Although the state radio stations, much to our surprise, offered great classical music that would have been at home on our own good music station, a steady stream of anti-American and anti-Israel propaganda and invective spewed out of the loud speakers followed by pro-Egyptian, pro-red Chinese, and pro-Russian editorial comment. This was in strange contrast to what we found on the street, in private offices, and even in government offices. The general sentiments appeared to be just the opposite. Admiration for America and Americans and appreciation for Israeli technical and agricultural training assistance was evident. Strange.

We arrived in Accra on January 20, 1965—Inauguration Day in Washington for Lyndon Johnson. Much newspaper space and TV coverage was devoted to Nasser's inauguration in Cairo. Very little was mentioned about Johnson's inauguration during the same period. And when it was mentioned, emphasis was on Washington's extreme security measures, the bullet proof glass, the abundance of troops in the parade, and Johnson's intention to overcome the "great poverty that exists in the United States." This last was in reference to Johnson's inaugural statement to declare "War on Poverty." Nothing good appeared in the media about the United States. We found such twisted coverage shocking. It was our first exposure to this type of journalism. Ghanaians seemed to recognize twisted propaganda when they heard it.

We had been warned that our hotel room would probably be "bugged." It was. One of the main lights in the room was not working. In a normal voice, I said to Flora, "You would think that in a first class hotel like this all of the lights would work." Following this we went to dinner. When we came back, the light was in perfect condition. This was no coincidence. We found other evidence of "bugs" during our stay.

Despite the anti-Israel propaganda on the state controlled radio, Israel, as it did in Sierra Leone, had a substantial economic investment in Ghana. Many of the larger Israeli trading and manufacturing companies had offices in Accra. In the course of our stay in Ghana we met numerous Israeli businessmen and government officials. Our impression was that the public Israel bashing was for the consumption of the Soviet agents in the country; that the real attitude of officials as well as businessmen was very pro-Israel.

PRIME MINISTER NKRUMA: UNITED AFRICAN APPEAL?

Possibly a year before our visit to Ghana, I had met the dictatorial Prime Minister Kwame Nkruma when he was in New York to address the United Nations Assembly. Bob Nathan and I had received a call from the African desk of the U.S. State Department asking us to meet with President Nkruma in his suite at the Waldorf Towers in New York. The purpose: to discuss the possibility of a United African Appeal which would be fashioned after the United Jewish Appeal (UJA).

The UJA was the amazingly successful fund raising arm of the Jewish Agency for Israel. The funds, donated principally by American Jews, were and are used to absorb and settle hundreds of thousands of new immigrants in Israel, to build infrastructure needed in the absorption process, and to develop economic opportunities for the newcomers. Nkruma was hoping to establish a pan African version of the UJA.

A representative from the African desk of the State Department, as well as the head of the Israeli Purchasing Mission in New York, Aryeh Manor, also attended the meeting.

We had been scheduled to meet in the prime minister's suite at six o'clock in the evening. Everyone was prompt except the prime minister. By seven thirty there had been no word from Nkruma, and we were getting hungry. Also Bob and I had wanted to get back to Washington the same evening. We horrified the State Department representative when we suggested leaving. "Oh, no, you can't leave. Being late is normal for African diplomats and businessmen. It would be an insult to leave now." We agreed to wait a bit longer, getting hungrier and thirstier, and no one offering to alleviate either situation.

By eight-thirty, despite the State Department, we determined to leave—just as Nkruma strode in, with no word of apology or explanation. He suggested that we might be thirsty and ordered beer for everybody. It arrived promptly, British style, warm. Nkruma opened the bottles, poured the beer into beer mugs, and remarked, "Oh yes, you Americans like your beer cold." Whereupon he called for an ice bucket and proceeded to put ice cubes in our beer. He had lived as a student for several years in Pennsylvania and should have known that Americans did not put ice cubes in beer.

As to his idea about a UAA, I am afraid that the water we diplomatically poured on this idea was colder than the ice cubes in our beer. It was clear at that time that the African-American community had not reached an asset resource level, nor a sense of oneness, that would sustain even a very modest appeal in comparison with the Jewish American community. There were also serious doubts about how such a program would be organized, operated, and funds doled out.

ISRAELI-GHANAIAN INTERESTS

Despite the Soviet influences, surprisingly, Israeli businesses, unions, and government had many close ties with economic, cultural, and government organizations in Ghana. Many Ghanaian students were studying modern operational methods, particularly in agriculture, in Israel. The parliament building in Accra was modeled after the Knesset[12] in Jerusalem. Most of the larger Israeli export firms had offices in Ghana. It was not unusual to hear Hebrew spoken in the street, and certainly in hotel lobbies and restaurants.

I was pleased to discover that Dov Gottesman was then stationed in Ghana. Dov had been the number one assistant to Carl Porat, when he followed Aryeh Manor as chief of the Israeli Purchasing Mission in New York. In the states, Carl and I made a good team in presenting to the American authorities the Israeli food procurement programs. Our success ratio was phenomenal. Of course, Dov and I knew each other well.

Dov was most anxious to discuss the possibility of a Public Law 480 program for Ghana similar to the one I had just worked out for Sierra Leone. Dov was not too happy when I told him that presently there was not a chance in hell of Ghana getting such a program. It would not be possible until there was a major sea change in the Ghanaian political climate and its announced anti-American stance. PL 480 was for America's friends, not its enemies.

The next morning Flora and I met another Israeli, Moses Boneh, the representative of Dizengoff West Africa, a large Israeli international trading company. In his office we met yet another young Israeli, Emmanuel Penn, the local manager of Dizengoff. Penn was a nephew of Rabbi Henry Segal, a Washington rabbi, whom we knew. Jewish geography!

Boneh took us on a delightful sightseeing trip around the business and official sections of the city. The city itself, with a population of about 500,000 people, had some beautiful sections with African Mediterranean architecture, some bad slums, very good roads, and excellent traffic control. The president's villa, surrounded by several protective fences, was high on a hill, protecting him from unexpected visitors.

Ghana was one country where the Israeli ambassador had a higher standing than the American ambassador. There was much close cooperation in trade, technical and agricultural training and industrial investment between Israel and Ghana. To the contrary, American interests in Ghana were deteriorating.

One of the high points of this trip was a most pleasant afternoon that we spent with Israel's ambassador, Mike Arnon, and his charming wife, Hadera. Mike had previously been press counselor at the Israel embassy in Washington. We had been quite friendly then.

Nothing could be accomplished in Ghana without 'dash'—a tip, a gift, or just plain bribery. Mike explained the system as coming from the tribal nature of the population. Officials were concerned about obtaining benefits for their tribe or clan. Accordingly, to have a project approved that would benefit a tribe or clan other than that of the official whose signature was needed for implementation, 'dash' was expected and given. However, as this practice was on the books as illegal, the official expecting dash had to exercise a certain care, and not extract too high a price. Levels were unspoken, but understood.

According to the local English language newspaper, *The Ghana Times*, a USIA documentary film on John Kennedy's life was privately shown while we were in Accra. It was not shown in public. The prime minister had expressly forbidden such showing, and according to Mike, the newspaper story, with pictures of prominent government officials attending the showing was a bad mistake. The officials pictured could be expected to hear directly from Nkruma.

ZIM AND THE BLACK STAR LINE

About a year later I was again in Ghana. I had been invited to join Naphtali 'Heinie' Wydra, managing director of ZIM Israel Navigation Company, in meetings to set up the Black Star Line, a Ghanaian shipping venture. ZIM had been asked to research the feasibility of such a venture (I worked on this aspect of the program), arrange for the purchase of ships, and train ships' crews as well as shore-side staff.

We met with Nkruma in Flagstaff House, his official residence and office. The immediate subject was to review contracts between Ghana and German ship yards for the construction of the first of the Black Star Line's new fleet.

As I was reading one of the contracts a particular paragraph caught my eye. I read it several times to be sure that it said what I thought it said. In brief, it provided that for every ton of new ship construction ten dollars was to be deposited in an Austrian bank account for Anna, the prime minister's favorite 'niece', an Austrian woman.

I called this paragraph to Heinie and the PM's attention, and said, "Mr. Prime Minister, you can't do this." To which he immediately said, "Why not? Nothing is hidden." Heinie gave me a signal to drop the question. I did. It was certainly not the time nor place for a discourse on public morality, on the improper dispersion of public funds to very private uses. And certainly not to the prime minister of Ghana.

COCOA SLURRY

In 1974, nine years after our first visit to Ghana, Flora and I returned to Ghana. I was invited as a consultant to Noe Drevici, a Rumanian businessman who had lived in Ghana for many years. He had made and lost several fortunes in his various ventures in that country. At the moment he was near the bottom of one of his fortunes, his factory producing busses having collapsed financially.

Always full of ideas, Drevici was looking to make another fortune. His latest idea was to develop a slurry pipeline whereby cocoa, the major crop of the country, could be processed up country where it was grown and moved to port or to a product processing center near the consuming or shipping points. Ula, his wife, a Swiss trained chemist, had developed a variety of highly nutritious food products from the by-products of cocoa production.

Drevici was convinced that such a pipeline would significantly increase the foreign currency earnings of the country, and would be very profitable for the investors. Potential bank backers demanded a feasibility study. My function was to develop the study for the project.

Drevici, of course, was very well known by all the Ghanaian authorities. I had no doubt that he was careful "to take care of them" when the occasion demanded to insure the ongoing success of his enterprises. Unfortunately, one of the problems he could not control was the all too often changes in government and who was on top. He was a fascinating man, extremely voluble, temperamentally on a hair-trigger, and constantly looking over his shoulder for the many potential enemies he might have made.

COLONEL ACHEAMPONG

By 1974, Nkruma was long gone. The current prime minister was Colonel I. K. Acheampong. I had been impressed with what I had heard about Acheampong and his plans for improving the economy of Ghana, with special efforts to improve living standards and output of the subsistence agricultural sector, and to reduce foreign debt. For the most part he was quite successful. I had hoped I would be able to meet him, and if not him, at least his minister of agriculture. However, with the limited time available, I made no effort to do so. Therefore, Flora and I were surprised and delighted to receive an invitation to lunch with the prime minister at his residence. We had no idea who or how many others were invited.

Mr. Drevici was ecstatic about our receiving this invitation. I am sure that in his mind he saw a direct line to the top government echelons that would surely result in the furthering of his projects. His wife had just prepared some samples of her cocoa product food stuffs. Drevici begged us to take them with us as gifts to the PM and request that his kitchen try them out. With some reluctance, we agreed to do so.

The lunch turned out to be a very small affair. Other than the PM,

Flora and myself, we were surprised and delighted to find our old friend from Washington, Moises Debra, the only other guest. Debra, now the secretary general of the prime minister's political party, had been during the Nkruma period, Ghana's ambassador to Washington where we knew him and his family well. It was a most pleasant reunion. While not specifically confirmed, we felt that this luncheon had been arranged by Debra.

I had originally met the ambassador several years earlier in Baltimore on the city owned vessel, 'Port Welcome.' The city of Baltimore annually entertains economic and commercial officers of various embassies aboard the vessel. These officials are exposed to a full day cruising Baltimore Harbor and parts of the Chesapeake Bay while the advantages of trading through the port of Baltimore are extolled. An excellent buffet lunch featuring Maryland food and drink specialties is served.

I had been on the invite list, as was, of course, the economic counselor of the Israel embassy, Avram Salomon. As we were enjoying our buffet luncheon, I noticed a dignified, slightly portly African gentleman who seemed to be very much alone—although there were several hundred people—almost all diplomats—aboard. After making the proper introductions, I asked him if he would like to join Avram and myself. He was Ambassador Moises Debra from Ghana. He was delighted to join us.

During the next several years, Flora and I saw a lot of Debra and his family. In addition to the usual Ghanaian Embassy affairs, we had even been invited to the wedding of one of his nieces. On several occasions Flora and I hosted him and Yitchak Rabin, ambassador of Israel, in our home. Since there were then no formal relations between the two countries, this gave both ambassadors an opportunity to meet and discuss items of interest to both countries. On such occasions it was not unusual for several secret service cars to be parked in front of our house and along Uppingham Street.

After Debra most graciously introduced us to the PM, the four of us sat down to an excellent lunch. With each course, Col. Acheampong rather firmly suggested that I have the first bite.

Was this African hospitality, or was I being used as a taster?

The PM, an easy conversationalist, was interested in knowing what brought me to Ghana. I had nothing to hide, and told him about Drevici's slurry pipe plan. He asked many questions, many to which I had no answers, it being too early in the study to have developed substantial information. But I had the feeling that the PM knew a great deal more about it than he let on. Debra said very little during the entire meal.

At one point an opportunity came up to mention Mrs. Drevici's new food products. When I mentioned her name, the PM remarked, "She is a very clever woman, but not always too practical." I did not pursue this idea, but did give the PM the sample bottles of the food stuffs, which he sent to his chef to evaluate.

The PM then asked me what our plans were for the next few days. I told him that we were flying to Lagos, Nigeria on the morning flight, spending two hours at a meeting and coming back to Accra on the late afternoon flight. The PM said, "You can't do that."

I showed him the schedule. He asked whether we had ever been in Nigeria. Learning that we had not, he again stated that it was impossible to do what I had planned, and explained why. How right he was, as we found out ourselves.

Before the lunch was over, the PM invited me to take a walk with him in his garden. Although he showed me some prize ornamentals, his main purpose was to give me an oral message to be delivered directly to Israel's Prime Minister Yitchak Rabin. After delivering the message Yitchak looked me directly in the eye and said, "Maury you never received this message."

The next day we flew to Lagos, Nigeria for several eventful days, not just one as originally planned, before returning to Ghana.

When we returned, I was again invited to meet the PM, this time in his office. We talked about my impressions of Ghana, and what the possibilities might be for a PL 480 program for Ghana, now that the country was no longer in the Soviet orbit.

I told him that the country and the people of Ghana had impressed my wife and myself very favorably. We had found the people industrious, able to adapt quickly to new situations and techniques, and that I found a spirit of 'nation' rather than tribe.

At this meeting, I had the temerity to broach a personal query to the PM. Every place I went in the country there was a picture of the

prime minister in full military regalia, sword, medals, gold lace—the
works. It was a stern looking photo. It was in every office, shop, and
store.

"Mr. Prime Minister," I said, "May I say something personal to
you?"

"Of course."

"Sir, you are a very handsome man. You are the leader of your people. But the picture of you I see everywhere in the country shows a
very stern military visage. You might consider a different picture."
What nerve I had, but I was still alive, as he slightly giggled, as the
Africans do, and simply said, "Thank you for your view."

FIGURE 19: Colonel I. K. Acheampong, Prime Minister of Ghana.
This is the new photo rushed to the author weeks before Acheampong
was executed. It was not a significant improvement.

That night, Flora and I were just leaving our hotel room to be
picked up by an American Embassy car which was to take us to the
Embassy for a party. The phone rang. "This is Major Mohammed

calling from the 'White House.' Will you be in the hotel for another half hour?" I told him that we were then waiting for an Embassy car to pick us up.

"I have a package that the prime minister wants me to deliver only to you this evening. Please wait. I will be there in ten minutes."

I knew that the 'White House' was a good fifteen miles from the hotel, but I agreed to wait fifteen minutes.

In ten minutes two motorcycles with screaming sirens, followed by a large Mercedes Benz, came racing up to the hotel. Flora and I were outside. The major jumped out, thanked us for waiting for him, handed me a large wrapped package. The Embassy car was, by then, also waiting for us

I did not take the time to open the package until we returned to the hotel later that night. It was a signed new photo of the prime minister. Better, but not by much, than the old one. It hangs in one of our guest rooms in Chevy Chase.

Several weeks after we returned home the Washington Post carried a story about a palace coup in Accra. Col. Acheampong had been taken to the beach and shot dead. I was never able to find out what happened, if anything to Mr. Debra. And of course, Drevici's dream pipeline went up in smoke.

Nigeria

In the mid-1970s I had reason to make two visits to Nigeria, one of Africa's largest countries, and potentially one of its richest. Flora joined me on both trips. The first trip, of only three days, was an interlude in our visit to Ghana in 1974, as mentioned previously. The second trip, in 1975, was for about two weeks.

Nathan Associates had a small development team in Lagos, Nigeria, working under a United Nations Development Program (UNDP) contract, on the Port Harcourt reconstruction. This was a major Nigerian seaport, but needed much renovation to bring it up to international commercial standards. Apparently there were some personnel problems among the team members that were impacting the work of the team. A report was wanted on the situation.

FIRST TRIP

Remembering Col. Acheampong's advice, we chose to go for three days rather than one. Our three day visit required much patience and ingenuity. To make a phone call from Ghana to Nigeria, it was necessary to call circuitously through London. The call would go to London, and from London to Lagos. Hopefully there would not be too much static on the lines and a conversation would be possible—but the odds were against this. There were no computers or e-mail in those days and the instant communication that these high tech tools provide was not available. Telephone service was at best inadequate.

Early the morning of October 23, 1974 we had a fast ride to the Accra airport, and took a 9:30 AM Ghana Airlines flight to Lagos. We were impressed with the efficiency and orderliness of the Ghanaian crew and ground staff. After a fairly short and comfortable flight, we arrived in another world—Lagos, Nigeria.

That Col. Acheampong was right about the impossibility of going and coming on the same day became rapidly apparent. No one hurried. The mobs were immense. Even with VIP credentials, getting baggage and clearing customs was tedious and time consuming. We learned quickly that the time factor could be corrected to a certain degree by using dash—a tip to anyone involved. Soldiers or police were very much in evidence, directing and controlling the crowds by the frequent use of their short handled, leather bound quirts.

The vehicular and pedestrian traffic from the airport to the city was beyond belief. Little or no traffic control was evident. Pedestrians, cars, trucks, animals, drays, cattle, motorcycles and bicycles all competed for the same space. A solid cacophony of horns, shouts, and motor noises beat on our ears for the entire ride.

To add to the congestion, the roads were lined with mountains of rusting scrap metal from five to ten feet high. The scrap metal was being 'warehoused.' The Russians had promised Nigeria a steel mill. The steel mill was never built. The approximately twelve-mile trip into Lagos took over three hours.

The hotels were full. Businessmen from all over the world were trying to make deals with government officials (mainly the abundance of highly placed generals). The deals involved the buying and selling of almost everything imaginable. Oil was the principal item being bought for export. Cement was the largest commodity being sold to Nigeria. The entrance to the harbor was jammed with almost two hundred anchored freighters loaded with bagged and bulk cement. Import licenses, mostly counterfeit, had been issued by a variety of 'wannabe' rich bureaucrats. At night, the lights of the vessels looked like a large town out on the water. Some of the vessels had been there for months. The cement in some of them had set, and could only be removed with jackhammers. It was a mess.

Because of the hotel situation, Flora and I stayed with the Nathan Associates mission chief, Sayre Schatz and his wife in their apartment. Flora found the street scenes from our bedroom entrancing. Sayre was a professor at Temple University in Philadelphia. Although long hours were spent being briefed on the staff problems and discussing possible solutions, we still had time in the two full days that we were in Lagos to see much of the over crowded city—two and one half million people—and to meet European members of international firms, consultants and some locals.

On this trip my function was to listen, record my impressions, and report back to Washington. The staff problems seemed to be aggravated by problems of communication between the field and the home office.

The principal outcome of the trip was our meeting Wilhelm ('Pim') and Carletta Roeske. Pim was the transportation specialist on a Ford Foundation team working in Nigeria. He was a Dutch national as was Carletta. She, however, had been raised in Indonesia. They were a most delightful couple. Maybe it was the affinity of Flora's Dutch background or something more indefinable, but we hit it off famously.

It so happened that Ford was dropping its Nigerian work, and Pim was 'in the market.' Nathan Associates needed a good transportation economist, and here was one already in the field. Further, as our contract was with the UN Development Program, Pim's not being an American citizen was no barrier. I was very impressed by him, received good references from all who had worked with him, and was delighted to recommend to the home office that he be taken on our team before someone else grabbed him. He was taken on, and stayed with the firm for many years.

SECOND TRIP

The following year, 1975, Flora and I returned to Nigeria on our way to Israel. Traffic was no better than the previous year. The harbor was still full of anchored ships loaded with cement. No dent had been made in the rusting piles of scrap metal. Indeed, the piles seemed to be larger. On this trip, we stayed at the one luxury hotel in Lagos. It was better than adequate.

While there were still team problems on the Port Harcourt contract, the atmosphere was better and the work was progressing. Most of the problems, as I remember them, were caused by administrative inefficiencies in the UN staff.

On our first week-end in Lagos, Pim, by then, head of the Nathan team, proposed a two day trip to the Ford Foundation rest facility in Abadan. Eager to see more of the country than just Lagos, we readily accepted.

It was a beautifully clear, not too hot day. The highway between Lagos and Abadan was one of the country's best. With Pim driving, Flora and I had ample opportunity to look around for the two and a half hour ride.

Judging from the number of cement-carrying ships in the harbor and the many 'wannabe' roads and overpasses along the highway, the government was intent upon covering much of the country with concrete. Every few miles there was a started ramp and/or overpass, seemingly unconnected and mostly going nowhere. Sheer waste. These started projects were basically monuments to bureaucratic corruption. They represented the fact that, while Nigerian government agencies had power to give generous contracts for supplies, there was no coordination of purpose or plan, and no accountability.

While the highway itself was excellent, numerous carcasses of wrecked cars, some very recent, some very old, lined the road. Any useful parts of the vehicles had been stripped off for sale. Pim was a careful driver. We arrived at the Ford Foundation facility safe and sound—and delighted.

The facility was like an oasis in the desert. Clean modern buildings, an inviting swimming pool, tennis courts, restaurants where one could eat anything desired without worrying about the consequences, and bedrooms that would have been at home in any good hotel.

Flora and I enjoyed our time, about two weeks, in Nigeria. We enjoyed the beautiful powdered sugar-like beaches. We enjoyed visiting the native markets. Flora became an avid and excellent hand at bargaining in the markets for Nigerian handicrafts and primitive musical instruments. And we thoroughly enjoyed the time we spent with the Roeskes, both professionally and socially.

The Roeskes and Atkins became fast friends and visited each other in our home countries. Later when Flora was interested in finding her Dutch roots, Pim was invaluable and made that search a memorable and successful activity.

And we also appreciated that the Nathan team, despite the operational difficulties, was doing good work.

In Nigeria, as in most other newly independent African countries political and social loyalty was to the tribe or clan, not to the national entity. This resulted in constant tribal jockeying for position and privilege, slowing down decision making to a point that progress in development and change was frequently stifled. Bribery in many forms appeared to be the way of life. Many large international companies, as well as small firms, adept at playing the game seemed to be prospering in the economic and commercial chaos that prevailed.

Africa was and is a troubled continent. It has uncounted riches and resources—oil, diamonds, lumber, palm oil, copra, minerals, arable land and water in many regions, beautiful beaches, and tourist potential.

But Africa also suffers from clan, tribal and religious rivalries, low public health standards, often primitive agricultural methods, low economic investment levels, and widespread corrosive, incipient corruption in much of the continent.

Over the years ahead, hopefully with massive help from industrial nations and world financial institutions, their problems will be eased.

14

Filipino Follies

BATAAN, MANILA, AND Corregidor invoke memories and feelings of World War II for many Americans. But not for me. My five visits to the Philippine archipelago were for peaceful purposes and development.

My introduction to the Philippines was through Zack Eastman, a Brooklyn born and Sephardic raised Jew, who would have been right at home in a Damon Runyan story. Zack was never without a 'pie-in-the-sky' idea or proposal that would make 'millions.' In the Philippines, shortly after World War II ended, Zack had made a few million dollars for himself producing handkerchiefs for export to the United States. He made fortunes and lost them as fast as he had made them. Somehow he had a knack for getting to know moneyed people—almost all new money. One of these was movie mogul Matty Fox whom Bob Nathan knew. Matty introduced Zack to Bob, and Bob introduced me to Zack.

Zack was a character. Not quite six feet tall, he weighed between two hundred and fifty to three hundred pounds. At times impeccably coiffed and manicured, at other times he looked like an unmade bed. Extremely voluble, particularly when talking about a new get-rich-quick scheme, of course using other peoples' money and influence. In short, he was a wheeler-dealer working on the fringe of influence. He could be fun. He could be charming. He could also be annoying as hell, and absolutely unrealistic about his pie-in-the-sky projects.

One of his Filipino contacts was Pablo Roman, a successful entrepreneur. Roman, in addition to being president of the Republic Bank in Manila, owned a large modern theater, The Cinerama, in the entertainment heart of Manila. He operated a small fleet of cargo and passenger boats that ran between Manila, Bataan, Corregidor, and some of the southern islands, as well as having large holdings around Lake Taal—and probably much more. His wife, Victoria, was a prominent medical doctor. They lived with their children and grand-children in a compound containing their own opulent home as well as those of their married children. A stone wall topped with embedded broken glass and barbed wire surrounded the compound. Armed guards were also evident.

This was the ambience, in which I found myself on my first trip to Manila in June, 1963. Zack had a new idea—utilizing one or more U.S. Government programs, to build a large modern piggery. This facility was to be on land owned by the Roman interests, abutting Lake Taal, a large lake which lies in the crater of Taal volcano. Another volcanic crater inside the large crater also had a lake. The site was about seventy miles south east of Manila. Both volcanoes were thought to be extinct.

My business-class seat mate on the flight to Manila was Frances Humphrey Howard, sister of Senator Hubert Humphrey who a year later would be elected President Lyndon Johnson's vice president. Frances, like her brother, was an interesting and indefatigable conversationalist. We had many common acquaintances in Washington. She was on her way to Manila for a women's rights conference.

On this first visit, with Pablo Roman as my client through Nathan Associates, I met the principal members of Pablo's group, his family, and his compadres, as well as many of his hangers-on, who, other than being 'yes' men, had no seeming function. Two men made a special impression on me; a Chinese-Filipino, Augusto 'Tito' Sunico, a very bright lawyer, and Perfirio Belgica, a boyhood compadre and a rich man because of Pablo. Belgica was very voluble, and hard to bring to the point of any discussion. Both were on the Lake Taal board. Belgica was chairman.

Eastman and Belgica met our plane at the Manila airport. It was quite obvious that Zack was very much at home in the milieu. He had convinced the Pablo Roman group that through Robert R. Nathan Associates' contacts in Washington, miracles could occur that would benefit the Philippines and not so indirectly, the Roman group. As

Francis Howard and I deplaned together, I introduced her to Zack and Perfirio. When Zack and Belgica learned of Frances' connection they were exuberant. After all, her brother was a powerful United States senator. I believe that they saw this as another road to millions of pesos in the sky. This resulted in lavish entertainment for me, as well as Ms. Howard. Filipinos delighted in using influence to gain ends. I found it necessary on occasion to tone down Zack's exuberance and over-promising as there was no way that his expectations could be met.

I was also concerned about Belgica's frequent references to the influence that some of Pablo Roman's people had with high government officials in Manila. It was apparent that he preferred to use influence instead of a well prepared and documented application to get the government aboard the program. It later became clear that corruption and political jealousies within the Philippine government (GOP) were blocking the forward movement of the program.

In meetings with Pablo's group, I described some of the Department of Agriculture programs, their purposes, limitations, and the responsibilities of host governments as well as participants in the programs. The common theme of these discussions was the possible application of the programs to a modern high-tech piggery. The Philippines was suffering a critical grain crop shortfall and meat shortage. There did seem to be an opportunity to apply for a PL 480 program. This entailed an agreement between the USDA and the Philippines wherein the U.S. would sell foodstuffs to private importers with payment in pesos, the local currency. These funds could then be made available to approved applicants for internal economic, agricultural or industrial, development.

After two weeks I left Manila with a feeling that I had gained a sense of the local business and commercial scene, that I knew who the actors were, that those who needed to know knew what had to be done in order to prepare a proper application, and that a lot of work was still needed. Yet, I doubted that it would get done.

Despite rich arable land and plenty of water, the country was suffering from shortages of the diet staple, rice, as well as corn, and feed grains for livestock. The general sense at the American Embassy was that these shortages were the result of bad policy and bad management. I never learned anything that might contradict this attitude.

٭

In January, 1964, six months after my initial visit, I made my second trip to the Philippines. This time it was to assist directly in the preparation by the Pablo Roman team of an application from the Philippine government to the U.S. Department of Agriculture for a PL 480 agreement such as I had previously developed in other countries. Such a program would provide for purchase from the USDA of special foodstuffs, surplus to U.S. needs, for sale or distribution in the Philippines. The purchases would be at concessional prices, and with Filipino currency. The 'catch' however, was that to avoid PL 480 commodities competing with normal commercial trade the quantity of concessional priced foodstuffs in the program had to be over and above normal commercial usage in the Philippines. This would be one of the sticky wickets of the program. What was "normal commercial" usage? To what extent would the current shortfall in grain production work against approval of an application? These were just two of the problems that loomed large to me. I thought they were surmountable if adequate and reliable statistics of supply and demand were available. I was assured by Belgica and Tito that this would not be a problem. Nevertheless, I had my doubts.

In any case the USDA was sufficiently interested to send John Dean and John Somers, officials of the Foreign Agricultural Service, to Manila to assess the situation. Dr. Robert Denne, an assistant secretary of agriculture, also came, for a variety of other reasons, but was interested enough in the PL 480 program to invite me, and later some of the Filipinos working with me, to discussion meetings with him. He was very helpful in getting across to Pablo's team some of the points on which I had been hammering.

The Lake Taal office had prepared many documents and drawings of its proposals. After examining them carefully, I made some suggestions, pointed out areas that might conflict with the intent of the U.S. program, and again emphasized the part that the Philippine government would have to play. Too casually for my taste, members of

Pablo's staff, particularly Belgica, were unshakably certain about their government being sure to be "on board."

One of the memorable experiences of this trip was a visit to the Lake Taal area in order to see where the proposed piggery would locate and to get a better idea as to how the project would fit in with the local agricultural and environmental scene. The lake itself was about twice the size of Deep Creek Lake in western Maryland. The lush tropical vegetation around the large clear, fresh-water lake was beautiful.

Departure for Lake Taal was scheduled for 7:30 AM sharp. And wonder of wonders, we actually left at 7:30 sharp, uncharacteristic of Filipino society. Three cars with twenty-one people, including Somers and Dean from the USDA were on this exploration. First stop was a church in Las Pinas. There was nothing unusual about this church or many others like it in every village on the route. Nor was there any comparison to the magnificence of the churches in the smallest Mexican village. But this church had an organ, the pipes of which were all bamboo. The organist, a nine-year-old boy, treated us to a variety of pieces. There was a mellow magnificence to the tone.

After touring the tropical, floral covered Lake Taal area, the whole group was invited to a nearby fishing village for a native lunch. Upon arrival at this little fishing village we saw fish weighing perhaps seven pounds jumping in the stream. What a place for spin fishing gear! Alas, none was available. Several ten or twelve year old boys dip-netted about ten of these mackerel look-a-like fish. As we watched, the boys scaled the fish, wrapped them in banana leaves and broiled them over coconut husks. Served on large banana leaves, we ate them by breaking off pieces of the white flesh with our fingers. A succulent appetizer!

We were then directed to one of the nearby huts. Made entirely of bamboo woven mats, and bamboo pole supports, they were about ten feet above the ground. Entrance was by a ladder, again bamboo, to two ten-by-fifteen foot rooms. The walls were lined with numerous diplomas and certificates, elementary, middle, high school, and specialized schools such as nursing, as well as for individual subjects, typing, carpentry, and history among others. It was clear that the occupants were very proud of their educational advancements. I wondered aloud if the floor would hold us. The Phil's found this amusing. It held.

We had more of this delicious fish with a tangy sauce that kept me thirsty for several days. We ate two kinds of rice, and a fish soup, along with soft drinks (the ever present Coke), scotch, brandy, and coffee, followed by bananas and coconuts a la mode. We ate and ate and ate, with our fingers, native style. This is an art, and requires a deft finger and wrist motion in a sweeping fashion. When properly done it is effective and attractive to watch. Our hosts dubbed me 'a compadre' as I demonstrated the knack of eating native style. After lunch, we were all given pillows and stretched out on the bamboo floor for a rest before the drive back to Manila.

A day or so later Pablo, Zack, and I went to Baguio, the Philippine summer capital. Baguio, about 6500 feet high in the northern mountains, was a four-to five-hour drive over crowded and tattered roads. Some of these so-called roads skirted 200 to 300 foot precipices with no railings. The area, settled by the Igorot tribe of wood carvers, was in the center of a lush pine forest. Before learning wood carving, the Igorot had been head hunters. They were also excellent self-trained civil engineers. Samples of their previous occupation, human heads, were available for purchase.

Given the nature of the highway, attested to by the carcasses of numerous wrecked cars, I made sure that our return to Manila occurred well before nightfall.

At the end of the second visit to Manila, I felt that we had made much progress, and that if the Roman team could concentrate on preparing the application properly, there was a good chance that an agreement could be reached and program initiated. I took off from Manila for Israel, via Bangkok, and Teheran. From Israel I headed home completing my first round-the-world trip.

❧

A year later, on January 8, 1965, Flora and I flew east on a round-the-world trip that would take us to west Africa, then Israel, Bangkok, Hong Kong, Manila, Tokyo, Honolulu before arriving home in mid February. For me, our stops in west Africa, Israel, Bangkok and

Manila were definitely work. Flora, in addition to experiencing new locales, had an opportunity to further increase her collections of folk stories and folk instruments, both of which she used in her work as a youth theater director, consultant, and playwright.

FIGURE 20: Maury with Pablo Roman in Manila. Maury is sporting a vandyke at the suggestion of the Secret Service because of his seeming resemblance to Secretary of State Henry Kissinger.

Upon arrival in Manila, my third visit, we were met at the plane by Belgica and Commodore Jose Andrada, the new chairman of the Lake Taal board. We were shocked to see the concentration of heavily armed guards everywhere. The country had been experiencing a crime epidemic along with almost uncontrolled smuggling and political unrest. Muggings, robberies, and assaults were commonplace. We were made to understand that to go out on the streets at night was not a good idea.

For some reason all the better hotels were full. We were taken to the Filipinos Hotel, where squads of huge cockroaches resided in our room with us. Only when we threatened to go to the lobby and sleep there, did the staff find a decent room for us.

Political opposition and bureaucratic pressure had built up against

Pablo Roman to the point that, although he owned 90 percent of the stock in his theater, he had to give up his CEO position. The same pressure required substantial changes in the board of the Lake Taal group. It also meant long delays in filing a PL 480 application. Commodore Jose Andrada, scion of a prominent Filipino family with extensive economic interests throughout the islands, was the new chairman of the board and general manager of the Taal Lake company. In addition to having been the first commodore of the Philippine navy, he was the first Filipino to have graduated from the U.S. Naval Academy in Annapolis. Andrada enjoyed a reputation as a serious, solid citizen and was respected for his ability to get things done without the usual corruption. I found him easy to work with. Unlike Belgica, who was given to long speeches, Andrada spoke thoughtfully and to the point. Belgica, formerly chairman of the board, was off the board. His function now was to entertain visitors, and this, in his fashion, he did well.

For the four days that we were in Manila my time was fully taken up with a variety of meetings including several with Dr. Adevose, Philippine minister of economic coordination, whom I knew from earlier sessions in Washington with Bob Nathan and Dave Chewning. I attended two meetings of the new board of directors of Lake Taal and had several briefings by invitation at the American Embassy with Economic Counselor Ernie Neal, whom I had known in Sierra Leone, where he had been AID Mission chief. He was quite interested in the potential of a PL 480 program in the Philippines. I also had the pleasure of spending a bit of time with Lee Paramore, the U.S. agricultural attaché. Lee and I had served together on the board of directors of Group Health Association in Washington, the first member-owned Health Medical Organization in the United States.

The problem of implementing a program lay with the Philippine government. Graft and corruption was growing and nobody seemed to be really concerned. There was a terrible shortage of food, which a PL 480 program could alleviate. Nationalism was on the march, and naturally, Uncle Sam was the boy to kick. While local groups were loudly complaining about the effect of Uncle Sam's military bases on Filipino society and economy, at least they weren't burning, stoning and throwing ink at the embassy. The many demonstrations were quite orderly.

The Lake Taal situation was thoroughly and openly discussed at the meetings of the board of Pablo's company that I attended. The board members were quite frank to admit that the problem had been with their government. Belgica had been politically identified with the anti Macapagal group, and Pablo Roman was running for congress on the Macapagal ticket. At every turn, I was getting the impression that political fencing was more important than results. The government seemed to have all the forms and trappings of democracy, and little of the substance. Presidential and congressional elections were scheduled for November, 1965. Political party conventions were held in December, 1964, and in January, 1965, the campaign was on in full force, insuring that there would be no progress on any economic development for at least another ten months. The locals had a saying that while the term is for four years, the officials run for two years, serve for two years, and get rich in four years.

Both Pablo and his wife, Victoria, were under the weather while we were in Manila on this trip. Pablo's daughter, Lucille Ramos, was most gracious in showing Flora the sights of Manila. Pablo also went out of his way to make his new fish-finned Cadillac and driver available to us. Not so incidentally, driving a large car through the streets of Manila was an art form. One had to weave between the 'jeepneys', the thousands of World War II surplus military jeeps that were a major means of city transportation. They had been refurbished to carry eight seated passengers, but many more would-be-passengers stood or hung on where ever they could. The picturesque, imaginative, and colored paint jobs were a photographer's delight. In addition to the jeepneys, motorcycles, small cars, an occasional team of oxen, and of course, military trucks crowded the streets.

We returned to the States via Honolulu and San Francisco. Both were welcome rest stops.

Three events occurred after I returned home that probably had an impact on the progress of a Philippine/U.S. PL 480 program.

In September, 1965, seven months after we were there, the thought-to-be-extinct Lake Taal volcano erupted with a great deal of damage and loss of life. Ashes from the eruption fell in the streets of Manila.

FIGURE 21: The ubiquitous jeepney

Two months later Philippine President Diosdado Macapagal was defeated in the elections of November, 1965 by Senator Ferdinand Marcos. This further complicated the progress of a Philippine/U.S. PL 480 agreement, while the playing teams realigned themselves in the new political calculus.

One day I had an unexpected visitor at my office in Washington. A tall Filipino gentleman came to my office and introduced himself. He wanted to talk about the PL 480 program. After several minutes of general discussion about the program's operation, "Once it is signed," he bluntly asked, "What's in it for me?" I was taken aback. I explained the value of the project to the Philippine economy—providing needed supplies of grain, rice, and possibly meat at concessional prices. Halfway through my recitation, he stopped me and said, "You don't understand." Pointing to himself, he repeated, "What's in it for me, I mean me?" That man was the Philippine secretary of agriculture.

This was the first direct awareness I had had of the probability of corruption in the program. I realized that little was accomplished in the local venue without some form of hanky-panky.

Eleven years later, in 1976, the matter of a Philippine PL 480 program again arose. I was reasonably confident that Zack Eastman's fine touch lay behind this re-interest. Also, Pablo Roman's team felt that Marcos' administration was ready to be serious about the project. His people also felt that they would like to use private financing for a Title IV program and for other development projects unrelated to PL 480. The invitation for me to come to Manila included Flora. The invitation also asked about the possibility of private financing, a timely request as Nathan Associates had been doing some work with a local venture capital company. Discussions with their principals indicated a solid interest in going to Manila and meeting with the board of Lake Taal.

On February 15, 1976, Flora and I again arrived in the Philippines. John Clark, a senior vice president of the venture capital firm, and his wife Ann, were already in Manila. This time, we were housed in the luxurious Intercontinental Hotel in Quezon City, an upscale suburb.

On this visit, there was a minimum of oratory and wishful thinking. Instead, John and I put in hours of solid work on several programs, including, of course, a PL 480 application ready for submission to the Philippine government. John expressed satisfaction with the viability of the projects for which financing was desired, and I was happy with the PL 480 application. This was now in the Philippines' court. My work was basically done. Once Marcos' people would approve, the documents would be sent to the American Embassy. Approval by Marcos' people generally meant by 'the lady', President Marcos' wife, Imelda. The U.S. Embassy would forward the application, with its comments, to the Department of Agriculture in Washington. When this occurred, it would be up to the Philippine Embassy in Washington, to follow through. I agreed to be available to help in expediting the U.S. approval.

✿

Although we worked hard, we also played hard.

On the first weekend, Pablo Roman took Flora and me and the Clarks on a high speed catamaran hydrofoil trip from Manila to Corregidor and Bataan. It was at these two points in World War II that out-numbered and out-gunned American soldiers and marines put up a heroic defense against the Japanese invaders, but ultimately had to surrender. Pablo owned the boat company. Aboard the vessel was a group of about seventy-five Japanese peasants going to Corregidor to say prayers for the souls of their sons and husbands who had died in the war. On the way from Manila to Corregidor they were noisy. On the way back, they were quiet and subdued.

The highlight of the trip was on Bataan at the palatial home of a member of the Philippine Senate. A whole bull and two large pigs were barbecued over a large open pit. Many side dishes, and much to drink, were also offered to the almost one hundred guests.

I also was able to squeeze in an afternoon of scuba diving in the Bay of Batangas, with its huge coral growths and multicolored tropical fish. Poisonous lion fish, hungry looking barracudas, and grasping moray eels made it a very exciting dive.

At the Intercontinental Hotel, daily breakfast on an outside patio included a delicious combination of mango and papaya perfectly served. On those few occasions when we were not invited out for dinner, we frequented a nearby Chinese noodle shop recommended by Tito Sunico. Generally, we were the only 'round eyes' in the place. The noodles and a choice of what seemed like a hundred toppings, were delicious and inexpensive.

We were entertained royally in some of the most posh restaurants and clubs in which I have ever been. In one of these private clubs, the waiters served platters of large Pacific lobsters, no claws, but with blinking red lights where the eyes had been.

The second weekend, Pablo invited Flora and me to join his family at Baguio, in the mountains north of Manila. The climate was delightfully cool, and the aroma of pines most pleasant. On Sunday morning, it was a revealing and heartwarming sight to see all thirty-five of the Roman grandchildren, dressed in their Sunday best, line up to greet their grandfather and receive his blessing.

The guests at the many dinner parties in very opulent homes were an interesting mixture. Often they were political enemies, but personal friends. In one case we were guests of the publisher of a large anti-Marcos newspaper. He was very articulate about Marcos' mismanagement and alleged corruption. Next to him was a leading member of Marcos judiciary, and several congressmen. The discussions were heavy with pro and anti Marcos statements flying. The atmosphere was tense with political anticipation. Yet all were close personal friends. An exciting evening. Did I sense that a crackdown was imminent?

⋰❧

My work being 'finished' we left for home, loaded with gifts and souvenirs, new ideas about the political and social structure of the Philippines and the sense that if a PL 480 program occurred, it would now be up to our friends in Manila.

The bottom line was that I never heard that any of the development projects, nor the PL 480 program, moved forward.

On our way back home, Flora and I spent and enjoyed a one day stop in Honolulu, with my aunt Zelda Hauser. We had run into her husband, Phil, in Manila. The next day we left for the island of Maui. Here we had the use for a week of my client Dick Levin's swank condo. Dick, a 6 foot 8 inch genial giant, operated an unusual gold and silver metal recovery business with a ship breaking sideline. Renting a car, we explored the island, and its volcanoes. A wonderful week before we returned to the mainland.

⋰❧

Ever expectant of a large payday for his exertions, Zack Eastman somehow arranged for a renewal of the attempts to consummate a PL 480 program with a new cast of Filipino characters—this time with a group "very, very close to Imelda and Ferdinand." So, in January 1984, twenty-one years after my first Philippine visit, Flora and I were again on our way to Manila, having received first class tickets on Philippine Airlines, and a satisfactory retainer.

We were met at the airport by Col. Rex Reyes and our old friend Belgica. Reyes was attested to be 'buddy-buddy' with President Marcos. It was clear from the way he was treated in the airport that he enjoyed some clout. Everyone seemed anxious to please him and his guests—us.

Around the airport runways, street approaches, and near the hangers were many strange looking military or police vehicles—mounted water cannons and half tracks manned by riot armed and armor clad personnel. We had arrived during a period of anti-Marcos political unrest and demonstrations. The cause of this enhanced security or show of force, I am not sure which or both, was the fatal shooting late in 1983, of Benigno Aquino, nicknamed Ninoy. He was a young very popular anti-Marcos politician. He was gunned down in view of a large crowd while deplaning in Manila. Marcos forces were blamed, but nothing was ever proven, and no one was charged with the murder. His sister, Corazon Aquino picked up her brother's opposition mantle. There were many large, noisy, but not violent, demonstration marches while we were there. Most of the demonstrators wore bright yellow tee shirts, with the printed slogan, WE LOVE NINOY. On several occasions we were not allowed to leave our hotel because of the possibility of violence. In 1986, Corazon Aquinos would be inaugurated as the new reform president of the Philippines.

As we had had, by this time, much experience in preparing PL 480 programs for Filipino projects, it was not necessary to spend much time on the application preparation. Each day Col. Reyes' aides promised an appointment with 'the lady', today, or tomorrow. The allotted days went by with little real work, and we never met with Imelda.

On a previous visit to Manila, Flora and I had met a charming young Filipino couple, Sonny and Lore Lagdemayo, distant cousins of Pablo Roman. It was pleasant to renew our acquaintance. On the second or third evening in Manila, they hosted a small dinner party for us at the Mandarin Hotel. On the table was a cake nicely decorated with "Happy Anniversary, Maury and Flora." Pleasantly surprised, we explained that our anniversary was several months earlier and that it was much more than our second. "Oh, this is the second anniversary of our meeting." We did enjoy their company.

Forty years after the end of World War II, jeepneys were still the conveyance of choice for thousands of Manila commuters. One day, Flora, boarding one of these vehicles, unfortunately, pulled a large back muscle, experiencing much pain. Treatment by a faith healer in our hotel room as well as by a medical doctor at a hospital owned by Reyes compadres was only mildly successful.

To make the flight home easier for Flora, Col. Reyes arranged for her to have a private, full length bed in the upper level of the Boeing 747. She slept most of the way across the Pacific and avoided jetlag.

Filipinos are delightful, gracious people. Their country is beautiful and enjoys bountiful natural resources. But somehow in the country's development, all the worst aspects of 'Coca-Cola-nization' were absorbed. The people love the United States, and our life styles, but in copying them, they adopted some of our worst aspects. And somehow, the challenge of accomplishment through influence and graft was a challenge to the Filipino, that added spice to one's economic life.

As might be expected, sadly, again nothing came of this latest attempt to refloat a PL 480 program. The Philippines could have benefited significantly from this program as had Israel and Sierra Leone.

The failure of the proposed PL 480 program to get off the ground, in no way discouraged Zack Eastman from coming up with further pie-in-the-sky projects, which, fortunately, we did not have the time—and I might say energy—to pursue.

15

Sri Lanka

I N JUNE 1982, we headed for lush, exotic Sri Lanka, with stops en route in staid buttoned-down Boston and highly manicured Switzerland.

—Boston, so that two exhilarated parents could attend their daughter Barrie's MBA graduation from Harvard Business School. We shall never forget the huge grin on her face when she was awarded a special silver cup for her performance as publisher of the 'B' school's weekly newspaper, *Harbus*.

—Geneva, for three days of meetings for me with officials of the International Refugee Committee, sightseeing for Flora. Although technically retired I sporadically worked on special projects for Nathan Associates.

Then on to Colombo, Sri Lanka where I was joining a Nathan Associates advisory team working under a USAID contract for the Sri Lanka Ministry of Finance. My function was as a 'natural resource and marketing officer.'

Sri Lanka is geographically situated to be a major player for air and sea travel, commerce and/or tourism. It lies between the Far East and Europe and the Middle East. It is liberally endowed with natural resources—magnificent scenery, beautiful beaches, the sea rich with fish, abundant fresh water for agriculture and industry, hard and softwood forests, arable land, rubber, rutile, palm trees of various types—copra, coconut, date palm, tea—green and black—and spices. The average temperature year round is 81 degrees, with almost always a pleasant cooling breeze. Sri Lanka also has the most desirable resource of all—a highly literate, able and hard working population.

The island could have and should have been an economic and social paradise.

So why wasn't it? Bureaucracy and ethnic differences.

The country had about twenty different ministries, each of which had to 'sign off' on each and every project. Even if there was no disagreement, this process alone was terribly time consuming. If any question arose it could take days, even months, for project approval to be forthcoming.

Most of the population is Buddhist. In the northwest corner of the island, the population is basically Hindu, originally from India. They have been fighting for generations for their own 'Tamil' country. Unfortunately, the fighting and bombing has not been restricted to only one part of the land mass.

Thousands of people have died in this guerrilla warfare. Among the casualties was a Nathan Associates' secretary, killed by a stray bullet while sitting at her desk in Colombo. Shortly after we left, widespread rioting, bombing, and burning occurred. The local lawyer assigned to our project was missing during the riots and considered dead.

Previous visits to other numerous exotic lands on four continents did not prepare me for the vibrant colorful culture found in this island nation. With independence from Britain the name had been changed from Ceylon to Sri Lanka. An island just off the southeast tip of India, with 25,300 square miles, is only slightly larger than West Virginia.

The population is one of the most literate in the world, with education free through the college level. The importance of English and education is stressed. Sri Lankans come in many shades of tan, brown and cocoa as well as a deep purple black and a charcoal ash. Features of all are Caucasian, with silky black hair generally straight, possibly with a slight wave.

Although western garb was becoming more prevalent, women generally wore multi-colored saris. Our office staff wore attractive saris during the work week, which give them a rather sensual appearance as they glided along. The frequently exposed bellybutton and midriff looked perfectly natural in that setting. One Saturday, needing to get out a crash report, we had our typing staff come to the office. All came wearing 'T' shirts and jeans. What a sartorial let-down! They looked like a small high school class in Washington's inner city.

The men wore either various colored shirts with either dark slacks, or a piece of striped cloth wrapped around their waists to form a sort of sarong skirt, which required constant adjustment.

One hundred and fifty years each of British, Portuguese and Dutch colonialism left their imprints on the people, economy, and culture of the country. The Portuguese brought tile roofs, the Catholic church, and many 'deSilva's' added to the four, five, and six syllable Sri Lankan names, such as Kumaratunga and Wickremasinghe, the president and prime minister respectively in 2003. The Dutch put in canals, were businessmen, and intermarried. The Brits cultivated the tea, introduced many of their ceremonies, such as 'changing of the guard', and brought public education.

Arrival and on to Kandy

We arrived early in the morning of June 12, at Colombo International Airport. Although we had flown first class we were tired, sweaty, and badly needing a shower and a bed.

But it was not to be.

Bob Johnson, RRN team leader, met us at the plane. We drove the hour to Colombo, the capital, and then were given forty-five minutes to shower and pack a small bag and be on our way for an overnight in the interior of the island. 'On our way' meant to Kandy, up in the hills, the second largest city in Sri Lanka, for meetings with Sri Lankan officials. The rest of the Nathan team had started out earlier.

The distance was about seventy miles—a full three-hour drive through lush tropical forests, over twisting curvy roads, alongside bubbling streams where work elephants were being bathed by their handlers. Very narrow, barely one-car-wide bridges, spanned the many streams.

Besides Bob Johnson and myself, the other Nathan Associates team members were Ed Hollander, a superb economist, writer and manpower specialist, Ted Wilde who covered demographic aspects, and John Glennie, responsible for the legal sections of the project. Joe Gunn, on his way back from another Asian assignment dropped in for a few days. All were regular RRNA staffers. Louise Hollander, Ed's wife, was also in Sri Lanka. Although she was not feeling well and was leaving for home with Ed in a few days, her presence made Flora's arrival and introduction to Sri Lanka more pleasant.

Kandy

Six thousand feet above sea level was a very special and pretty city, Kandy, looking like an Asiatic setting for a make believe children's fantasy or a Gilbert and Sullivan operetta. It had been the center of one of the three kingdoms in the country until rather recently. Its ceremonies, temples, lakes, costumes, drums, religious processionals, engaging people—the ancient and the present—all blurred together in our jetlagged condition. The gentle shaking of the head, side to side meaning "yes" constantly confused us.

We stayed at the old and picturesque Hotel Suisse. Ceiling fans, primitive bathrooms, no air conditioning, dust rose (double entendre intended) mosquito netting over our bed. Dinner in a marvelous high ceilinged and balconied room, included many graciously served courses.

In Kandy in addition to discussions with Sri Lankan officials about our program, we visited spice, cocoa, coffee, and palm farms. We were able to talk to farmers, members of the agricultural marketing boards and observe some of the equipment used in production and processing. We were advised that while walking through the spice (and other) fields never to be the third person in line along the paths. "Why?" we asked. The reply, "The first person wakes up the cobra, the second person agitates it, and he hits the third person." We made sure that we never were number three.

I was particularly interested in government plans for major expansion of productive acreage. Regrettably, there did not seem to be a coordinated well-thought-out plan for this expansion and for product marketing. Our immediate program would nibble at the edges, but by no stretch of the imagination would it substitute for a full time advisory team to develop a solid program. Aside from the plans that we were told about, the World Bank had made a major agricultural loan to Sri Lanka for the Malaweli Ganga River area. The bank had a small resident team in Colombo working with Sri Lankan specialists on this project. Thousands of acres along Sri Lanka's major river were being planned to produce large quantities of fruits and vegetables in addition to those products produced in other parts of the country. In a later private meeting with the Bank project leader, he confided to me that the program was very much behind schedule—mostly for administrative foot dragging reasons.

After Kandy we returned to Columbo with task related stops along the way.

Colombo

Colombo is an Asian city. It has elements of Manila, Cairo, Singapore, Bombay and Bangkok, but smaller and less sophisticated. It is not Sri Lanka anymore than New York is the U.S.A. In abundance are Germans, Chinese, Japanese and Russians all trying to "do business." But few Americans. Dance, music, art, drama and film are important parts of the cultural life. The museums, unlike those in Cairo, are not just dusty storehouses of priceless objects, but house many attractive educational exhibits. They are well attended by Sri Lankans, as are the many fine bookstores. Flora took full advantage of the cultural opportunities, attended educational films, dance concerts, and children's theater. She met with prominent local personalities active in the arts, whom she later remet in national youth drama conferences in other countries. She also lectured on children's theater at Colombo University. As a guest of Dick Schifter, U.S. assistant secretary of state for human rights, and a friend from Washington, Flora even sat in on the UN Human Rights Conference meeting in Sri Lanka.

We visited the 'free trade zone' outside Colombo. Here many very up scale American women's clothing firms were producing expensive sweaters, blouses suits, lingerie etc en masse, paying about one dollar a day to the hundreds of girls and women operating the sewing machines, cutters, pressers, and packaging equipment. These products were not for Target or Sears. They were for the most upscale stores in New, York, London, and Paris.

We also visited a variety of factories producing industrial products principally for the local market, but also some for export. It was obvious, even to an untrained eye, that many of these plants could have benefited by an infusion of more modern and efficient equipment. We were surprised to learn that Sri Lanka had no facility in the country to produce bottles for packing fruits and vegetables—although there was excellent raw material for such production. Bottles were imported from other Southeast Asian countries.

Our exposure to Sri Lanka's economy took us to a trade school that trained men in fishing, particularly long-line fishing. This was the then accepted way to fish for tuna and other desirable fish that had a big market, especially in Japan. However, while young men were being taught long-line fishing, Sri Lanka had no long-line fishing vessels. The only employment in this area for the trade school graduates was on Japanese vessels.

Ted Wilde, Flora and I went to the finals of the prestigious annual city wide (Colombo) high school Shakespeare dramatization contest. The plays were held in a non-air-conditioned hall of a Catholic church. Despite the heat, the place was packed. We got in the auditorium by Flora's using her wiles and going in on the coattails of a priest headmaster of a boys' school. All of the performers were male, regardless of the role. It was an intriguing evening.

The streets cluttered with busses, cars, tri-shaws, bicycles, trucks, lorries, motorcycles, cows, dogs, pedestrians, bullock carts, and an occasional elephant, were full of potholes. Traffic, British style, driving on the left side, did not make it easy to cross a street without being super careful.

American Ambassador Reed, political appointee, held the obligatory Fourth of July party at the Embassy. Flora and I represented our team. All of the AID people that we worked with during the week as well as the Sri Lankan officials with whom we were working were in attendance. The party was held outside in the garden. A Sri Lanka navy band performed creditable renditions of the "Washington Post March" and "The Star Spangled Banner," but had less success with "Dixie" and other American tunes.

It was a very hot tropical night. Ambassador Reed wore a Hawaiian loose fitting shirt. Most of the guests were also tieless. However, Mr. Reed had ordered that the Marine Guard be present—in full dress blues. This meant jackets with tight collars. Several of the marines fainted from the heat. Their buddies were furious with the ambassador, but had no immediate recourse.

Dinner at the home of Ranjith Gunawerdenas, a fiberglass boat manufacturer, was an opportunity to learn more about the country's mores and customs. Our hosts were a sophisticated and interesting family. As with nearly all of the elite of the country, their children went to private schools. The young ladies of this family attended Ladies College which spans preschool to university. Much in demand, we were told that it took only children of 'Old Girls.' There were about 5,000 students.

As we entered the dimly lit house, we were almost overcome by the odor of frying coconut oil—a cooking staple—that permeated the house, and at meal time much of the residential areas of the city. The menu consisted of deep fried fresh tuna sticks, which despite the oil, were fairly tasty; tough and scrawny chicken; a salad of mixed vegetables heavily seasoned with garlic, cinnamon, and ginger, and mixed with buffalo curd, the popular Sri Lankan yogurt. Generally food was *very* highly seasoned, almost to the point of being, for a westerner, non-edible. This may be a contributing factor for the high rate of stomach cancer in the country.

Conversation was enlightening. All was not sugar and spice in the Sri Lankan populace. We learned about what our hostess called 'slave children.' Poor parents in the villages would 'sell' their children to city people to 'work' as servants. Often they were beaten, overworked, and generally mistreated. We heard about 150,000 street children in Colombo, whose parents had come from the villages, lived in tiny hovels, had large families and literally did not have enough space for the whole family to lie down at night. Often they took turns, some roaming the city at night and sleeping during the day.

So despite having an abundance of raw materials, a smart and willing population, it was obvious that there was much to do and much that would make a difference. Inquiry into why the gap between ample raw materials, an educated population, and a sluggish economy almost always echoed the same answer. "Too many bureaucracies, politics, some corruption and lack of investment capital."

The Tea Board

One of the most interesting invitations and experiences we had was a weekend visit to the Tea Board Research Institute in Talawkelle in the hills near the Tamil region.

Sri Lanka produces highly prized teas, the two principal types,—green tea and black tea. The green tea was considered premium and higher priced. It came from bushes high on the hills. The black tea until recently considered of poorer quality was produced in the lower hillsides. The market for green tea was basically Germany and Britain, for the black tea it was the middle east. As the Arabs developed purchasing power their demand for black tea tipped the economic scales so that the price of black tea soon became better than that of green tea. At that time there were no decaffeinated teas. This was a project that the laboratories, a building near the guest house, was working on.

The Tea Board guest house was high on one of the highest hills with a beautiful view over thousands of acres of tea plants. It was a typical British colonial upper class house, fully staffed with the requisite servants, who, barefooted, padded about doing their work silently, but oh so efficiently. Well trained.

During our visit and my meetings with Dr. P. Sivapalan, Director of the Tea Board, we sampled many different types of drinks; beer, lemonade, wine tea, tea soda, various flavored teas, and of course, following the British tradition, after dinner whiskey (scotch) and soda.

Visiting the tea fields, we heard the singing of the pickers, hundreds of women plucking the two pale green leaves off of each plant.

Flora and I had the guest house to ourselves, except for 'Gunga' and 'Din', our names for the two white-clad serving staff. Dinner was served in a high ceilinged dining room at a large table elegantly set. Anthuria was abundant and beautiful. The dessert pineapple was more than luscious. In front of me a bell cord hung from the ceiling. A touch on the cord brought either 'Gunga' or 'Din' on the run—quietly.

Following after-dinner tea in the sitting room, 'Gunga' asked us what time we would want our 'bed-tea' in the morning. Our large airy bedroom had twin beds covered by large ceiling to floor blue mosquito netting. At seven AM promptly, our bed tea was delivered. We had a sumptuous breakfast in the dining room. This included perfectly ripe papaya wedges, followed by an attractive platter of fried eggs, grilled tomatoes, and bacon with toast and marmalade. While it was a relief to have some food in Sri Lanka that was less spicy than dynamite, the eggs were fried in coconut oil. Flora dared me to touch the buzzer. I did. 'Gunga' and 'Din' were promptly beside me. We requested one of the mangoes on the sideboard. In no time we had a succulent ripe mango that could have competed with the best of those we had experienced in Manila.

By 8:00 AM we were on our way, with the staff and their families all lined up in the driveway waving, smiling, and calling out good wishes bidding us goodbye. We left with a very warm feeling. The first two hours of a different route back to Colombo had us hanging on to our seats as we went down hairpin curves, passing trucks and busses as well as pedestrians along precipice edges. This was the area where the film *Bridge on the River Kwai* was filmed. Our immediate target was Nurelya Eilya (City of Light), formerly a British resort and retreat.

There we visited the exquisite Hakgala Botanic Garden and lunched at the super elegant Grand Hotel. An additional couple of hours of a harrowing ride down plunging stomach-turning mountain roads brought us back to our hotel in Colombo. Fortunately our driver was excellent, helped by the Buddha on the dashboard, flashing on and off, during the journey.

Final Thoughts

With its abundant natural resources and an educated populace the economic potential is enormous. However, it must deal with its over loaded bureaucracy and corruption.

The food is terribly spicy, and one must be careful. As in many developing areas, drinking the water can be dicey. The country is quite clean and efforts are made to keep trash under control.

The monetary unit is the rupee. One rupee was worth about five cents American. The most common paper currency was a two rupee piece (10 cents, Sri Lankan). These often looked as though they were used kleenex. Coins were as small as one rupee (5 cents). There were 100 Sri Lankan cents in a rupee

Saudis, Indonesians, and Europeans were recruiting for Sri Lankan workers for their countries at salaries many times those available in Sri Lanka.

A world so different from ours—so different from any we have visited before—in the Far East, Mid East, or Africa. We were fortunate to have had the opportunity to experience Sri Lanka. We hope that Sri Lanka, in some small way, was fortunate to have had us.

FIGURE 22: The author and Sri Lankan
agronomists examining a cinnamon tree, 1982.

PART IV

Safe Moorings, Back Home

16

Shore-side Problems . . . and Solutions

IN ADDITION TO foreign firms and countries, Nathan Associates' clients included domestic companies and institutions. Many had problems with Federal agencies. Situated in Washington, Nathan Associates' staff with contacts in government agencies, often knew which button to push. In addition, the firm's reputation for integrity and excellence brought us many clients with "Washington problems." They were generally with administrative and regulatory bodies and almost always involved a practical economic approach. Characterizing our clients and our work as 'diversified' would be an understatement.

My domestic clients included American-Hawaiian Steamship Co., American Export Lines, American-Israeli Shipping Co., Arditi Export Corp., Chilewich Corp., Commercial Metals Co., Dreher Leather Manufacturing Co., Dunbar Shoe Co., Institute of Scrap Iron and Steel, Levin Metals, Judith Leiber, Kromex Manufacturing Co., Killark Electric Manufacturing Co., Meals for Millions, Tony Lama, as well as serving as an expert witness for law firms in connection with breach of contract and negligence suits.

The challenging and exciting aspect of such diverse clients necessitated learning a great deal about new businesses and industries in a short time. Accordingly, I became more than somewhat educated about the practical aspects of international trade, the economics and marketing structure of the highly volatile scrap industry, the structure of the domestic leather markets, as well as the pros and cons of the shipping world.

Kromex Manufacturing Company

One of the first Nathan Associates clients that Bob Nathan put on my desk was the Kromex Manufacturing Co., a small Cleveland, Ohio company that had developed a method for retooling surplus aluminum and brass shell cases into stylish kitchen canisters for flour, sugar, spices and other kitchen staples. It also made coat racks on wheels. Kromex needed allocations from the government to purchase brass, copper, and aluminum. The application had to demonstrate that an allocation would not interfere with or constrain the Korean War effort. It was necessary to show that it was in the national interest to grant an allocation.

Loquacious Manny Asquith, president of Kromex, spewed out ideas like a machine gun. It was often difficult to follow his thought trends. Despite this, it was fun to work with him. He was a marketing whiz. Using some 'creative' economic concepts I was able to get Kromex its needed allocations. Our billings to Kromex were promptly paid.

In the December holiday season a large truck stopped by our home and unloaded three large packages. These included an outboard motor for me, a tricycle for our three year old son, and a variety of Kromex kitchen products for my wife. This was a new experience for me, and accepting these gifts would have been a "no no" if I were still in the U.S. government. I asked Bob what I should do about them, pointing out that Manny had paid his bill and was giving the firm other work.

"What to do about them?" Bob said, " Write Manny a nice note of thanks, and enjoy them." This we did.

Killark Electric Manufacturing Co.

Joe DeLoge, president of Killark Electric Manufacturing Co., St. Louis, Missouri, had a problem. Killark had won a contract award to supply some specialized parts to the U.S. Navy. Too late to withdraw his offer, DeLoge realized that fulfilling the contract would practically bankrupt the company.

DeLoge was an immensely wealthy and proud man. He had been president and CEO of several Fortune 500 companies. Killark, a producer of small electrical fittings, was a play toy for him. His home was a Tudor castle brought over from France stone by stone and reassembled on the banks of the Mississippi River, where it was joined by the Missouri River. From the mansion a manicured, tree-lined lawn extended about one hundred yards toward the Mississippi. Beneath the lawn was an auditorium that could seat several hundred guests while they enjoyed a concert by the St. Louis Symphony Orchestra. In addition to being a major donor to the orchestra, he had given the city the Ferdinand DeLoge Memorial Hospital in memory of a deceased brother. Once, over lunch at his home, on gold, yes gold as in metal, dishes, he once explained to me, that only a fool bought a new car. He never did. "Let some one else take the first year's depreciation," he stated.

We had been recommended to Killark by another client. Mr. DeLoge called me from St. Louis. In a long telephone conversation he explained Killark's problem. I told him that I was not a lawyer, but could participate in an administrative law matter.

The next day Killark's senior vice president flew to Washington in the company's Cessna 172 bringing all the relevant documents. I did not see where I could be helpful as my contacts at the Department of Defense were fairly thin, and I made no secret of this. "Okay, but see what you can recommend."

I spent three days at the U.S. General Accounting Office (GAO) law library poring over all the regulations and cases I could find on government contract terminations. I found practically nothing that might help.

I decided to write an economic appeal, rather than a law brief, requesting relief and contract adjustment on the basis that to enforce the contract would be contrary to the interests of the U.S. government and the war effort.

Enforcement would create the following hardships:

- Killark might have to declare bankruptcy;
- Several hundred workers would be unemployed;
- The specialized manufacturing facilities of Killark would not be available for subsequent military needs;
- Federal and state governments would lose tax revenues;

- The needs of the Navy for the products would be delayed;
- In short, enforcement would be 'unconscionable.'

With Killark's approval, this appeal with a great deal of statistical and financial data, was submitted to the GAO.

A week later, I was called to a meeting with the accountant general of the GAO, Mr. Staats. Together with several of his staff, my statement was discussed. Then Mr. Staats said, "You have developed a new concept for contract termination or adjustment. We accept it."

It was the concept of 'unconscionable enforcement.'

Killark was allowed to renegotiate its contract.

A few days later I was invited to the AG's office again. I was greeted with the news that there was an associate counselors position open. "Would you be interested?"

There was considerable surprise when I said, "I am not a lawyer."

Commercial Metals Company, Inc.

Commercial Metals Co. (CMC), based in Dallas, Texas, a large 'big board' Fortune 500 scrap metal firm, was one of Sid Lerner's clients at Nathan Associates. When Sid left RRNA to move to Dallas to become a vice president of Commercial Metals, the job of Washington representative was assigned to me.

My knowledge of the scrap business was extremely limited. I was aware of some of the nomenclature as my maternal grandfather, Barnett Abrams, and my uncle Harry Abrams, had both eked out modest livings accumulating Washington area scrap metals and reselling to larger yards. But guided by CMC officials, I learned a great deal in a short while about the overall industry.

CMC collected scrap, both ferrous and nonferrous, from worldwide sources. Sales of prepared scrap to domestic mills and foundries, as well as a large export trade, were the engines of bottom line success.

Margins in the trade were generally very narrow, and with changing technologies, scrap collection and processing became more and more capital intensive. Although dominated by a few large companies, competition in the industry was intense.

Jacob Feldman, president and CEO of CMC, had taken over a

small operation from his father and had built it into a significant presence in the scrap industry. Jake, as he was known throughout the industry, was a tall, very intense and focused man. In college he had been a star tennis player. A leader in the Dallas Jewish community, he was greatly concerned about events in Israel and was one of the largest contributors to the American Israel Public Affairs Committee (AIPAC). My Dallas visits always included a brain storming session on Israeli developments and the Mideast situation. A Sunday morning call to me at home to discuss the Israeli news story of the day was not unusual.

Charles Merritt, senior vice president and later president, was one of the few non-Jewish top officials in the industry. He described himself as a southern "country boy." He had a delightful lazy southern drawl, but a very sharp mind. His favorite phrase, "There are no free lunches" meant, "Do what you have to do to get the job done." Emphatically, one thing Nathan Associates staff would never do was anything that would even hint at offering a bribe. We were quite sure that some competitors did not observe the same standards.

Harry Bauer, a refugee from Nazi Germany, a senior official with CMC and later president of the firm's New York chemical and bulk trading office, was a hard driving, smart and demanding individual. Harry kept a sign on his desk proudly attesting to his lack of humility. He did make money for the firm. He was also a hard worker and major contributor to the New York Jewish charities.

Bert Romberg, head of non-ferrous operations, was a pleasure to work with. Smart and always pleasant, he was very effective and taught me much about non-ferrous metals.

Stan Rabin, one of the younger CMC officials, did not fit the mold of a scrap metal executive. He was quiet, thoughtful and personally considerate. His responsibilities were to develop corporate policy rather than trading. When Jake Feldman and Charlie Merritt retired, Stan became president and CEO of the company.

My work for CMC required frequent meetings in Dallas to discuss domestic and international market trends, government regulations and export controls. CMC was a major player in the international movement of scrap metals. The United States, with its huge economy, generated enormous amounts of scrap metal. For many years scrap metal exports from the U.S. were rigidly controlled by the export division of the U.S. Department of Commerce. This was to insure that American mills and foundries had adequate supplies of scrap to produce the steel and brass needed for the domestic market. My responsibility was to prepare the economic rationale to support CMC's export applications. Molly Tatel, my assistant, performed yeoman service in working with Department of Commerce personnel processing these applications and obtaining export licenses. It was no easy job. The government licensing officers in the metal export division were too often former mid-level employees of mills and foundries, and had a strong institutional bias against scrap metal exports and exporters.

Intensity and high tension were often the hallmarks of top CMC officials, often demanding and getting the impossible, and just as often reluctant to pay adequately for it. However, it was a good client relationship that lasted for many years.

Over the years we were consultants to eight scrap metal companies of various sizes and specialties. As they frequently had competitive aspects we had one dominant rule that applied to each of our scrap clients: "Never ask questions about any of your competitors with which we also work." If they did they were no longer a client. We in Nathan Associates leaned over backwards to be scrupulous about protecting clients' information and treating each one as if it were the only client in the business. Only once in my experience did a company ask about a competitor. Our answer was, "Sorry, you are no longer a client." The president of that company complained to Bob Nathan, who backed me up with the statement, "That is company policy. That was spelled out when you became a client."

The Institute of Scrap Iron and Steel

The Institute of Scrap Iron and Steel (ISIS), a national trade association watched over the interests of the ferrous side of the scrap industry in Washington. It was ably directed by Dr. Herschel Cutler. As RRNA represented different scrap firms across the country, we had numerous occasions to discuss projects, problems and programs with Herschel. It was a pleasure to work closely with him. He was very smart and had an open mind as well as a quick grasp of changing situations.

During the Korean 'police action,' the American iron and steel producers complained bitterly to the Department of Commerce and to their Congressional contacts that scrap exports were interfering with domestic steel production. Ferrous scrap was a needed ingredient in new steel production. And the mills had powerful political clout. With a realistic probability that an embargo would be imposed on exports of ferrous scrap, ISIS retained Nathan Associates to analyze domestic ferrous scrap demand, country wide scrap generation in response to price, and the impact of an export embargo on the domestic iron and steel industry. As I had the responsibility for the firm's scrap metal clients, the case fell on my desk.

I assembled a small statistical and economic analysis staff for this project. The firm had just hired a bright young man, Richard Blankfeld, as a research associate for me. Richard had recently earned his Master's degree in economics at Boston University. With some misgivings from some of my colleagues, I turned him loose on the ISIS project. Much of the success of the work was due to his competence and imagination.

Our approach to the problem was first to develop a method for measuring the potential volumes of scrap iron and steel through an analysis of iron and steel production over a long period of years. We then applied estimates of life expectancies to iron and steel products. We set liberal allowances for economically uncollectible scrap such as sunken ships in deep ocean waters. By measuring the actual scrap collections against this theoretical supply we were able to develop a tabulation over a long period of time showing how much more scrap it might be possible to locate and collect.

Part of the analysis consisted of a study of what price was needed to encourage the thousands of small collectors all over the country to collect scrap rather than use their trucks "to haul watermelons." We found that if the price of scrap declined significantly, haulers would rather use their trucks and time for other activity than scrap collection. An analysis of our data indicated that an export embargo might actually drive the price of scrap down thus discouraging scrap collection. The result could be less ferrous scrap for the American mills than they were presently getting unless they raised their paying prices substantially. Further, there was no evidence that any of the mills were having problems acquiring scrap supplies.

The study was entitled *The Marketed Supply of Scrap Iron and Steel*, and was released in October 1978. It received national attention and publicity. No embargo was imposed.

Our billing for the report to ISIS was an interesting example of non-economic pricing. ISIS had commissioned a major iron and steel sculpture by the artist, Marc di Suvero, as a gift "to the people of the United States." It was being erected on the grounds of the Hirshhorn Museum and Sculpture Garden of the Smithsonian in Washington, D. C. During the erection process, Dr. Cutler invited me to join him on one of his inspection visits as the huge art work was being assembled. On one of these trips, Herschel asked me, "What are you going to charge us for your study?"

"What are you paying Marc for this sculpture?" I asked.

Looking at me, Herschel said, "Two hundred and fifty thousand dollars."

"That is what the study is going to cost you."

Herschel looked at me for about thirty seconds, laughed, and said, "It's a deal."

And that is what ISIS paid Nathan Associates for the study!

American-Hawaiian Steamship Company

With the exception of bulk commodities, i.e. coal, ores, fuel oil, and grains, ocean movement of commercial cargoes is mostly by container ship. Not so forty years ago. Movement of domestic coast to coast commodities by vessel was almost entirely in 'break bulk' vessels. This was also true of international shipments.

Sam Moerman, was a prominent Washington practitioner of maritime law. He had been retained by the American Hawaiian Steamship Company to prepare a ship mortgage insurance application to be submitted to the Department of Commerce, Maritime Administration. American Hawaiian needed mortgage insurance for the construction in American shipyards of three 900 foot long container ships to serve the intercoastal trade between the U.S. east and west coasts via the Panama Canal.

For this purpose the Maritime Administration required information covering the following issues:

1. Whether the project was economically sound; and
2. What the impact of the grant would have upon other water carriers in the intercoastal trade.

Nathan Associates was retained by Moerman to prepare this part of the application. My colleague, Dr. Franz Wolf, directed the study. I was part of the research team.

In addition to developing some of the statistical data, I met with officials in the U.S. Departments of Agriculture and Commerce, as well as industrial shippers to obtain data regarding potential cargoes, and also attitudes toward containerization. Despite some obvious advantages, I found a great deal of skepticism regarding the economic and technical aspects of using containers for either intercoastal or international commerce. One officer at the Department of Agriculture referred to containerization as "a crazy idea."

The report, *The Cargo Potential for Movement by Containerized Vessels between California and the North Atlantic States*, was an eye opener. Since 1962, when this report was issued, ocean freight carriage by containers has become the worldwide norm rather than the exception.

Judith Leiber

Judith Leiber, probably the country's most imaginative designer and manufacturer of women's elegant handbags, called me one day at the suggestion of another client, Gordon Choisy of Paris, France. Leiber bags were expensive. Five thousand dollars was not an unusual price for one of her purses. (Several are in the Smithsonian.)

"Mr. Atkin, I have a problem. Fish and Wildlife wants to put me out of business." she stated. "One of its agents has gone into the Dallas Neiman Marcus store, attempted to confiscate my display of handbags, and when the clerk refused to open the display, threatened to kick in the glass."

Many of the Leiber handbags contained exotic leathers, principally alligator, lizard, and snake. Many exotics were on international lists prohibiting their use. Most American producers of leather products such as shoes, wallets, handbags, and briefcases were very careful to only use skins that were legal. There were some who would try to take advantage of 'a good buy.' Judith Leiber was not one of them.

I immediately contacted officials of the Fish and Wildlife Service of the Department of Interior in Washington, told them the story as I had heard it, and asked them to look into the situation from their point of view. At the same time, I collected all the information that I could about the agent in question; his training in exotic skin recognition, his history in the F&W Service, whether he entered the store with a search warrant, and an affidavit of the conversation between the F&W agent and the Neiman Marcus clerk. Fortunately, there were several witnesses to the occurrence, including store customers. We obtained collaborative statements from them. I also arranged for a seasoned herpetologist to examine the bags in the store and prepare a report as to whether or not in his opinion there were forbidden skins in the bags.

When all of the data were assembled, I wrote a brief to F&W protesting in the strongest terms the uncalled for strong-arm tactics of its agent. Following its own investigation, F&W concluded that its agent had acted improperly, apologized to Judith Leiber and the case was closed.

Several weeks later, Flora and I were in New York on a short theater vacation. As a courtesy we visited the Leiber work rooms. Mrs. Leiber was most gracious about my work on her behalf and expressed thanks for the fast resolution of her problems. She then surprised us by presenting Flora with a beautiful Judith Leiber bag. I protested as we had been well paid for our efforts and that her gesture was appreciated but unnecessary. Mrs. Leiber graciously replied, "You saved me a great deal of inconvenience and embarrassment. Please enjoy this."

This was hardly economics. There was a fine line between law and economics in many of our activities. They earned me the accusation "of practicing law without a license."

Expert Witness

I enjoyed working with lawyers and serving as an expert witness in trials. There were often many surprises in addition to the economic presentations for which I had been retained. Two such incidents are worth telling.

One case involved a 'wrongful death.' I had been retained to evaluate the economic loss to the plaintiff family. The dollar amount that I presented to the jury was based upon the deceased's income level, expected future earnings, had he lived, given his age and profession with appropriate adjustments for inflation and certain special circumstances. The gross figure was not questioned. However, the defendant's lawyers vigorously challenged the current value of the gross amount.

To be conservative, I had used a discount factor based upon investments in U.S. government bonds and notes. Defendant's lawyers argued strongly for a larger discount factor based upon stock market returns, an approach that would have meant a much lower cash award to the plaintiffs.

Under cross-examination, the lead attorney suggested that it was more realistic and proper to invest the funds in sound American corporations that would provide a higher rate of return than government bonds. "For example," he said, "why not invest in an old line solid company like Pennsylvania Railroad? It pays a very good dividend."

I asked the judge if the bailiff could bring me my briefcase. There was a paper in it that would answer the question asked. He agreed, but asked that I show him the paper first.

The bailiff brought my briefcase. I opened it and gave the judge that morning's *Washington Post*. He looked at it, and said, "Please proceed."

The two inch bold type headline across page one of the newspaper said "PENNSYLVANIA R.R. BANKRUPT"

It was obvious that the lawyer had not seen the morning paper. The jury totally accepted my recommendation that the discount factor for the future earnings should be the interest rate on U.S. government bonds.

Case Closed.

Another case with a surprise was in a Florida court. It involved the relationship between wholesale travel and retail travel agencies. It was 1970, before the Israel-Egyptian peace agreement.

I was on the stand. The opposing lawyer was pro-forma questioning my competence as an expert witness while examining his legal pad and not looking up at me. "Now, Mr. Atkin," he said, "you understand that this is a case involving wholesale versus retail travel."

"Yes sir," I answered.

"Now," he proceeded, "if you and your wife were to ask your client to arrange travel for you to Egypt, what would that be? Would that be wholesale or retail?"

"That would be ridiculous," I said.

Somewhat annoyed the lawyer repeated his question to me. I gave the same answer. At this point he asked the judge to request that I give a "civil" answer to his question.

The judge, who had paid attention to my statement of qualifications said, "Mr. Page, if you had been listening to Mr. Atkin when he gave his background statement instead of studying your papers, you would have heard that he was a former diplomat for the Israeli government. A request by Mr. Atkin to go to Egypt would have been ridiculous."

Case closed.

FIGURE 23: As Senior VP of Robert R. Nathan Associates, Inc. the author enjoyed many opportunities to solve problems for clients, aid Israel and contribute to community pro bono projects.

17

Pro Bono
(Do unto Others . . .)

As we 'hunt and gather' for ourselves, it is important also to 'hunt and gather' for society, to give back to the community, without regard to material compensation—for the public good—*pro Bono*. Such activities can and do return great psychological benefits.

My primary goal was never the accumulation of wealth. It was more directed toward an interesting career that would have value for me and my family and contribute to society in meaningful ways. Now, looking back over eighty plus years, I am enjoying the psychological and material rewards of my career.

In addition to working, raising a family, attending to the many chores of home ownership, and civic responsibilities, I have managed to allocate substantial time to pro bono activities—for which I have no regrets.

Group Health Association (GHA)

Can you imagine the American Medical Association (AMA) blocking doctors from seeing their own patients in hospitals? It could and did. This precipitated a fight that changed the way medical service was delivered.

In 1938–39, a small group of economists and lawyers in the U.S. Department of Agriculture banded together and organized a medical co-op in which the consumer members would control the policies, arrange for physical facilities, and hire the medical staff which would be salaried. Except for a few specialties such as dentistry and psychiatry, full medical service would be provided to members for a flat monthly fee which would vary depending upon family size. Group Health Association (GHA) was born.

The medical establishment, particularly the AMA, was anything but gracious about this radical departure from the way medical services were delivered. GHA doctors were blocked from hospitals. Their patients could be admitted, but had to be serviced by a non GHA doctor. Anti-GHA ads were placed in newspapers. AMA publications carried stinging editorials against this 'socialized medicine.' The GHA lawyers went to court. The case eventually reached the U.S. Supreme Court. The court ruled against the AMA.

As a very early member of GHA I was considered a founder. I also served on the finance, complaint, and consumer policy committees. In 1954, I was elected to the board of directors. Two years later, I was elected treasurer.

GHA was not without growing pains. Despite a captive patient list, the pharmacy was an annual money drain. Raising prices was not an option to me as treasurer. To have done so would have encouraged members to patronize outside pharmacies anxious for the business. At this point, Sam Bialek, an elementary school friend of mine and proprietor of a small chain of pharmacies, called on me. He had a proposal. With GHA's membership then about 75,000 persons, he felt that the pharmacy should show a good profit. He offered to add the pharmacy to his chain, pay a fair rental, and guarantee an annual profit to GHA.

I immediately thought, "If Sam thinks that he could make it profitable, why can't we? What were we doing wrong?" For several days I pondered this question, while discussing it quietly with other trusted board members. Several days later, I notified the accounting firm that had been auditing the records of the pharmacy since the beginning of GHA that their contract would not be renewed. Simultaneously, I retained another firm to audit the pharmacy books promptly. The head pharmacist submitted his resignation as did his number one assistant. The resignations were accepted. From that day the pharmacy was profitable.

In 1994, the board of GHA decided to sell its facilities and membership to HUMANA. After several years HUMANA sold its Washington operations to Kaiser-Permanente.

March of Dimes (MOD)

Polio, poliomyelitis, or infantile paralysis—all names for the same affliction, has afflicted mankind for centuries. Hieroglyphics in ancient Egyptian tombs indicate that polio was a known disease more than two thousand years ago. Principally affected were children, but not exclusively. The cause was a mystery. There was no cure, and it was often fatal. When not fatal, it often left the patient with crippled limbs, or unable to breath without mechanical assistance.

President Franklin D. Roosevelt, as an adult, lost the use of his legs to polio. His infirmity, frequently hidden by an accommodating staff, moved several of his influential friends to try to do something about the disease. During his presidency, the Mothers' March of Dimes was born. Symbolically, and appropriately the March was set for January 30th, Franklin Roosevelt's birthday. Mothers throughout the United States went from door to door, office to office, collecting dimes, and larger donations, to finance expanded research into the cause and cure for polio. In addition to raising public awareness of the impact of polio epidemics, private and government funds became available to find the cure. States, counties, and cities across the United States organized to participate in the March.

The successful search for protective vaccines is now history. Nationwide inoculation of all children during the late forties and early fifties virtually wiped polio off the American medical map. Unfortunately, almost at the end of the 'polio season', 1949, and before the vaccine was available, our three children and Flora contracted the dreaded disease.

It would be easy to write a book about our experiences, our mental states and concerns for the future, community reactions, and visits to various 'gurus', including the facilities at Warm Springs, Georgia, where Roosevelt spent vacations to ease his polio-damaged legs. Suffice it to say that we were fortunate in that our children and Flora had relatively mild cases—although each was left with some residuals.

Four cases in one family was a rarity. The media across America as well as in Europe, picked up the story, embellished it, and often 'reported' interviews with Flora and me that never happened. Aside from the media insensitivity, there were many wonderful letters, notes and acts of encouragement and well wishes. Total strangers offered assistance of various types, including financial. Time and space doesn't permit a total report. However, I do want to mention one particular telephone call. It was from Henry Kaiser, the world renowned California industrialist who revolutionized methods of building cargo ships for the war effort. Mr. Kaiser invited our whole family to come to his Kabat-Kaiser Foundation in California for treatment. He made it clear that the invitation included transportation, housing, medical services, and that we were to be his guests. I thanked him profusely, pointed out that I had job responsibilities in the Washington, D.C. area. He replied that he had checked out my background and he had a position in his industrial organization for me. I expressed my thanks, but indicated that we would not take his offer.

Thirty years later, Flora wrote a play, *Hold That Tiger*, based upon the experience. It was produced by Connecticut College, performed as staged readings by American Association of Theater and Education, and by the Post Polio Society in Washington. This was her catharsis.

After passage of the contagious period, I began to be active on the Montgomery County MOD planning committee. In 1951, I was elected chairman for the county drive. We were very successful in raising a larger amount that year than had been raised previously.

Democrat Precinct Chairman

In 1948, Flora and I and our young son Joseph, moved from Washington, D.C. to Silver Spring, Montgomery County, Maryland. A by-product of our move was that we could vote in local, state, and national elections. Silver Spring was the bedroom mecca for young educated professionals, many of whom had come to the area with the New Deal's expanding agencies. Local politics, not a choice in non-voting Washington, D.C., became a natural outlet for ideas and energy. In 1949, along with many other young professionals who were dubbed 'the young turks', I became active in the largest voting precinct, 13-12, in the county, This political unit had been one of the strongholds of the Col. E. Brooke Lee political machine. By 1951, I was elected precinct chairman. Our home, painted white brick, became known as the precinct White House.

Within a few years, we 'young turks' in our area as well as like-minded groups in other precincts were campaigning strenuously. We knocked on doors, set up meetings, found inspirational speakers and upset the Lee machine, and successfully elected our candidates to the county council and the school board. In 1956, the Atkin family moved to the western part of the county and I gave up the chairmanship.

The experience taught me that while local politics was hard work, organization and persistence could make a difference.

Potomac Cooperative Federation

Through my GHA activities, in 1956, I was appointed to the board of the Potomac Cooperative Federation, an association of thirteen cooperatives serving over 100,000 persons in the District of Columbia, Maryland, and Virginia. In addition to GHA, other members included Rochdale Cooperatives (grocery stores and gasoline stations), Potomac Federation of Co-op Schools, Community Arts Association, and the Pan American Cooperative. The Federation also sponsored Nationwide Insurance Co., the nation's largest cooperative insurance company. In September, I was elected president of the Federation which gave me automatic membership on the Nationwide Insurance Co.'s advisory board, meeting in Columbus, Ohio.

American Veterans Committee (AVC)

"Citizens First, Veterans Second," the motto of AVC, appealed to me. I had not intended to join any special interest group after receiving my Honorable Discharge from the Marine Corps Reserve. But I did join AVC in 1944, as I found many like-minded friends had joined, and I sympathized with its views on current problems of the day. Many of the members were middle to senior level policy people in President Roosevelt's expanded government agencies. I became chairman of the membership committee of the Washington chapter. The president and a leading policy maker was Bob Nathan, whose consulting firm I later joined.

AVC was a small liberal organization open to all races and creeds. Its members believed in and worked for political and social equality in the United States. In its club house on New Hampshire Ave., N.W., AVC was proud to have the only restaurant in the entire city open to African Americans as well as whites. AVC was especially active in the fight with the National Theater on E street in Washington, to allow tickets to be sold to blacks. The National Theater, then the only live drama theater in Washington, was strictly segregated. NO BLACKS. AVC mounted a campaign to break this situation. Pickets paraded daily in front of the theater. Support was sought and found in the *Washington Post* newspaper. Church groups were approached to help in the fight for equality. Some did, many did not. Rather than open its doors to mixed audiences, the National closed, and stayed closed for several years. When it reopened it was reopened to all. I was proud to have had a part in that struggle.

During the period the National was 'dark,' there were violent discussions between two competing sectors of the organization; one, the liberal democrats who had started and built the organization, and the other, the johnny-come-lately communists who attempted to hijack AVC. In a national convention in Milwaukee, Wisconsin, in 1947, the fight was bitter and venomous with many all night meetings and strategy sessions. The insurgent group, very bright, very leftist veterans, attended George Washington University. Sadly, from my perspective, they were mostly of Jewish descent. The communists were defeated, but the effort almost wrecked AVC as a national institution. I am pleased to have been a member of the anti-communist sector of the Washington delegation.

AVC limped along with its aging members, attracting very few new veterans from later wars. It never regained the political clout that was enjoyed before Milwaukee, but it still makes points in various policy arenas.

District of Columbia Auxiliary Police

During the years just preceding the U.S. entry into World War II,

CHAPTER 17 / *Pro Bono (Do unto Others . . .)*

and the war years, if one was not in the service one tried to give time and effort to a civilian activity supporting the war effort. I enrolled in the District of Columbia Auxiliary Police. Because of my interest and experience on the water I was assigned to the Harbor precinct on Maine Avenue and given a billyclub, a black raincoat, and a gold badge. The badge had inscribed across its face "Lieutenant." This was my rank as commander of the volunteer auxiliary police of the precinct. Our responsibilities were, with the regular force, to patrol the Potomac and Anacostia rivers rendering help where needed, and particularly to observe activity under and around the various bridges spanning the two rivers. We police auxiliarists were not armed and had no arrest authority.

The harbor precinct had a variety of small boats. The largest, a 55 foot tug, had a 100 horsepower diesel engine. This motor, about the size of a full size family sedan, and weighing close to 7,000 pounds, compares with present diesel equipment of about 250 horsepower which weighs less than a thousand pounds.

Very little occurred to require much activity on the part of the auxiliarists, or indeed, of the regulars. It was more watching and waiting than action. I also found the company of the paid force of the D.C. Harbor Precinct, less than stimulating. But it did provide a little opportunity to be on the water, and to learn a bit more about boatmanship.

Selby Bay Yacht Club (SBYC)

In the late 1950s my close friend, Herman Taetle and I bought a much used, and abused, 24 foot wooden boat. It was equipped with a Ford Model T motor which ran surprisingly well. However, the seams along the side, fortunately above the waterline, had gaps that one could see through and any size wave had little trouble coming through. The vessel also sank at its dock in the Rhode River several times. It didn't take us long to have had enough of that boat. We sold it, bought a 24 foot Steelcraft, and became members of Selby Bay Yacht Club, on a small bay off the South River, about six miles south of Annapolis. It was the only club on the Chesapeake Bay then that accepted Jewish members. Its membership included Jewish and Gentile boaters—a good mix over the years.

During Flora's and my over fifty years of SBYC membership we bought and sold about twelve different craft, going up to a 42 foot trawler, and back down to a 31 foot Tiara before becoming non-resident members in 1999. During those active years, I was elected to the "bridge," the board of directors, and in 1978 was elected Commodore. As commodore, I succeeded in having individual electric meters installed for each slip. This was not too popular with the owners of the large vessels which used considerably more power than the average boat. Until meters were installed the annual electric bill was divided by the total number of slips and each slip holder was billed the same amount, never mind whether the boat was twenty-four feet long or fifty.

Given my frequent trips to Israel, members of the club asked Flora and me, in 1978, to arrange and conduct a trip to Israel. This we did with great success. With ex U.S. Army Chaplain Walter Zanger as our guide, we traveled the length and breadth of the country. With a Bible in one hand and a copy of Josephus in the other, Walter made the rocks, hills and valleys of Israel come alive for us. The Haifa Yacht Club and the Tel Aviv Yacht Club, as well as the Israeli navy, royally entertained us. We had many private sessions with leading government and business personalities, including Teddy Kollek, Reuben Hecht, Yitzhak Shamir, then Speaker of the Knesset, (Parliament) and the consul general of the American Embassy. Again, in 1980, Flora and I lead another group from SBYC to Israel and this visit included Egypt. This trip gave our tour group a chance to compare life in Egypt and in Israel, and provided memorable experiences for all hands.

We have many fond memories of this very active family club—cruises, fishing, sailing, club house parties, and personal friendships. Flora and I felt that the boating and other club activities contributed substantially to enriching our children's lives.

United States Coast Guard Auxiliary (USCGA)

SBYC was the base for Flotilla 24, U.S. Coast Guard Auxiliary. Members of the flotilla were all members of SBYC. I also joined the flotilla.

FIGURE 24: Commander Maury relaxes on duty

The principal missions of the Auxiliary, a civilian, volunteer arm of the U.S. Coast Guard are boating safety and education. It is not necessary to own a boat to be active in the Auxiliary. It is necessary to have a solid interest in its missions and to devote some considerable time to carrying them out.

My particular areas of interest were safety patrols, vessel inspection, and teaching small boat handling to community classes. For almost nine months of the year my boat, with a trained auxiliary crew, and I would be available for weekend patrols between Annapolis and the West River on the western shore of the Chesapeake Bay; and between Bloody Point Light and the east end of the Bay Bridge on the eastern shore. Each year I was responsible for six to ten such patrols. The Coast Guard paid for the fuel used, and a small, but inadequate, amount toward crew meals. Tours of duty were for at least eight hours, but if we were on a 'case', the time could exceed the eight hours. Cases consisted of dead batteries, out of fuel, or grounding. Less frequently, accidents, drowning, fire, sudden sickness, and reckless operation of a boat would require an auxiliary patrol's attention. While we had no police authority, generally the boating public cooperated with our patrolling vessels.

Mel Foer, my very close boyhood friend, and Irv Title were my favorite crew. Both auxiliarists and good seamen, they knew what to do on the boat and on patrol. Another favorite in the Auxiliary was Charles "Buck" Walck, who incidentally received his first training in classes held in our home. Buck was a bear of a man, about six feet four, close to three hundred pounds. He was a strict instructor, examiner, and mentor. While he was tough to the point that he frightened new members, actually he was a pussycat. He was devoted to the Auxiliary and put in many thousands of hours of volunteer time. Unfortunately he crossed the bar in 2002. Almost the full complement of the Annapolis and Baltimore Coast Guard regulars, as well as many auxiliarists attended his funeral at Arlington Cemetery.

The inspection program, voluntary on the part of the boat owner, checked vessels for state and federal required and recommended equipment and documentation. If the vessel met all equipment and document requirements, a decal indicating compliance was issued. Boat owners wanted these decals because it meant that their vessels had complied with specific safety standards. I earned many awards for the most inspections for our flotilla, and sometimes for our division also.

In one case, I offered to examine a boat at the gas dock in Marco Island, Florida. The owner, in a hurry to get to the fishing grounds, said he did not have time for an inspection. I mentioned that an inspection would not take any longer than it would take to fill his gas tank. I did not tell him that he could not fill his tank while I was conducting the inspection. His wife asked him to have the examination.

Grumbling about the loss of fishing time, he agreed. The inspection revealed a dangerous leak in his gasoline line. I pointed it out, and told him that had he started his engine, he would probably have blown up the boat and possibly himself. He went white, thanked me profusely, and definitely did no fishing that day.

Yearly, the CGA held seamanship training classes. I enjoyed teaching small boat handling and marlin spike (knots and their uses).

In order to take responsibility in each Auxiliary activity area, it was necessary for the auxiliarists to have attended training courses, and to have passed exams on the subjects. I qualified in communication, small boat handling, operations, and vessel examinations. I also earned the coveted coxswain rating. Auxiliarist boat captains operating under Coast Guard orders were required to have this level of training.

For various reasons Flotilla 24 dwindled in membership. This was also true of another nearby unit. CG headquarters decided to merge the two flotillas, and form Flotilla 72, effective January 1, 1965. I was registered as a charter member. In 1977, I was elected Commander of Flotilla 72.

When I had joined the Auxiliary, its members were all Caucasian. Flotilla 72 was the first unit to train and enroll African-Americans. Flora and I hosted several integrated basic seamanship classes in our home. The Coast Guard and the Auxiliary are now fully integrated.

During the years of my active service, I accumulated enough award certificates to paper all four walls of a good sized room. I also received awards and medals, some of which I had doubts about whether I had earned, such as the Persian Gulf medal. Most, I know I earned.

In 2002, the flotilla presented me with a clock mounted in a walnut case. The inscription stated that it was for 40 years of dedicated service to the Coast Guard Auxiliary from "Floatilla 72." I would not let the spelling be corrected. The Auxiliary membership was a valuable experience. It helped me hone my skills at boat handling, provided opportunities for hands-on public service, and brought me into contact with many wonderful dedicated men and women, all interested in making the water safer.

In 2003, I retired from the U.S. Coast Guard Auxiliary. Division VII recognized my retirement with a citation and a gift of a second clock. Weems & Plath Martinique Flag Quartz Ship's clock for "41 Years of Superior Performance."

Jewish Community Council (JCC)

For ten years, 1978–1988, I served on the board of the Jewish Community Council, the coordinating body and community relations and public affairs arm for almost all Jewish organizations in the Washington Area. Executive directors during my tenure were Danny Mann, Mike Berenbaum, and Rabbi Sydney Schwartz. My principal activity was chairing the public relations committee. In November, 2003, I was given the Council's Annual Community Service Award.

Jewish Council for the Aging (JCA)

Recognizing that older people frequently need assistance to maintain levels of independence, and that family members often need assistance in caring for the elderly, in 1973, Julius Sankin, a friend and neighbor, organized the Council for the Aging of Greater Washington. JCA programs for the elderly today include Transportation, Fitness 55, Senior Aid, Adult Day Care, Home Care, Retirement Planning, Senior Net Computer Learning Centers, and Senior Employment Services. With a paid staff of 50, and 500 active volunteers, JCA serves almost 30,000 senior citizens a year.

At the urging of my friend, Sam Gorlitz, then president of JCA, I became an active member in 1985, and was soon elected to the board.

Only partially funded by the Jewish Federation of Greater Washington, most of JCA's operating funds had to come from other sources. For several years I directed JCA's largest fundraiser, an annual raffle of a new four door sedan. The irony of this is that I am philosophically "anti raffle." However, I was able to overcome my bias and raise money to fund JCA's various programs providing 'Resources for Aging Well.' Joyce Reisman and Jeanette Okin, both volunteers, deserve most of the credit for the success of the raffles.

Recognition of my activities resulted in being named a "Life Member" of the board, and, in 1998, I was awarded the "Rosalie and Leon Gerber Distinguished Senior Award."

Foundation for Jewish Studies (FJS)

A generous, anonymous grant of $1,000,000 enabled Joshua Haberman, Rabbi Emeritus of Washington Hebrew Congregation to establish the Foundation for Jewish Studies. The purpose was to develop new opportunities for adults, using local, national, and international sources, to expand their knowledge and understanding of Judaism— its history and philosophy.

Many of the lectures and classes are free. However, reasonable charges are made for group studies abroad, special retreats, open university classes, lunch and learn sessions. In addition, in order to maintain a high academic program level, donations from private individuals are necessary and solicited. No funds are received from the Jewish Federation of Greater Washington.

I have been a participant in its programs since the Foundation started in 1983. During the past several years I have been an active member of the board of directors, assistant treasurer, and treasurer. For myself, a Foundation trip to Spain, a week in England at Cambridge University, week end retreats, and lunch and learn sessions opened new vistas for me regarding the economic, social, and political history of the Jews.

National Defense Executive Reserve, U.S. Department of Commerce

During times of national emergency it was often necessary for the government to allocate scarce material and equipment to insure that there would be an adequate supply for military needs as well as to meet civilian needs. This required a cadre of experienced industrial executives, economists and lawyers from the civilian economy.

FIGURE 25 Maury receiving certificate of designation, NDER, from Wilson Sweeney, U.S. Department of Commerce, 1968

To insure that there was a reliable, trained and ready cadre to fill these professional positions, the Federal Emergency Management Administration organized National Defense Executive Reserve chapters in the defense agencies. I enrolled in the chapter at the Department of Commerce. The training schedules called for one or two days a month of active duty operational exercises.

My candid reaction to the training and the personnel being trained was that if the country had had to depend upon us, the country would have been in real trouble.

In 1997, the Executive Reserve was 'discharged.' I received a bronze medallion recognizing my service.

Additionally

My community service has also included serving on the executive of the Committee for Accuracy in Mid-East Reporting (CAMERA), chairman of Adas Israel Congregation's first Shem Tov award committee, the board of America-Israel Public Affairs Committee (AIPAC), participant in Big Brothers Organization, and member of Bannockburn Cooperative Development Committee. More recently I have joined the boards of the Golan (Israel) Fund, and the Robert Nathan Memorial Foundation.

᎐

Would I do it over again? Yes, but probably with some minor modifications such as concentrating on fewer organizations and possibly accepting greater responsibility within an organization. While I gave much time and effort to public activities, I gained more than I gave, psychologically and spiritually.

While these community activities took much time, my family responsibilities were not neglected.

18

Fascinating Personalities

A MONG THE FRINGE benefits of my efforts in Israel, was the opportunity to meet and work with many of the Israeli builders and movers of the state. The following are a few anecdotal incidents, as I remember them, about some of those.

David Ben Gurion

It was February, 1967. I had been in Israel about a week when I received a telephone call. "Could you make a trip to Sde Bokr for a visit with David Ben Gurion?" The call had come from his secretary, a Mr. Kimche. Ben Gurion, the architect of the new state and its first prime minister during the hectic and feverish days of 1948 to 1953, was the George Washington of Israel. He was in retirement then in Sde Boker, in the Negev south of Beer Sheva. For a short time during 1954 he had 'retired' but returned as prime minister until 1963. It is no exaggeration to say that without BG's steadfast leadership and iron-will as secretary-general of the pre-state Jewish Agency, there would have been no state of Israel. His secretary said that the PM had heard of the work I had done for Hadassah, and would like to talk to me. I was thrilled. We agreed upon a meeting place and time, the place being Sde Boker. As I suspected that the question of a grant for one of Mr. Ben Gurion's favorite projects might come up. I asked if Dr. David Frost could accompany me. No problem.

In early February, 1967, I had received a call from an assistant administrator of AID's medical and school grant programs, Dr. David Frost. He informed me that he was going to Israel to inspect some of the facilities that had received AID grants. As the facilities, such as the Hadassah hospital and schools, were those with which I had been instrumental in securing the grants, some of my clients with Israeli interests, such as Hadassah and American Mizrachi Women felt that I should be in Israel when Frost was there. I agreed.

FIGURE 26:   In Ben Gurion's study in Sde Bokr

FIGURE 27:   Maury and Ben Gurion examining a document

David Frost was a pleasant enough person to be with. Although Jewish, he had little background knowledge of Judaism, knew almost nothing about Zionism and the dream of a Jewish homeland. In addition to my proudly showing off Jerusalem and the various institutions in which he had a direct concern, I undertook a low level educational campaign. My main tactic was to make sure that the officials of the institutions, and of the Israel government with whom he met were, without pushing, able to fill in a lot of historical and Biblical background for him. Secondly, I wanted Frost to be aware of the tremendous advances that had been made in the country in such a short period of time. Some of the advances were the direct result of the AID grants. Frost recognized this and appreciated it.

Two days after Kimche's phone call to me, with a rented car, Frost and I were on our way to Sde Bokr. I drove from Jerusalem through Bethlehem, Hebron, and Beer Sheva to Sde Bokr. The drive down, about 160 kilometers, was beautiful with the topography and scenery changing constantly.

We arrived at the appointed time. Kimche answered our knock on the door. He started to apologize for our having made the trip and explained that the prime minister was not feeling well and could not see anyone. However, before the full sentence was completed a voice in the back said, "I'll see them. Vera isn't here." It was David Ben Gurion. After greeting and welcoming us he explained that he did have a slight fever and that Vera, his wife, was very protective. He did look a bit flushed, and was wearing a heavy red woolen bathrobe.

His office/library was covered floor to ceiling with shelves of books—Hebrew, Yiddish, English, Russian, classical Greek, German, Polish and probably more in other languages. Books were also stacked on the floor, on chairs, and on anything else that would support some. Ben Gurion's small cottage was situated near the rim of a large crater, and was well into the Negev. It was a very modest building with Ben Gurion's library/study/office, a bedroom and bath, an entry foyer, and a kitchen with a small table and chairs—all comfortable, but nothing elaborate.

As I suspected, he was anxious to talk about the University of the Negev. This was still to be built. Using details from the Bible, BG, as he was affectionately called, talked at some length about the special desert disciplines that would be studied and researched at this school. He pointed out references in the Bible to flora, fauna, and minerals in the Negev. And of course, he wanted to know what grants might be available for 'his' school. The University of the Negev was established a few years later. Renamed Ben Gurion University, it is a pillar of research and scholarship in the Mideast.

Exploring AID grant criteria, neither David Frost nor I could find any AID grant programs for which the Negev school could qualify. For example, one of the major AID programs available, and the one under which I had obtained a five million dollar grant for Hadassah, was AID to American Schools and Hospitals Abroad. This was part of Public Law 416. This Act requires that the American organization control and direct the overseas facility, and also have a physical presence in the foreign country to supervise the school's or hospital's activities. Clearly, the structure of the University of the Negev could not meet this requirement, among others.

After several hours of wonderful conversation, the PM suggested that it was time for lunch. Frost and I thought that this was the indication that the meeting was over, and started to say our goodbyes. BG would have none of this. He insisted that we stay for lunch. We were delighted to agree, but wondered who was going to prepare the lunch. Kimche had disappeared, and there was only the three of us there.

We all went into the kitchen and while Frost and I drank juices, Ben Gurion prepared delicious salad lunches for the three of us. It was a delightful experience.

About an hour later we insisted that we had to leave. We wanted very much to get back to Jerusalem before dark as winter days are short in Israel. There is really no dusk, just daylight then darkness. We rushed back to Jerusalem before night fell, exhilarated and full of wonderful memories.

I had bought and brought with us Moshe Pearlman's book, *Ben Gurion Looks Back*. As BG was autographing the book for me, copies of which were on a nearby chair, he asked, "Is this one of mine or one you brought?" I replied that it had been bought in Jerusalem. "Good," he said as he wrote my name, signed his name, and dated it, in Hebrew.

Teddy Kollek

Teddy Kollek, the long time legendary mayor of Jerusalem, was one of the most fascinating and versatile personalities that I met during my whole career.

As a young man Teddy immigrated to Palestine from Austria in the early forties. He became active in politics and in the Haganah. It did not take him long to become an aide to David Ben Gurion, then secretary general of the Jewish Agency—the Jewish self-government structure in Palestine.

In addition to being a super diplomat Teddy was a cracker-jack salesman. In the mid forties he was sent to the States to raise desperately needed funds for the Haganah. Possessed of rare charm and an equally rare smile it was almost impossible to resist his pleas. He could also be tough when the occasion demanded. His twinkling blue eyes could turn hard. An excellent raconteur, he was able to turn awkward situations into victories by telling a story—often Biblical, often ribald.

Following World War II, scrap metal, ferrous and non-ferrous, became scarce, and market prices escalated. Accordingly, the American scrap metal dealers, many if not most being Jewish, were enjoying great prosperity.

It was with this group that Teddy was very effective in raising funds for the Jewish Agency, which had the responsibility of moving Jewish survivors of the Holocaust out of the camps in Europe to Palestine. Once in Palestine, they needed food, shelter, training for a new life and a new culture. The Agency also raised funds for the defense of the Jewish settlements—for Haganah.

Teddy visited various cities in the U.S., got the local Jewish community to arrange for private meetings of five to fifteen prominent and wealthy Jewish leaders—making sure that there was good representation from the scrap and liquor industries.

Teddy made a pitch about conditions in Palestine, the work that the Agency was doing and why a great deal of money was needed. Near the end of the meeting, Teddy locked the door to the room, and ask the men to unbutton their belts and take out their money belts. He would make a statement about how the scrap-induced sales resulted in large cash transactions, many questionable. He pled that the cash in the money belts be donated.

It was amazing how thousands of dollars came out of the money belts. Teddy had a knack of making the donors feel that he was doing them a favor by taking their money.

BEFORE INDEPENDENCE

I had met Teddy Kollek in 1946 prior to the establishment of the State of Israel. When I decided that I wanted to get involved with the Jewish effort in Palestine I visited Gottlieb Hammer. He sent me to meet Teddy. This was my introduction to the activity in the Hotel Fourteen. Under Teddy's direction and inspiration a small group of young, dedicated Jewish men and women, almost all from Palestine, were buying, getting as gifts when possible, a wide variety of goods, both hardware and software, urgently needed by the growing farms, villages, and the Jewish defense forces. Hotel 14, as the operation became known, was also responsible for the safe shipment of the material collected to Jewish Palestine. These operations required much ingenuity and often skills that were new to the 'operators.' If one of the group developed an idea that Teddy liked, his usual comment was, "Okay, do it." If the reply to this was "I don't know how" Teddy's answer was "Learn." And learn we did!

At that time, still many months before Independence, my function with the Hotel 14 group was to keep in touch, get to know operating members, and to be helpful with suggestions and advice when possible. However, when on May 14, 1948 Israel attained statehood and I became a member of the Washington Embassy staff, my real work with Teddy's group changed. I became the liaison between the Israeli diplomats, Materials for Israel, operated by 'Rusty' Jarcko, and U.S. government offices—excluding the U.S. State Department.

MAYOR OF JERUSALEM

After the State of Israel was declared, Kollek became a personal aide to David Ben Gurion, Israel's first prime minister. Following this he ran for and was elected mayor of Jerusalem, a post which he held for almost forty years. During his tenure he did much to beautify and develop cultural activities in the city. Teddy was a gracious host to political, artistic and tourist groups from all over the world. He truly made Jerusalem one of the outstanding capitals of the world. He also went out of his way to cultivate the Arab population of Jerusalem and make them feel that they had a stake in the city's development.

THE WALLS CAME DOWN

During Israel's War of Independence the Old City of Jerusalem was occupied by the Jordanian Legion. A few hundred feet away, but well within rifle shot, was the western, or new, city occupied by the Jews. The No Man's Land separating the two sections, a distance of possibly two hundred feet, was marked by two concrete walls two to three feet thick, each about forty feet wide, and about thirty feet high. These walls effectively divided the old city from the new city. In 1952, after a truce was enacted, it was decided to tear down the walls. Teddy invited me to join him to watch the walls being destroyed. It was an exciting few moments. Well placed dynamite, ignited on signal, soon made these awesome barriers piles of rubble.

The street on which the walls were built, Rehov Mamilla, led almost directly toward the Jaffa Gate of the Old City walls. On one side of this street were deserted stone houses which had been abandoned by the Arab occupants during the fighting. The other side was open toward the Old City walls. It was almost surrealistic to walk around the walls while a Jordanian soldier, patrolling the Old City walls a few hundred feet away, watched, and occasionally pointed his gun toward the Jewish side.

Destruction of these walls also signified hopes for a broadening of relations between east and west Jerusalem and a united Jerusalem. The Rehov Mamilla buildings, which had no water, nor other utilities. were quickly occupied, illegally, by sephardic Jewish immigrants from Arab countries. Despite the presence of Jordanian soldiers less than one hundred feet away, many children were playing in the street in front of these units. The area is now a very upscale housing, shopping and restaurant mall.

ARMED GUARD

On one of my trips to Jerusalem, probably in the early sixties, Shosh, the mayor's long-time, incomparable, and efficient secretary phoned.

She asked if I could be available the next morning to accompany two prominent anthropologists to a dig at Revivim, a kibbutz in the northern Negev. Of course, I said "Yes."

At seven A.M. the next morning, in the mayor's office, Teddy introduced me to two Americans, a Dr. William Foxwell Albright and another Ph.D. At the time, the names meant nothing to me. Later I learned that Albright was one of the most illustrious anthropologists in the United States.

As we prepared to leave for the day's trip Teddy beckoned me into his private office, handed me a small Berreta automatic, 8mm. "Why," I asked.

"Just in case. Don't let the Americans know that you have it. If you come back after dark, it may be needed."

"Thanks a lot," I said. "But there is no clip in it."

"Oh, the driver has the clips, and will give them to you if you have to come back in the dark."

While at the dig site, I picked up a piece of dark colored rock about three inches long. One long edge was thin and sharp, the other edge about an eighth of an inch thick. As I started to throw it to see how the strange shape would act, Dr. Albright stopped me. He said that what I had was a paleolithic razor. We left Revivim after a most interesting day in which I learned more about a dig than I thought I ever wanted to know. I have never tried shaving with the 'razor.' I still have it, and we did not come back in the dark.

THE PLEDGE

I was preparing to leave for one of my frequent trips to Israel. Charles Slater's book, *The Pledge*, was just about to be released. I was able to get several pre-release copies to take to Israel with me.

Arriving in Jerusalem, I called Teddy's office and told Shosh that I had the book for Teddy and would bring it by the office the next day. "Fine," she said.

At five o'clock the next morning a pounding on my hotel door awakened me. It was Teddy. "Put on a robe, let's go to my office where we can talk and have some coffee. And bring the book with you." It felt strange walking through the King David Hotel in a bathrobe with the mayor to his official car. But I learned that this was pure Kollek.

SBYC SPEAKER

In 1979 and in 1981, at the request of members of Selby Bay Yacht Club, I led two tours to Israel for about thirty club members. The 1981 trip included a tour to Egypt.

When I was setting up the programs, I wrote to Teddy, asking him to speak to the group about his vision for the future of Jerusalem. He agreed.

We met in a side chamber of the mayor's office. Coffee was served. Teddy came in, greeted the group and announced, "I never speak to tour groups. But I could not say 'no' to Maury." The SBYC members were duly impressed. Teddy proceeded to give a most impressive talk and lead a discussion based on questions from the group.

FLUORIDE

On my visits to his office the mayor sometimes used the opportunity to get my reaction to something that was bothering him, or to a new problem that had just developed. One such instance was the question of fluorine additives to the city's drinking water.

For a relatively small investment that would pay substantial dividends in better health for all citizens, a fluorine program could be installed that would add just enough of this chemical to almost eliminate cavities in children's teeth. This was a program being adapted in cities throughout the world.

But there were objections, not from dentists fearing loss of patients and business, but from the ultra-religious sectors of the community. They were concerned about adding chemicals, possibly non-kosher, to the water that they drank. They argued that it was contrary to religious law. Another problem was that the approved budget had no allocation for the program, and Teddy wanted to install it as soon as possible. He needed $250,000 to install a system.

We discussed possible funding sources, including local Israeli businessmen. We also talked about the religious aspect. Teddy thought he could handle this without too much of an uproar.

I am not sure where he found the funds. I never asked if he approached some of the businessmen that I suggested. But he did install the system. After a few years it was clear that it had made a difference in the incidence of cavities among the youth.

JERUSALEM FOUNDATION

Teddy's vision was to make Jerusalem the most attractive city in the world. To this end he established the Jerusalem Foundation. Its purpose was to raise funds to clean up the slums, renovate where necessary, beautify everywhere, and build parks throughout the city. The Foundation also established a series of annual cultural activities that became the envy of the artistic world—art galleries, museums, a world class symphony orchestra, and symposia of every discipline.

It was the rare visit to Israel that I did not spend some time with the mayor. Teddy was well aware of my activities with a wide variety of Israeli institutions; government, philanthropic, and private. He was not adverse to taking advantage of these contacts to discuss or promote some of his ideas and programs. He always made me feel welcome in his office, as did his staff.

Yitzhak Rabin, General, Ambassador,
Prime Minister and Fisherman!

In 1968, Yitzhak Rabin came to the United States as the Israeli ambassador. As the general credited with winning the 1967 Six Day War that opened the Sinai, the Golan Heights, the West Bank, and most important of all, Jerusalem, to Israel, his reputation preceded him.

After his service as ambassador to Washington, Rabin years later became the youngest prime minister of Israel. In September, 1985, he signed the ill-fated Oslo Peace Agreement on the White House lawn along with Yassir Arafat, leader of the Palestine Authority. Prime Minister Rabin was assassinated by a disgruntled Jewish religious student on November 4, 1995, in Tel Aviv.

When he first came to America, Ambassador Rabin, a serious chain smoker, was taciturn, not given to small talk and spoke poor English. He was considered somewhat standoffish and cold by the Washington Jewish community. However, as he rapidly mastered English idiom and presentation, as well as developing a better than average tennis game he became quite popular in Washington and around the country.

I was fortunate at the time to be very much involved with Israeli economic matters. Accordingly I was a frequent visitor at the Israel

Embassy. Many of these visits involved consultations with Yitzhak. Over time we became rather good friends. Several times I would arrange for him to meet at our home ambassadors from West African countries that had broken relations with Israel after the '67 war. I was also, on occasion, the conduit for private messages from these ambassadors to Rabin.

As ambassador he was especially effective with the military at the Pentagon, and with the Nixon White House. He enjoyed ready access to both. Despite Nixon's known snide remarks about Jews, Rabin had great admiration for the man, and considered him to be the best friend that Israel had ever had in the White House.

His admiration caused him to make a major diplomatic and political faux pas during President Nixon's 1972 campaign for reelection. Yitzhak made a speech calling for Nixon's reelection. All hell broke out in the print and wire media. There were big headlines across the country. News anchors and commentators had a feeding frenzy. The State Department was beside itself. For an ambassador of any country to get involved in American elections was a definite no-no. To say that the media was anxious to reach the ambassador for 'clarification', for a statement, for an interview, would be a major understatement.

The night after his undiplomatic statement, Leah Rabin, Yitzhak's wife, phoned me at home. I believe it was a Thursday evening.

"Maury, what are you doing this weekend?" she asked.

"I will probably go fishing, and putter around with my boat." I replied.

"Could you take Yitzhak on the boat with you for a few days?"

Of course I could and did.

The next day Yitzhak, and his young son Yuval joined me and Barry O'Brien, a youngster, about Yuval's age. As a member of the Big Brothers Organization I had taken Barry under my wing. The Big Brothers provided adult male companionship and guidance for young boys who have no other adult males, brother or father, to turn to.

The four of us went to Selby Bay Yacht Club where our 42-foot cruiser, the *Serenade*, was docked.

We had provisions for four days; food, drink, fish bait, tackle, reading material and Scotch. usually I did not permit smoking on board. However, for Yitzhak Rabin I was prepared to make an exception.

The boys had the forward stateroom. Yitzhak and I used the aft stateroom. He volunteered to do the cooking. I accepted.

While the media was fruitlessly trying to reach Rabin, we cruised the South, Severn, and West Rivers in addition to the Chesapeake Bay. The fishing was just so so. But the cruising and swimming were great. One evening we tied up at Carol and Isadore Lubin's dock on the South River. Isadore, who had been U.S. Commissioner of Labor Statistics under President Roosevelt, and was now an advisor to the United Israel Appeal, had a summer home on the river. With guests not connected to any media we had a lively evening of discussion and dinner. We also consumed more than an adequate quantity of Scotch.

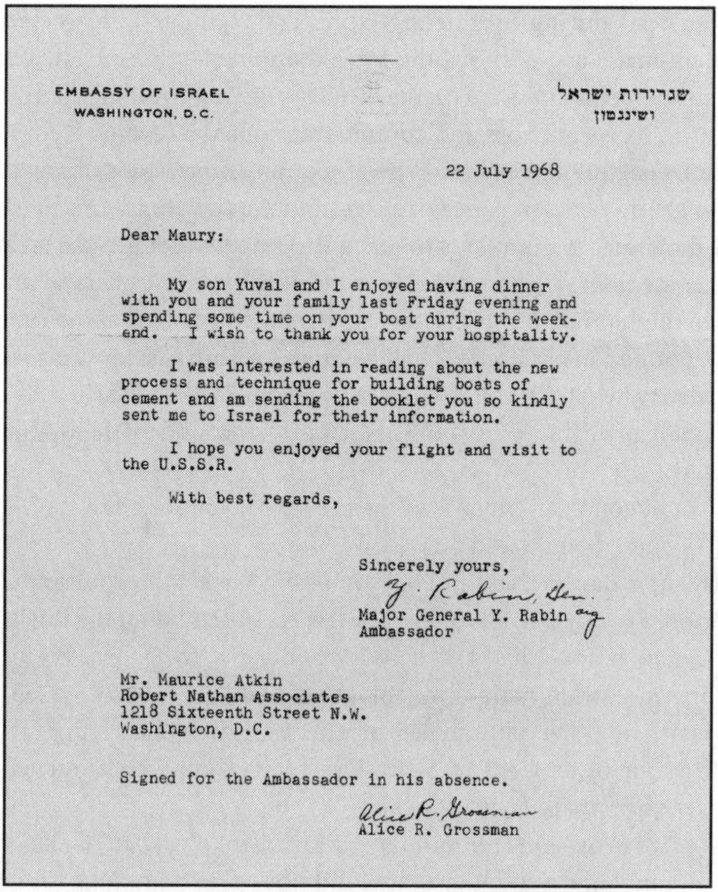

EMBASSY OF ISRAEL
WASHINGTON, D.C.

שגרירות ישראל
וׁשינגטון

22 July 1968

Dear Maury:

My son Yuval and I enjoyed having dinner with you and your family last Friday evening and spending some time on your boat during the week-end. I wish to thank you for your hospitality.

I was interested in reading about the new process and technique for building boats of cement and am sending the booklet you so kindly sent me to Israel for their information.

I hope you enjoyed your flight and visit to the U.S.S.R.

With best regards,

Sincerely yours,

Y. Rabin, Gen.
Major General Y. Rabin
Ambassador

Mr. Maurice Atkin
Robert Nathan Associates
1218 Sixteenth Street N.W.
Washington, D.C.

Signed for the Ambassador in his absence.

Alice R. Grossman
Alice R. Grossman

FIGURE 28: Letter of thanks from Ambassador Rabin

At one point in Yitzhak's escape from the media he asked to use the ship marine radio to call the embassy. I showed him how to use it, no cell phones then, and paid no further attention. Several days after the call, which was almost all in Hebrew except for the ship to shore connection, I received a 'Violation Citation' from the Federal Communication Commission for improper use of the marine radio. Yitzhak had made the entire call on emergency Channel 16 instead of shifting to another channel. An explanatory letter to FCC brought an 'excused.'

The next day, our last on this voyage, we fished for Norfolk Spot just off the Thomas Point lighthouse in the Chesapeake. With the sun beginning to hang low, we prepared to head back to Selby Bay Yacht Club. Yitzhak volunteered to pull up the anchor. I fired up the engines, and slowly moved up on the anchor while Yitzhak pulled. Simultaneously, I was taking movies of the operation for posterity.

It was no great deal to raise the anchor. But as it cleared the water's surface there was an unusual appendage on one of the flukes. A fish, a large Norfolk Spot was impaled on the fluke. This was the first and only time that in all my years of fishing I have seen a fish caught on an anchor fluke. It was really a "fluke."

I caught this on film.

Reuben Hecht—Renaissance Man and The Dagon Silo

Reuben Hecht was an institution unto himself. I have never met another person with such diverse interests and all on a professional level—businessman, artist, photographer, collector, philanthropist, economist, publisher, writer, soldier, dreamer and idealist.

On one of my early trips Israel in the 1950s I was introduced to Dr. Hecht by James Sassower, a Haifa freight forwarder, and "Heinie" Wydra, Managing Director of ZIM—Israel Navigation Co., Israel's flagship shipping line. Reuben Hecht the CEO and managing director of the Dagon silo in Haifa, was tall and thin in his late thirties. A salt and pepper goatee trimmed just right added to a very dignified appearance. His clothes were very proper but not flashy in any way. Rarely did he wear a tie. He had a strong handshake, and usually a fairly formal mode of address. His desk, at any of the frequent times that I was in his office, was absolutely clear of papers and clutter. Except for his closest friends, he was 'Dr. Hecht.' The doctorate, from a German University, was in law and economics.

Hecht was the scion of a wealthy Swiss family which owned and operated a large fleet of freight barges that cruised the various canals and rivers of Europe, especially the Rhine. The principal cargoes were various bulk shipments, particularly grain and coal moving across Europe for both local consumption and export. The Lines' barges also carried packaged freight, wine, and any other commodity that could efficiently move by water. It was an immensely successful and far flung operation.

Unhappy with the idea of joining the family's business and becoming a rich Swiss businessman, at an early age he broke with the family and went to Palestine in 1936.

Reuben was in love with Zionism, a devotee of Theodore Herzl, and an incurable idealist—but with both feet on the ground. He was also a hardcore revisionist. During Menachim Begin's term as prime minister of Israel, Hecht was Begin's closest confidante and economic advisor.

In Palestine, he organized, built and ran the most efficient and low cost grain silo in the world. He was the main supporter of the Haifa Symphony orchestra. He was also a competent art photographer and painter. He wrote and published frequently. His beautiful tribute to Theodor Herzl, the publication of a special edition of *Herzl's Alte Neuland,* is a classic. His collections of primitive and ancient agricultural implements, clay shipping and storage amphora, and centuries old grain seeds are the basis for an unusual grain museum in Haifa which he created. Devoted to the history of the production of grain from the beginning of time, it is replete with dioramas, time-line charts, three dimensional scenes, and priceless agricultural artifacts.[13]

His employees both loved and feared him. While he paid the best wages in Israel, his word was law. He would brook no inefficiency, but he rewarded innovation. He was always generous to employees on occasions of weddings, births, bar mitzvahs, as well as in times of illness or disstress.

In the late fifties Dr. Hecht became a client of mine. Initially, my work for him was basically keeping him informed about U.S. government programs that might impact on his interests, and when in Israel, to spend some time discussing some current Israeli topic of interest. These sessions, in addition to myself, were generally attended by one or more of his board members.

One of the U.S. programs of great interest to Dr. Hecht was the Cooley Loan Section of Public Law 480, a part of the United States Agricultural and Assistance Act. Named after Senator Cooley, (D) South Carolina, funding for these loans came from the large surplus of soft currencies that the United States government had accumulated selling surplus agricultural commodities to developing countries with repayment in local currencies.

The Cooley Loan program allowed these excess local currencies to be loaned out on very liberal terms for economic projects in developing countries. Israel, a major importer of wheat, corn, rice, and barley under PL 480 had generated large holdings of Israeli pounds in the U.S. Treasury. These local currencies could be made available to firms whose development projects would be of benefit to the United States. Interest was a low 5.5 percent, and payment was over a period of eight years. Since Israel was buying increasing quantities of grains from the United States, the Dagon silo seemed to be a natural for such a loan.

In 1962, Dr. Hecht retained me, specifically, to prepare and process through the U.S. Export Import Bank a Cooley loan application for several million dollars in Israeli currency. The money was to be used to expand the capacity of the DAGON silos threefold, and install state of the art grain handling equipment.

I was successful in this project. As a result of the DAGON rebuilding and expansion, these silos became the most efficient and low cost silos in the world. Hecht's operating techniques and detailed supervision were major factors in the efficiency levels reached.

❧

There was one encounter with him that remains in my mind above any other. Levi Eshkol was prime minister. Hecht, the Revisionist Party[14] member, had no use for Eshkol nor the Labor party. He was an unapologetic right winger, who hated government regulations, and even more, bureaucratic stupidity.

On one of my trips to Israel he asked if I could see him in his office at a certain time. Of course I could. James Sassower took me to the office. He was invited in with me. In Hecht's private office were seated his personal lawyer, and about five members of his board, including Heinie Wydra, and Dr. Justin Heidecker, Hecht's life long friend and personal assistant, as well as Zvi Edelman, managing director of Dagon.

Wow! I wondered what was going on? Was I in for a grilling? What did I do wrong?

Dr. Hecht greeted me as affably as always, and ordered fruit juice for all present. He then took off on Levi Eshkol and the Labor government, particularly as its actions affected him and the silo. There were a few perfunctory remarks from those present, some of whom were members of the Labor party. I said nothing, but wondered what I was doing there.

Then Dr. Hecht gave me a multi-paged letter in English to Levi Eshkol. Hecht's English and German were excellent, not his Hebrew. He asked me to read the letter. It took me about twenty minutes to do so. The room was quiet as I read the letter. The loudest noise was the hum of the air conditioner.

The document was a detailed chapter and verse statement of all the mistakes—as Hecht saw them—of Eshkol's stewardship, particularly as related to the overloaded bureaucracy of the Ministry of Commerce. It was an anti-Labor, and anti-Eshkol diatribe. In fairly formal, but precise language, he was accusing Eshkol and his bureaucrats of stupidity, political malfeasance, failure to keep promises and enforce contracts. In short, it was an amazing document.

When I had finished reading and looked up, there was absolute silence in the room. The air conditioner, still humming, sounded as if it were roaring. By this time I realized that the others had already known the contents of the paper.

I looked around at all of them, took a deep breath and said, "Dr. Hecht, this is quite a statement. You probably want my reaction. It is well documented. You may be absolutely right about the incidents discussed. If you send this to Eshkol you are going to develop an enemy for life and will probably accomplish nothing." The silence in the room grew thicker, if possible. No one was used to hearing anyone challenge Hecht's judgment. When I realized that I was still alive, I continued. "You want to know what I would do with this? I would do this." With that I tore the paper in half.

Even the breathing stopped. Dr. Hecht's face got red, then almost purple. I expected a physical assault for such chutzpah. This lasted for about fifteen seconds which seemed like fifteen minutes. Then Hecht said, "Mr. Atkin you are right. Will you help me write a more appropriate letter?" The relief in the room was indescribable but very audible. Everyone started talking at once. I was drenched in sweat.

I spent the next two days, using Reuben Hecht's immaculate desk to rewrite the letter, making the same points but in a non-belligerent manner. After the letter was finished, signed and sent, Hecht asked me what he owed me for the time. I gave him an amount in Israeli currency which I could use for my expenses on that trip. He called his bookkeeper and had him give me a check for the fee in local currency. He then said, "To come here you had dollar expenses." I said that the fee received would be fine. Nevertheless, he called his bookkeeper back and, in German, asked him to write a check in dollars. When the check was brought back and given to me it was for the largest single fee, relative to time, that I had ever received. Dr. Hecht had trumped my ace.

&

In 1979, when Flora and I led a group from Selby Bay Yacht Club to Israel, we were Dagon's guest for lunch at the facility's boardroom. Dr. Hecht, joining us for lunch, invited the group to take a special tour of the silos and the handling equipment. However, before we did this he gave a short talk about the growth of the plant and the business. He was most kind in his remarks about my part. He stated, "The work that Mr. Atkin (he never called me anything but Mr. Atkin) did for Dagon resulted in savings to the Israeli economy of millions of dollars annually."

Sheik Sa'aloman Tarif

Sollie Friedman, chief auditor of Soleh-Boneh, a Jewish Agency controlled construction and development firm, and an Israeli client of Nathan Associates, invited me to visit Piqin, a village, somewhat northeast of Haifa, the residence of Sheik Sa'aloman Tarif, spiritual and lay head of the Israeli Druze[15].

Sheik Tarif was tall, dignified, and strikingly handsome. He was a regal figure in his flowing robes, gold-embroidered skull cap and full white beard. As I was on the trip more or less as a tourist, I did not participate in the fairly short business part of the session. And of course, following protocol, we joined the Sheik and several of his staff for an elaborate lunch in the large parlor of his home/office. The main decor in that room was a beautiful oriental rug. In the center of the rug was a brass platter about six feet in diameter. In the middle of the platter were a roasted sheep and chickens surrounded a variety of beautifully displayed fruits and vegetables.

Lunch participants sat on the rug in a circle around the platter. We sat with legs crossed. Not an easy position to hold for any length of time for westerners used to putting their legs under a table. It was a very pleasant and tasty meal. The Sheik included all present in the conversation. Through an interpreter, he queried me about the food program, although he seemed to have a good knowledge of it.

The guest immediately on my right conversed with various of the other guests and the host in a variety of languages. He seemed to be very well traveled, and amazingly knowledgeable about events in the United States. I expressed to him an interest in meeting him later in Tel Aviv for lunch or dinner. I wanted to get to know more about him than was either diplomatically or pragmatically possible at the lunch.

However, he told me that he was leaving the next day for an overseas trip, and had no idea as to when he would be back in Israel. I thought that I was getting the brush-off, but said nothing. He gave me his name and said that he hoped we might meet on a future trip of mine to Israel, or in the States. His name was Tuvia Friedman. He did leave Israel for the Argentine the next day. Tuvia Friedman was the Mossad agent sent to Argentina to bring German SS Colonel Eichmann back to Israel for trial.

Before we left his home, Sheik Sa'aloman pinned an enameled badge, about an inch and a half wide, onto my sweater, and thanked me for coming, and thanked Sollie for bringing me. I took his picture, and later sent him an enlargement of it. I was later told that he had it hanging in his sitting room. Obviously a fascinating day.

Two days later, I was sitting on a bench in Tiberias. Two Druze men walked by. One of them noticed the badge. They came to me and in Arabic indicated that they wanted to do something for me, almost anything. I was with the American agricultural attaché who spoke Arabic. He said that the badge I was wearing indicated to the Druze that the wearer was to be treated with great respect, and to be given help whenever possible.

I declined their offer of assistance with sincere thanks.

James Sassower—Consular Agent

It was Flora's and my fortune, in 1951, that James Sassower and his wife Leni were assigned to be our guides and hosts in Haifa. Together they had built up a successful freight forwarding business, based on integrity, efficiency, and service. They did this without political or economic clout. In 1963, I received a call from Leroy (Roy) Atherton, chief of the Middle East desk at the U.S. State Department and later U.S. ambassador to Egypt. Roy and I had known each other since my earliest days with the Israel Embassy. We had developed a solid respect for each other, and while we did not always agree on program or policy we did agree more often than not.

Roy said that for budgetary reasons the State Department was going to close its Consular office in Haifa. In its place there was talk about opening an honorary consular agents office in that city to provide what would ordinarily be consular services. This position, to be filled by an Israeli, would be non-salaried.

I was asked for recommendations for someone to be offered this position. One qualification, in addition to competence, was that the persons recommended should be non-political.

Without hesitation, I gave James's name to Roy. I stated that he was one of the most scrupulous and conscientious persons that I knew anywhere in the world. In 1964, James Sassower was named United States Consular Agent in Haifa. For more than thirty years, he with Leni at his elbow performed this function with great pride and distinction.

Over the years he received many awards recognizing his and Leni's service to the United States and to Israel.

I personally have always taken much satisfaction in knowing that I had a hand in that appointment.

Henry Kissinger—My Look Alike

Clearly not an Israeli, Henry Kissinger, national security advisor and later secretary of state to the Nixon administration, was a frequent visitor to Israel and much involved in the peace negotiations at the time. Kissinger was a controversial figure in Israel, as well in many other parts of the world. We just happened to know each other peripherally, and while we agreed that we looked nothing alike, I was frequently mistaken for him in Washington, in Egypt, in Italy and, of course, in Israel.

It is true that our hairstyles are similar, and when we both wear a certain type of horn-rimmed eyeglasses there is a slight resemblance. When I occasionally put on extra pounds, a week hardly goes by when someone who does not know me says, "Has anyone ever told you that you look like Henry Kissinger?"

Occasionally we have been together, and at such times it is clear that we do not look alike. One such occasion was a party at the Embassy of Israel. Flora and I were there as were Henry and Nancy Kissinger. We mentioned to the Kissingers that people often mistook me for Henry. Nancy Kissinger said to me, "I don't think so. But you are better looking." Clearly, a side by side, face to face, comparison showed little look-a-like traits.

Nevertheless, as a result of this supposed look alike situation, I have had some amusing experiences here and abroad. Thinking back now, I recognize the possibility that what I now see as an amusing experience, could well have resulted in a situation far from amusing.

One day, following a meeting at the State Department, a Department staffer, came hurriedly out of an office, placed his hand on my elbow as he said, "Mr. Secretary, we have been looking for you. Your helicopter is waiting." One Germanic unaccented word out of me was enough to convince the gentleman that a mistake had been made. Shortly thereafter, the Secret Service suggested to me that I should grow a beard, "For your protection, sir." So I did grow a rather jazzy looking vandyke which I wore for about a year.

In the winter of 1981, during one of our two assignments in Cairo, Egypt, Flora and I were walking along the Corniche. A well dressed Egyptian rushed out of a nearby building, and threw his arms around me in a typical Egyptian cordial greeting. In thick Arabic accented English he exclaimed, "Henry, you have come back, and you didn't call me." The first words of surprise out of my mouth were enough to produce profuse apologies for the mistaken identity.

On another occasion when we were in Cairo Congressman John Anderson, then a wannabe presidential candidate, was on a fact finding mission in Egypt and the Middle East in general. While in Egypt he and his entourage were quartered at the Hilton Hotel, as were we.

One evening, as his motorcade was lining up and filling up with his staff, Flora and I were watching the activity along with other on-lookers. I guess that we were about thirty feet from the limos, and having just dressed to go to a party I was wearing a suit and jacket. Just after the congressman came through and got into his car, one of his aides approached me saying, "Will you please get in the car, sir, we are running late." I have often wondered what would have happened if I had gotten into one of the limos. Oh, well, another missed opportunity.

At Dulles airport, while Flora and I were waiting in the United Air Line's Red Carpet lounge prior to flying to Europe several years ago, two men came in, passed my chair, saw me reading, nodded toward me and said, "Good to see you Mr. Secretary" and walked on before I could open my mouth.

On a Russian River cruise in July 2000, several passengers, Americans, asked if I were Henry Kissinger, and afterward, jokingly, they continued to call me "Henry."

In Annapolis, Md., at a synagogue wedding several women across the aisle, as soon as the bridal party went by on its way to the reception, rushed over and asked for my autograph. Were they ever disappointed!

In Washington, on the streets, or in theaters, and even while in my car stopped at a traffic light, strangers have made comments to me or pointed to me and whispered to each other, actions that might have been appropriate for the real Henry, but not for me. These were never nasty nor snide, often funny given the context.

In Florida, California, New York, Italy, France, and Israel similar encounters have occurred.

Although Kissinger is not in the news as prominently as he was during his federal heyday, in almost every situation where I am at an affair (social, theater, or meeting) I am constantly asked, "Did anyone ever tell you that you look like Henry Kissinger?"

Given the unstable world situation and the great number of crazies running around, I retroactively appreciate the Secret Service's advice to grow a vandyke. I shudder to think of what some unhappy anti-American with a Kissinger grudge, might have done.

19

Miscellaneous Incidents
Some Revealing • Some Amusing

Are You Jewish?

D URING FLORA'S AND my first trip to Israel, in 1951, I was invited to attend a meeting of the Export Promotion Committee of the Ministry of Trade and Industry. The meeting was held in one of the second floor patched-up rooms of a bombed out former Arab hotel on the corner of Aza and King George Streets, in Jerusalem. The first floor was still unusable. It has since been rebuilt as a modern office building.

The subject was "How to expand Israeli exports in order to earn hard currency" (dollars). As I recall, there were about six or seven participants. Michael Tzur, secretary general of the ministry was chairman of the session. In addition there were representatives from the ministries of Agriculture and Finance. During the first part of the meeting the discussion centered on Israel's trade deficit. Principal exports were citrus and diamonds. Imports were everything imaginable needed for a new country with a major part of its population penniless immigrants.

I was the new boy on the block. They didn't know me. They didn't seem to know that I had been a member of the Israel Embassy staff in Washington. They only knew that I had been brought over by the Israeli government as a consultant and that I was from a prestigious American firm. Accordingly, they addressed me as "Mr. Atkin." The general tone was formal and 'correct.' After a while, with everyone else being called by their first names, I suggested that they use my first name.

"What is your first name?" I was asked.

"You have the choice of Maury, Moshe, or Moish."

"Moshe? Moish? Are you Jewish with the name Atkin?"

I explained that Atkin was a Russian name, that I was certainly Jewish, had been Bar Mitzvah, and also had the physical credentials of a Jewish male. It was amazing how the tone of the discussion, as far as I was concerned, changed.

Levy's Canned Chicken

During the same meeting a discussion developed about the export prospects to the United States of kosher boned and cooked canned chicken produced by the Levy Company in a Tel Aviv suburb. Several cans of the product were on the table. Part of the discussion was whether the American Jewish religious authorities in New York, the target market, would accept the 'hecksher' (kosher certification) of an Israeli rabbi. At that time, and possibly still today, meat certified by a Tel Aviv rabbi was not considered kosher in Jerusalem, and vice versa. (We have the same problem today between Baltimore and Washington kashruth authorities as far as meat is concerned.)

My opinion was requested. I certainly was no expert on kashruth practices. But I did know that products with a 'hecksher' or the accepted symbol of 'U' or 'O', as well as a visible hecksher label as is used on wine and other kosher products were accepted throughout the United States. I also pointed out that the market in America was much larger than just the Jewish population of New York. However, I was adamant that the product had to be good. It had to have uniform color, weight, moisture content, and taste. It had to be attractively packaged and competitively priced. Having seen some Israeli canned products I had some doubts about Levy's chicken meeting the standards necessary for the American market.

At this point the meeting was recessed for lunch. My appointed guide and escort was a young Englishman from the ministry of Finance who had made aliyah several years earlier. He constantly smoked a curved stem pipe, rarely took it out of his mouth. Accordingly, his speech, with a British accent was to me a mumble. I had great difficulty understanding him for quite a while. However, he proved to be knowledgeable and most helpful.

After I discussed with him an idea I had, he enthusiastically took me to three stores. We bought two cans of Levy's canned chicken at each one. We then bought a can opener. He then introduced me to a favorite Israeli lunch—and still a favorite of mine—a falafel pita bread sandwich and a can of cold Maccabbi beer. Delicious.

Back at the meeting, I again repeated my statement about the American market and the need for a quality, uniform product. I pointed out that a trial shipment of Levy chicken to New York would certainly sell out. But if the quality was not good, forget about another shipment.

So, at that point my Brit friend opened the six cans of chicken we had just bought plus the two cans that were already on hand. The result was illuminating. Among the eight cans there was absolutely no uniformity. Some were predominantly white meat, some predominantly dark meat, some only white meat, some only dark meat. All had varying amounts of moisture or 'soup.' On the whole not an appealing display. I had made my point.

Roll Out the Barrel

In the beginning there was light and there was darkness; there was water and there was earth—but there were no bottles.

In the beginning the fledgling state of Israel started its economic and cultural life with many shortages—money, tires, money, paper, money, food, and bottles. Along with its manifold problems of coping with the 'friendly' neighbors, intent upon its destruction, and thousands of basically penniless immigrants arriving daily there was an acute shortage of glass bottles.

Bottles were needed for a wide variety of fluids for both commercial and, most urgently, for plain housekeeping needs for home use. Prepackaged liquids—kerosene, water, sodas, milk, juices, liquid extracts, etc. just did not exist in Israel. Most homes cooked and heated the premises with kerosene-burning equipment. The kerosene itself was generally delivered by a hawker from a donkey-drawn cart. A fifty-five or forty-two gallon oil drum was mounted horizontally on the cart. There was a spigot on one end of the drum to fill bottles.

The housewife had to supply her own bottle to receive kerosene needed for the cooking stove, generally a two burner primus, for the space heater and for the hot water heater. But glass bottles for these purposes as well as for other uses were one of the items in very short supply.

While I was still at the embassy, a request came to try to find a cheap supply of bottles. The request landed on my desk. Inquiring around I found that one of the biggest users of plain glass bottles, as distinguished from trademark bottles such as the familiar Coca-Cola shape, were breweries. One of the largest national breweries—at least it had the most radio advertising (no TV then)—was the Schaefer Brewery. Its catch phrase " Schaefer's is the one to have when you are having more than one" was well known. And Schaefer had a facility in New Jersey close to shipping points.

A phone call to Schaefer struck oil. Correction, struck beer. It seems that the company had an excess supply of over-aged 12 ounce bottled beer in cases containing 24 bottles each taking up valuable warehouse space in New Jersey. Management was interested in disposing of these non-income producing assets.

I 'bought' five thousand cases of beer, 120,000 bottles for the government of Israel (GOI). The bottled beer was free. The GOI arranged to move the cases from a warehouse in Newark, N.J. to a port of the same city. The contract with the brewery required that the bottles had to be empty upon arrival in Israel. Schaefer did not want its over-aged beer to be sold or consumed in Israel or any other country. The Schaefer management was properly concerned about the potential marketing impact of off-flavor beer.

No problem!

The 5,000 cases of beer were shipped out of Newark, New Jersey aboard a ZIM Navigation Co. vessel. ZIM, jointly owned by the government of Israel and the Jewish Agency, made an attractive freight rate available. During the three week sea voyage, the deck crew was kept busy opening and dumping the contents of 120,000 bottles of lager into the Atlantic. The ship's log did not reflect how much of the brew passed through the crew before going into the sea. In fact, the crew was under strict orders prohibiting drinking the beer. But seamen being seamen...

Nor was there any record of wild and woozy fish. The arrival of the bottles in Israel was most welcome.

Rusty Jarko and the FBI

While on the Israel Embassy staff, I had reason to visit the Newark, N. J. office of Materials for Israel frequently, and in particular, Julius Jarko, director of that organization. Known far and wide as 'Rusty', he ran an especially efficient and effective operation. Its function was to accumulate and ship to Israel a broad variety of supplies and equipment needed for absorption, resettlement, and protection of the new struggling country and its inhabitants. Rusty was most helpful in coordinating the beer shipment from Newark to Israel.

Often as not, these shipments included items desperately needed in Israel, but on the Department of Commerce's embargo list. Most of such items were therefore shipped as 'agricultural equipment'. While Rusty's operation was certainly not approved by the FBI, for the most part the Bureau, conveniently, preferred to look the other way. One summer day in 1948, I was in his office. He had a visitor, the head of the regional FBI office. Rusty introduced him to me. Let's call him Mr. O'Riley. That is not his name, but he was certainly Irish and it was quickly obvious that he and Rusty knew each other very well.

"Rusty," he said, "I have to talk to you privately."

"Anything you have to say to me, you can say in front of Maury." was Rusty's immediate reply. I offered to leave, but was asked to stay. O'Riley then said, "Rusty, we have to pick up that ship you are loading."

Rusty was horrified. At that time the particular goods on the ship being loaded in Newark harbor were desperately needed by Israel's defense forces. Asked why this ship in particular, and at this time, O'Riley took out a newspaper clipping and placing it on Rusty's desk said, "We don't mind turning our back to your operations, but we don't like being kicked in the ass."

The clipping described a fundraising meeting that Bergson's Stern Gang group had held in the Hollywood Bowl the previous night, at which the principal speaker, Ben Hecht, announced that that very evening they—Bergson's people, were loading a ship in Newark. He named the ship and said that it was with the knowledge of the FBI. The ship's $5,000,000 cargo was confiscated by the FBI.

Was this a deliberate ploy by the Stern Gang to embarrass the government of Israel, or was it just a case of a "big mouth?"

Rabbinical Pickets

It was 1950. I was in Baltimore trying to purchase a suit at one of that city's 'wholesale' men's factory stores. It was a Saturday afternoon. I was paged to pick up a telephone. It was a caller from the Israel Embassy, giving me the unwelcome news that a ZIM line ship loading urgently needed foodstuffs in Newark was being picketed by a group of orthodox rabbis carrying Torah scrolls. The picketing was preventing the ship's loading.

I took the next train to Newark. The scene at the pier was surreal. A group of six bearded men in Williamsburg (Brooklyn) garb, carrying Torah scrolls were marching back and forth along the pier, preventing any cargo loading. I never found out whether or not they were rabbis, but it did not matter.

I found the ringleader, explained the need to load the vessel and send it on its way. The food being loaded was desperately needed. His reply was to scold me unmercifully. "How could we desecrate the Sabbath by loading a Jewish ship on the Sabbath?"

We made a deal. I guaranteed that there would be no Jewish stevedores working on the loading gangs. I knew that there were no Jews on those gangs. And I knew that he knew it too. But he agreed to the deal, and the loading proceeded—after I also agreed to reimburse him and his 'buddies' for their costs of transportation.

The ship sailed on time. It was all in the day's work.

I often wondered how these orthodox men justified their riding on the Sabbath from Brooklyn to Newark. Certainly they had not walked.

The Eye of the Sheep

I believe it was early 1967. I was in Haifa in connection with Dagon Silo and ZIM matters. I was invited to join a Jewish Agency official on a day's trip to Nazareth. We were to meet the Arab mayor of that ancient city in connection with some Agency business.

To my surprise, we didn't go to the city hall, but to the mayor's quite comfortable home with a beautiful view over the valley south of the city.

The mayor, a Christian, was most hospitable and was fashionably dressed in suit and tie. He introduced our group of three to his wife and to several other local dignitaries—all Arabs. After some discussion about an Agency program in the area, we were invited to lunch. It was a sumptuous and delicious meal.

All present, men only, sat around a large brass/copper tray about five feet in diameter. On the tray was a whole roasted sheep, several roasted chickens, numerous raw and cooked vegetables, pita bread, little bowls of humus, olives, small cucumbers, and small demitasse cups for very strong coffee.

While we ate, various citizens of the town, all Arab, who had business with the mayor, sat on low stools around us. They were very quiet, not saying a word to any one at the 'table' or to each other. This was slightly uncomfortable for me, but no one else seemed to care.

As we progressed through the meal the mayor plucked one of the eyes from the roast sheep, held it up and made a flowery speech to me about the work I was doing and the importance of it to the whole community. Needless to say, I was more than slightly embarrassed. But, with a flourish he presented the eye to me. As I gingerly took it, I whispered out of the side of my mouth to the Agency representative, "What do I do with it?"

He whispered back, "You eat it!"

"I can't," I whispered.

Obviously I was going to get no help from him. Thinking as fast as I could, I turned to the mayor, repeated to him some of the things that I had heard on the ride up from Haifa, what he had done for his community and his people, and most importantly, what he had done to facilitate smooth relations between Arab and Jew. I then presented the eye back to him saying, "You will do me great honor if you will accept this as a token of my esteem for you and the good things that you are doing for your people."

He smiled broadly, accepted the eye, and ate it with great relish. Fortunately, no one commented that there was a second eye.

Hava Nagila

Flora and I, were flying into Lagos, Nigeria aboard a Nigerian Airline plane. As we were preparing to land, music suddenly filled the cabin. It sounded most familiar.

It was Hava Nagila, (Let Us Rejoice) a favorite Israeli song played almost invariably at American Bar Mitzvahs and Jewish weddings.

We later learned that the plane had recently been reconditioned at AIA, Israel Aircraft Industries.

Silver Cuff Links

You can never tell!

Yes, you never know who your customers are.

In Mexico City, on one of my frequent trips there, I hankered to buy some Mexican silver cuff links. I had a fondness for this somewhat primitive jewelry. I already had several sets, but decided that I would like one or two more.

I was in Ciudad de Mexico on behalf of the Israel government. My hotel, the Prado, was close to several of the local silver stores. Taking advantage of an hour's free time and a beautiful day for a short walk, I visited one of the stores.

The proprietress and her teenage daughter were behind the display counters. Both spoke excellent English. After explaining my interest in some Mexican silver cuff links, I was shown several trays of links, but none that suited my taste.

As I started to leave, Señora Proprietress said to me in English, "I have more links in the back. I will get them." In Yiddish, she said to her daughter, "Keep your eye on the 'goy' (gentile). I will be right back."

I pretended not to understand, and said nothing about her obvious distrust of a stranger.

Señora came back with new selections, from which I picked several that I liked. Still no comment from me.

That evening a large meeting of the Mexico City Jewish community was held at the sprawling campus of the Jewish Community Center. Representing the government of Israel, I was the guest of honor.

As the chairman, Dr. Adolpho Fastlicht, presented me with a beautiful tooled leather Mexican briefcase, I became aware of a very red faced Señora Proprietress sitting in the first row of the audience.

You can never tell.

20

In Retrospect—Roundup

A S WITH MANY personal memoirs, this one started because close friends and family, some of whom were partially aware of snippets of my career and life, urged me to "put it in writing" for our children, grandchildren, and great grandchildren.

It has been said that behind every successful man there is an anxious mother-in-law. I would like to think that alongside every man there is a loving family.

Sixty-three years ago while still doing graduate work I married Flora Rose Blumenthal. At the time I could not and did not promise her a great material life. I did however, promise that our lives would never be dull. While there is no complaint about our material rewards, our days and years together have never been boring. And we look to the future with expectations that it will continue in the same manner.

Flora and I are proud of our expanding family. We are pleased that all are pursuing activities that they like, and contributing to society in a meaningful way. Our time and effort in raising a family has been most rewarding.

Flora, a fourth generation Washingtonian, has a BA, cum laude, 1940 from Syracuse University in English and music education, and did graduate work at Bennington College, and Catholic University in dance and drama. She pursued successful careers in dance, music, recreation, education, and later in theater for youth as a director, choreographer, and playwright. Ten of her plays have been published, and presented in 49 states and 6 foreign countries. In 1982, she was listed in *Who's Who in America*.

FIGURE 29: L–R, back row, Stephen Berkeley, Maury Atkin, Joseph
Atkin, John Vondra. Front row, Judy Berkeley with Benjamin, Flora
Atkin, Sam Vondra, Carol Atkin, Lisa Vondra with Ethan.

Our immediate family consists of our children, Joseph Raymond
and his wife, Carol Ann (Friedman), Barrie Joan, and Jonathan Barry.
It now also includes two grand daughters, Lisa Ilene and Judith Lyn—
children of Joseph, and their husbands, John Vondra and Stephen
Berkeley as well as three great grandsons; Samuel Barrett Vondra,
Ethan Ross Vondra, and Benjamin Jacob Berkeley.

Here, I must make a confession.

While I am pleased to be a great grandfather, I did have difficulty accepting that our son Joseph—Joey in earlier years—was a grandfather.

In raising our children during the difficult 50s and 60s, years of
Vietnam, drugs, violence and student rebellion, we tried to inculcate
high standards of moral and ethical conduct, an appreciation of the
value of "doing unto others" and of public service, as well as a knowledge and love of Judaism. We have tried, also, to give them the tools,
via education, for successful economic careers. We are proud of what
they have done and are doing. All have graduate degrees.

Joseph earned his BA in 1967 from Washington University, St. Louis, and an MBA in 1969 at Indiana University, Bloomington. In 1971,
he added CPA to his name. In June, 1967, he married Carol Fried-

man, of DuQuoin, Ilinois, whom he met at Washington University. Carol, a junior year Phi Beta Kappa, a former teacher, is a wonderful wife, mother, and grandmother. To Flora and myself she is more of a daughter than a daughter-in-law.

Joe used his academic skills in real estate, accounting, and art gallery management. In September, 2002, he accepted a position as senior vice president and chief financial officer of the Chicago Council for the Jewish Elderly. In September, 2004, he was promoted to executive vice president of CJE. He loves the not-for-profit economic area, and the short commute from home in Glencoe, Illinois, to office.

Barrie earned both a BA from Brown University, Providence, Rhode Island, and a M.S.ED from the University of Pennsylvania in 1971. Harvard awarded her an M.B.A in 1982. With the degree she received a silver cup for outstanding service as publisher of *Harbus*, the 'B' school newspaper. After responsible positions with Rodale Press, *The Miami Herald*, and *TV Guide* she decided to become her own boss. As such she is a freelance consultant to the publishing industry. Barrie has homes in Provincetown and Waltham, Massachusetts. In September, 2003, she lost her partner of twelve years, Roberta Lasley, to cancer.

Jonathan, Barrie's twin brother, earned his BA from Lake Forest College, Lake Forest, Illinois, in 1971, and his MFA from Rochester University, Rochester, New York in 1973. He is a widely published freelance photo-journalist, and thoroughly enjoys living in New York City.

Our granddaughter, Lisa, earned her BA from University of Wisconsin, 1993, and her Wisconsin Teachers Certificate, 1997. Mother of two young boys, she teaches part time at the Jewish Community Center, Milwaukee, along with managing her household. Her husband, John, is a regional manager for Anderson Windows. They and their two boys live in Whitefish Bay, Wisconsin.

Our other granddaughter, Judy, in 1995 received a BA from University of Pennsylvania; in 1997, a MSW from University of Southern California, and a MA in Jewish Communal Service from Hebrew Union College, Los Angeles. With motherhood and a long daily commute to Chicago, Judy resigned as director of the Schools and Synagogue Divi-

sion of the Chicago Jewish Federation and took a position as development director of Am Shalom Synagogue, Glencoe, Illinois. Steve, her
husband is a partner in Neal, Gerber, and Eisenberg, a Chicago law
firm. Judy and Steve live in Glencoe, Illinois with their son.

❧

This memoir was not intended as a comprehensive autobiography.
I think that I made a difference, particularly where much of my professional interest and time was concentrated—Israel. In other places
such as West Africa, Egypt, the United States or the Far East, you the
reader must be the judge.

❧

We, like many others, are concerned about the kind of world
that Sam, Ethan, and Ben will live and work in. Global warming, the
depletion of the seas' bounty, rainforest depletion, new deadly no cure
diseases as well as the resurgence of old ones, worldwide terrorism,
and government mismanagement are only some of the problems
that their generation will confront. These very problems also offer
challenges to our future generations. They present opportunities
for exciting and untested careers and interesting lives. Previous
generations have faced and conquered equally daunting problems.
Let us look forward to the coming generations to do the same.

FIGURE 30: Maury and Flora relaxing on Chesapeake Bay

FIGURE 31: Two that did not get away

FIGURE 32: Great grandsons

Top left: Samuel Barrett Vondra,
born July 29, 2000
Top right: Ethan Ross Vondra,
born June 17, 2003
Lower left: Benjamin Jacob Berkeley,
born August 17, 2003

Chronology

Year	Event
1917	Born, Hobart, NY. Moved to Washington, D.C
1934	Graduated Central High School, Washington, D.C.
1938	BS, University of Maryland, Graduate Fellowship
1940	MBA, University of Maryland
1939–48	Economist, Marketing Specialist, USDA
1941	Married Flora Blumenthal, Enlisted USMCR
1942	Honorable Discharge, USMCR
1945	Son, Joseph Raymond born
1948	Resigned USDA, Appointed EO and Agricultural Advisor Israel Mission (later Embassy) Washington, D.C. Moved to Silver Spring, MD
1949	Twins born. Jonathan Barry and Barrie Joan. Three children and Flora contacted polio
1950	Resigned from embassy. Joined economic consulting firm of Robert R. Nathan as senior economist
1951	First of 87 trips to Israel
1955	Moved to town of Somerset, Chevy Chase, MD
1950–85	Overseas assignments and professional travel to Israel, Mexico, Canada, Italy, France, Switzerland, Germany, Denmark, Norway, Sweden, Greece, Sierra Leone, Ghana, Nigeria, Egypt, Japan, Philippines, Trust Territories, Sri Lanka, Thailand and Caribbean Islands
1971	First granddaughter born. Lisa Ilene Atkin
1973	Second granddaughter born. Judith Lyn Atkin
1980	Commodore, Selby Bay Yacht Club
1981	Commander, U.S. Coast Guard Auxiliary
1983	Retired, Senior Vice President RRNA
2000	Great grandson, Samuel Vondra, (born to Lisa)
2003	Great grandsons, Ethan Vondra (born to Lisa) and Benjamin Berkeley (born to Judith)

Notes

1. Following World War I, the League of Nations gave the governing mandate for Palestine to Great Britain. Lord Balfour, Britain's foreign minister, on November 2, 1917 wrote a letter to Lord Rothschild, the president of the English Zionist Federation, declaring "His Majesty's Government views with favour the establishment in Palestine of a national home for the Jewish people."

2. For a vivid and personal account of the maneuvering at the UN see *The Birth of Israel*, by Jorge Garcia-Granados, Alfred A. Knopf, 1948

3. Atkin was the family name in Russia. It was my father's name and his father's. However, transliterating from the Yiddish, in English it might have been Etkin or Itkin. Israeli genealogists suggest that the name Atkin could have been derived from "Etty's Kin."

4. Lee Pennington, son of one of the Golden Company founders, subsequently assistant director of the FBI under J.E. Hoover was a witness on Joseph's naturalization papers.

5. Literally, the village. Government functions were split between Tel Aviv and Jerusalem.

6. See Chapter 6 "The American Cheese—Is It Kosher?"

7. Southern area of the state.

8. A fully equipped plant, ready to operate.

9. Exotic skins included crocodile/alligator, lizard, snake, ostrich, frog, and shark.

10. Cajun was the French dialect spoken by the descendants of the Arcadians who migrated from Eastern Canada to the Louisiana Territory. The term is now used for the people, their music, and foods.

11. Ex-Pats. Former officials of the British colonial period who had run the country until independence from England, now working as advisors to the current government.

12. Israel's parliament.

13. For more information about the Hecht family and the development of the Dagon Silo see *The River and The Grain*, Zvi Herman, Herzl Press, NY, 1989.

14. A minor extremely right-wing political party.

15. The Druze are Arabs whose religion is a variation of Islam, who look to Moses' sister Miriam and his father-in-law, Jethro, as their religious antecedents. Druze clans live in Israel, Syria, and Lebanon. The Israeli Druze are furiously defensive of Israel and serve in its armed forces.